FAR AWAY AND LONG AGO

Photo by Opie Ltd. Redruth

Yours sincerely

W. H. Hudson

FAR AWAY AND LONG AGO

A HISTORY
OF MY EARLY LIFE

BY
W. H. HUDSON

AUTHOR OF "IDLE DAYS IN PATAGONIA," "THE PURPLE LAND,"
"A CRYSTAL AGE," "ADVENTURES AMONG BIRDS," ETC.

NEW YORK
E. P. DUTTON & COMPANY
681 FIFTH AVENUE
1925

CONTENTS

CHAPTER I

EARLIEST MEMORIES

CHAPTER II

MY NEW HOME

CHAPTER III

DEATH OF AN OLD DOG

CONTENTS

CONTENTS

CONTENTS

CHAPTER X

OUR NEAREST ENGLISH NEIGHBOUR

CHAPTER XI

A BREEDER OF PIEBALDS

CHAPTER XII

THE HEAD OF A DECAYED HOUSE

CONTENTS

CHAPTER XVII

A BOY'S ANIMISM

CHAPTER XVIII

THE NEW SCHOOLMASTER

CHAPTER XIX

BROTHERS

CONTENTS

CHAPTER XX

BIRDING IN THE MARSHES

CHAPTER XXI

WILD-FOWLING ADVENTURES

CHAPTER XXII

BOYHOOD'S END

CONTENTS

CHAPTER XXIII
A DARKENED LIFE

CHAPTER XXIV
LOSS AND GAIN

FAR AWAY AND LONG AGO

FAR AWAY AND LONG AGO

CHAPTER I
Earliest Memories

Preamble—The house where I was born—The singular
Ombu tree—A tree without a name—The plain—The
ghost of a murdered slave—Our playmate, the old
sheep-dog—A first riding-lesson—The cattle: an evening scene—My mother—Captain Scott—The hermit
and his awful penance.

IT was never my intention to write an autobiography.
Since I took to writing in my middle years I have,
from time to time, related some incident of my boyhood, and these are contained in various chapters in
*The Naturalist in La Plata, Birds and Man, Adventures
among Birds,* and other works, also in two or three
magazine articles: all this material would have been
kept back if I had contemplated such a book as this.
When my friends have asked me in recent years why
I did not write a history of my early life on the
pampas, my answer was that I had already told all
that was worth telling in these books. And I really
believed it was so; for when a person endeavours to
recall his early life in its entirety he finds it is not
possible: he is like one who ascends a hill to survey
the prospect before him on a day of heavy cloud and

shadow, who sees at a distance, now here, now there, some feature in the landscape—hill or wood or tower or spire—touched and made conspicuous by a transitory sunbeam while all else remains in obscurity. The scenes, people, events we are able by an effort to call up do not present themselves in order; there is no order, no sequence or regular progression—nothing, in fact, but isolated spots or patches, brightly illumined and vividly seen, in the midst of a wide shrouded mental landscape.

It is easy to fall into the delusion that the few things thus distinctly remembered and visualized are precisely those which were most important in our life, and on that account were saved by memory while all the rest has been permanently blotted out. That is indeed how our memory serves and fools us; for at some period of a man's life—at all events of some lives—in some rare state of the mind, it is all at once revealed to him as by a miracle that nothing is ever blotted out.

It was through falling into some such state as that, during which I had a wonderfully clear and continuous vision of the past, that I was tempted—forced I may say—to write this account of my early years. I will relate the occasion, as I imagine that the reader who is a psychologist will find as much to interest him in this incident as in anything else contained in the book.

I was feeling weak and depressed when I came down from London one November evening to the south coast: the sea, the clear sky, the bright colours of the afterglow kept me too long on the front in an east wind in that low condition, with the result that I was laid up for six weeks with a very serious illness. Yet when it was over I looked back on those six weeks as a happy time! Never had I thought so little of physical pain. Never had I felt confinement less—I who feel, when I am out of sight of living, growing grass, and out of sound of birds' voices and all rural sounds, that I am not properly alive!

On the second day of my illness, during an interval of comparative ease, I fell into recollections of my childhood, and at once I had that far, that forgotten past with me again as I had never previously had it. It was not like that mental condition, known to most persons, when some sight or sound or, more frequently, the perfume of some flower, associated with our early life, restores the past suddenly and so vividly that it is almost an illusion. That is an intensely emotional condition and vanishes as quickly as it comes. This was different. To return to the simile and metaphor used at the beginning, it was as if the cloud shadows and haze had passed away and the entire wide prospect beneath me made clearly visible. Over it all my eyes could range at will, choosing this or that point to dwell on, to examine it in all its details; and, in the case of some person known to me as a child, to follow his life till it ended or passed from sight; then to return to the same point again to repeat the process with other lives and resume my rambles in the old familiar haunts.

What a happiness it would be, I thought, in spite of discomfort and pain and danger, if this vision would continue! It was not to be expected: nevertheless it did not vanish, and on the second day I set myself to try and save it from the oblivion which would presently cover it again. Propped up with pillows I began with pencil and writing-pad to put it down in some sort of order, and went on with it at intervals during the whole six weeks of my confinement, and in this way produced the first rough draft of the book.

And all this time I never ceased wondering at my own mental state; I thought of it when, quickly tired, my trembling fingers dropped the pencil; or when I woke from uneasy sleep to find the vision still before me, inviting, insistently calling to me, to resume my childish rambles and adventures of long ago in that strange world where I first saw the light.

It was to me a marvellous experience; to be here, propped up with pillows in a dimly-lighted room, the night-nurse idly dosing by the fire; the sound of the everlasting wind in my ears, howling outside and dashing the rain like hailstones against the window-panes; to be awake to all this, feverish and ill and sore, conscious of my danger too, and at the same time to be thousands of miles away, out in the sun and wind, rejoicing in other sights and sounds, happy again with that ancient long-lost and now recovered happiness!

During the three years that have passed since I had that strange experience, I have from time to time, when in the mood, gone back to the book and have had to cut it down a good deal and to reshape it, as in the first draft it would have made too long and formless a history.

The house where I was born, on the South American pampas, was quaintly named *Los Veinte-cinco Ombues,* which means "The Twenty-five Ombu Trees," there being just twenty-five of these indigenous trees—gigantic in size, and standing wide apart in a row about 400 yards long. The ombu is a very singular tree indeed, and being the only representative of tree-vegetation, natural to the soil, on those great level plains, and having also many curious superstitions connected with it, it is a romance in itself. It belongs to the rare Phytolacca family, and has an immense girth—forty or fifty feet in some cases; at the same time the wood is so soft and spongy that it can be cut into with a knife, and is utterly unfit for firewood, for when cut up it refuses to dry, but simply rots away like a ripe water-melon. It also grows slowly, and its leaves, which are large, glossy and deep green, like laurel leaves, are poisonous; and because of its uselessness it will probably become extinct, like the graceful pampas grass in the same region. In this exceedingly practical age men quickly lay the axe at the root of things which, in their view, only cumber the ground; but before other trees had been planted the antiquated and grand-looking ombu had its uses; it served as a gigantic landmark to the traveller on the great monotonous plains, and also afforded refreshing shade to man and horse in summer; while the native doctor or herbalist would sometimes pluck a leaf for a patient requiring a very violent remedy for his disorder. Our trees were about a century old and very large, and, as they stood on an elevation, they could be easily seen at a distance of ten miles. At noon in summer the cattle and sheep, of which we had a large number, used to rest in their shade; one large tree also afforded us children a splendid play-house, and we used to carry up a number of planks to construct safe bridges from branch to branch, and at noon, when our elders were sleeping their siesta, we would have our arboreal games unmolested.

Besides the famous twenty-five, there was one other tree of a different species, growing close to the house, and this was known all over the neighbourhood as "The Tree," this proud name having been bestowed on it because it was the only one of the kind known in that part of the country; our native neighbours always affirmed that it was the only one in the world. It was a fine large old tree, with a white bark, long smooth white thorns, and dark-green undeciduous foliage. Its blossoming time was in November—a month about as hot as an English July—and it would then become covered with tassels of minute wax-like flowers, pale straw-colour, and of a wonderful fragrance, which the soft summer wind would carry for miles on its wings. And in this way our neighbours would discover that the flowering season had come to the tree they so much admired, and they would come to beg for a branch to take home with them to perfume their lowly houses.

The pampas are, in most places, level as a billiard-table; just where we lived, however, the country happened to be undulating, and our house stood on the summit of one of the highest elevations. Before the house stretched a great grassy plain, level to the horizon, while at the back it sloped abruptly down to a broad, deep stream, which emptied itself in the river Plata, about six miles to the east. This stream, with its three ancient red willow-trees growing on the banks, was a source of endless pleasure to us. Whenever we went down to play on the banks, the fresh penetrating scent of the moist earth had a strangely exhilarating effect, making us wild with joy. I am able now to recall these sensations, and believe that the sense of smell, which seems to diminish as we grow older, until it becomes something scarcely worthy of being called a sense, is nearly as keen in little children as in the inferior animals, and, when they live with nature, contributes as much to their pleasure as sight or hearing. I have often observed that small children, when brought on to low, moist ground from a high level, give loose to a sudden spontaneous gladness, running, shouting, and rolling over the grass just like dogs, and I have no doubt that the fresh smell of the earth is the cause of their joyous excitement.

Our house was a long low structure, built of brick, and, being very old, naturally had the reputation of being haunted. A former proprietor, half a century before I was born, once had among his slaves a very handsome young negro, who, on account of his beauty and amiability, was a special favourite with his mistress. Her preference filled his poor silly brains with dreams and aspirations, and, deceived by her gracious manner, he one day ventured to approach her in the absence of his master and told her his feelings. She could not forgive so terrible an insult to her pride, and when her husband returned went to him, white with indignation, and told him how this miserable slave had abused their kindness. The husband had an implacable heart, and at his command the offender was suspended by the wrists to a low, horizontal branch of "The Tree," and there, in sight of his master and mistress, he was scourged to death by his fellow-slaves. His battered body was then taken down and buried in a deep hollow at some little distance from the last of the long row of ombu trees. It was the ghost of this poor black, whose punishment had been so much heavier than his offence deserved, that was supposed to haunt the place. It was not, however, a conventional ghost, stalking about in a white sheet; those who had seen it averred that it invariably rose up from the spot where the body had been buried, like a pale, luminous exhalation from the earth, and, assuming a human shape, floated slowly towards the house, and roamed about the great trees, or, seating itself on an old projecting root, would remain motionless for hours in a dejected attitude. I never saw it.

Our constant companion and playmate in those days was a dog, whose portrait has never faded from remembrance, for he was a dog with features and a personality which impressed themselves deeply on the mind. He came to us in a rather mysterious manner. One summer evening the shepherd was galloping round the flock, and trying by means of much shouting to induce the lazy sheep to move homewards. A strange-looking lame dog suddenly appeared on the scene, as if it had dropped from the clouds, and limping briskly after the astonished and frightened sheep, drove them straight home and into the fold; and, after thus earning his supper and showing what stuff was in him, he established himself at the house, where he was well received. He was a good-sized animal, with a very long body, a smooth black coat, tan feet, muzzle, and "spectacles," and a face of extraordinary length, which gave him a profoundly-wise baboon-like expression. One of his hind legs had been broken or otherwise injured, so that he limped and shuffled along in a peculiar lopsided fashion; he had no tail, and his ears had been cropped close to his head: altogether he was like an old soldier returned from the wars, where he had received many hard knocks, besides having had sundry portions of his anatomy shot away.

No name to fit this singular canine visitor could be found, although he responded readily enough to the word *Pechicho,* which is used to call any unnamed pup by, like pussy for a cat. So it came to pass that this word *pechicho*—equivalent to "doggie" in English— stuck to him for only name until the end of the chapter; and the end was that, after spending some years with us, he mysteriously disappeared.

He very soon proved to us that he understood children as well as sheep; at all events he would allow them to tease and pull him about most unmercifully, and actually appeared to enjoy it. Our first riding-lessons were taken on his back; but old Pechicho eventually made one mistake, after which he was relieved from the labour of carrying us. When I was about four years old, my two elder brothers, in the character of riding-masters, set me on his back, and, in order to test my capacity for sticking on under difficulties, they rushed away, calling him. The old dog, infected with the pretended excitement, bounded after them, and I was thrown and had my leg broken, for, as the poet says—

> Children, they are very little,
> And their bones are very brittle.

Luckily their little brittle bones quickly solder, and it did not take me long to recover from the effects of this mishap.

No doubt my canine steed was as much troubled as any one at the accident. I seem to see the wise old fellow now, sitting in that curious one-sided fashion he had acquired so as to rest his lame leg, his mouth opened to a kind of immense smile, and his brown benevolent eyes regarding us with just such an expression as one sees in a faithful old negress nursing a flock of troublesome white children—so proud and happy to be in charge of the little ones of a superior race!

All that I remember of my early life at this place comes between the ages of three or four and five; a period which, to the eye of memory, appears like a wide plain blurred over with a low-lying mist, with here and there a group of trees, a house, a hill, or other large object, standing out in the clear air with marvellous distinctness. The picture that most often presents itself is of the cattle coming home in the evening; the green quiet plain extending away from the gate to the horizon; the western sky flushed with sunset hues, and the herd of four or five hundred cattle trotting homewards with loud lowings and bellowings, raising a great cloud of dust with their hoofs, while behind gallop the herdsmen urging them on with wild cries. Another picture is of my mother at the close of the day, when we children, after our supper of bread and milk, join in a last grand frolic on the green before the house. I see her sitting out of doors watching our sport with a smile, her book lying in her lap, and the last rays of the setting sun shining on her face.

When I think of her I remember with gratitude that our parents seldom or never punished us, and never, unless we went too far in our domestic dissensions or tricks, even chided us. This, I am convinced, is the right attitude for parents to observe, modestly to admit that nature is wiser than they are, and to let their little ones follow, as far as possible, the bent of their own minds, or whatever it is they have in place of minds. It is the attitude of the sensible hen towards her ducklings, when she has had frequent experience of their incongruous ways, and is satisfied that they know best what is good for them; though, of course, their ways seem peculiar to her, and she can never entirely sympathize with their fancy for going into water. I need not be told that the hen is after all only step-mother to her ducklings, since I am contending that the civilized woman—the artificial product of our self-imposed conditions—cannot have the same relation to her offspring as the uncivilized woman really has to hers. The comparison, therefore, holds good, the mother with us being practically step-mother to children of another race; and if she is sensible, and amenable to nature's teaching, she will attribute their seemingly unsuitable ways and appetites to the right cause, and not to a hypothetical perversity or inherent depravity of heart, about which many authors will have spoken to her in many books:

> But though they wrote it all by rote
> They did not write it right.

Of all the people outside of the domestic circle known to me in those days, two individuals only are distinctly remembered. They were certainly painted by memory in very strong unfading colours, so that now they seem to stand like living men in a company of pale phantom forms. This is probably due to the circumstance that they were considerably more grotesque in appearance than the others, like old Pechicho among our dogs—all now forgotten save him.

One was an Englishman named Captain Scott, who used to visit us occasionally for a week's shooting or fishing, for he was a great sportsman. We were all extremely fond of him, for he was one of those simple men that love and sympathize with children; besides that, he used to come to us from some distant wonderful place where sugar-plums were made, and to our healthy appetites, unaccustomed to sweets of any description, these things tasted like an angelic kind of food. He was an immense man, with a great round face of a purplish-red colour, like the sun setting in glory, and surrounded with a fringe of silvery-white hair and whiskers, standing out like the petals round the disc of a sunflower. It was always a great time when Captain Scott arrived, and while he alighted from his horse we would surround him with loud demonstrations of welcome, eager for the treasures which made his pockets bulge out on all sides. When he went out gunning he always remembered to shoot a hawk or some strangely-painted bird for us; it was even better when he went fishing, for then he took us with him, and while he stood motionless on the bank, rod in hand, looking, in the light-blue suit he always wore, like a vast blue pillar crowned with that broad red face, we romped on the sward, and revelled in the dank fragrance of the earth and rushes.

I have not the faintest notion of who Captain Scott was, or of what he was ever captain, or whether residence in a warm climate or hard drinking had dyed his broad countenance with that deep magenta red, nor of how and when he finished his earthly career; for when we moved away the huge purple-faced strange-looking man dropped for ever out of our lives; yet in my mind how beautiful his gigantic image looks! And to this day I bless his memory for all the sweets he gave me, in a land where sweets were scarce, and for his friendliness to me when I was a very small boy.

The second well-remembered individual was also only an occasional visitor at our house, and was known all over the surrounding country as the Hermit, for his name was never discovered. He was perpetually on the move, visiting in turn every house within a radius of forty or fifty miles; and once about every seven or eight weeks he called on us to receive a few articles of food—enough for the day's consumption. Money he always refused with gestures of intense disgust, and he would also decline cooked meat and broken bread. When hard biscuits were given him, he would carefully examine them, and if one was found chipped or cracked he would return it, pointing out the defect, and ask for a sound one in return. He had a small, sun-parched face, and silvery long hair; but his features were fine, his teeth white and even, his eyes clear grey and keen as a falcon's. There was always a set expression of deep mental anguish on his face, intensified with perhaps a touch of insanity, which made it painful to look at him. As he never accepted money or anything but food, he of course made his own garments—and

what garments they were! Many years ago I used to
see, strolling about St. James's Park, a huge hairy gentleman, with a bludgeon in his hand, and clothed with
a bear's skin to which the head and paws were attached.
It may be that this eccentric individual is remembered
by some of my readers, but I assure them that he was
quite a St. James's Park dandy compared with my hermit. He wore a pair of gigantic shoes, about a foot
broad at the toes, made out of thick cow-hide with the
hair on; and on his head was a tall rimless cow-hide
hat shaped like an inverted flower-pot. His bodily covering was, however, the most extraordinary: the outer
garment, if garment it can be called, resembled a very
large mattress in size and shape, with the ticking made
of innumerable pieces of raw hide sewn together. It
was about a foot in thickness and stuffed with sticks,
stones, hard lumps of clay, rams' horns, bleached bones,
and other hard heavy objects; it was fastened round
him with straps of hide, and reached nearly to the
ground. The figure he made in this covering was most
horribly uncouth and grotesque, and his periodical visits
used to throw us into a great state of excitement. And
as if this awful burden with which he had saddled himself—enough to have crushed down any two ordinary
men—was not sufficient, he had weighted the heavy stick
used to support his steps with a great ball at the end,
also with a large circular bell-shaped object surrounding the middle. On arriving at the house, where the
dogs would become frantic with terror and rage at
sight of him, he would stand resting himself for eight
or ten minutes; then in a strange language, which might
have been Hebrew or Sanscrit, for there was no person

learned enough in the country to understand it, he would make a long speech or prayer in a clear ringing voice, intoning his words in a monotonous sing-song. His speech done, he would beg, in broken Spanish, for the usual charity; and, after receiving it, he would commence another address, possibly invoking blessings of all kinds on the donor, and lasting an unconscionable time. Then, bidding a ceremonious farewell, he would take his departure.

From the sound of certain oft-recurring expressions in his recitations we children called him "Con-stair Lo-vair"; perhaps some clever pundit will be able to tell me what these words mean—the only fragment saved of the hermit's mysterious language. It was commonly reported that he had at one period of his life committed some terrible crime, and that, pursued by the phantoms of remorse, he had fled to this distant region, where he would never be met and denounced by any former companion, and had adopted his singular mode of life by way of penance. This was, of course, mere conjecture, for nothing could be extracted from him. When closely questioned or otherwise interfered with, then old Con-stair Lo-vair would show that his long cruel penance had not yet banished the devil from his heart. A terrible wrath would disfigure his countenance and kindle his eyes with demoniac fire; and in sharp ringing tones, that wounded like strokes, he would pour forth a torrent of words in his unknown language, doubtless invoking every imaginable curse on his tormentor.

For upwards of twenty years after I as a small child made his acquaintance he continued faithfully pursuing

his dreary rounds, exposed to cold and rain in winter
and to the more trying heats of summer; until at last
he was discovered lying dead on the plain, wasted by
old age and famine to a mere skeleton, and even in
death still crushed down with that awful burden he had
carried for so many years.   Thus, consistent to the end,
and with his secret untold to any sympathetic human
soul, perished poor old Con-stair Lo-vair, the strangest
of all strange beings I have met with in my journey
through life.

CHAPTER II
My New Home

We quit our old home—A winter day journey—Aspect of
the country—Our new home—A prisoner in the barn—
The plantation—A paradise of rats—An evening scene
—The people of the house—A beggar on horseback—
Mr. Trigg our schoolmaster—His double nature—Imper-
sonates an old woman—Reading Dickens—Mr. Trigg
degenerates—Once more a homeless wanderer on the
great plain.

THE incidents and impressions recorded in the preceding chapter relate, as I have said, to the last year or
two of my five years of life in the place of my birth.
Further back my memory refuses to take me. Some
wonderful persons go back to their second or even their
first year; I can't, and could only tell from hearsay
what I was and did up to the age of three. According
to all accounts, the clouds of glory I brought into the
world—a habit of smiling at everything I looked at and
at every person that approached me—ceased to be vis-
ibly trailed at about that age; I only remember myself as a common little boy—just a little wild animal
running about on its hind legs, amazingly interested in
the world in which it found itself.

Here, then, I begin, aged five, at an early hour on
a bright, cold morning in June—midwinter in that south-

ern country of great plains or pampas; impatiently waiting for the loading and harnessing to be finished; then
the being lifted to the top with the other little ones—at
that time we were five; finally, the grand moment when
the start was actually made with cries and much noise
of stamping and snorting of horses and rattling of
chains. I remember a good deal of that long journey,
which began at sunrise and ended between the lights
some time after sunset; for it was my very first, and I
was going out into the unknown. I remember how,
at the foot of the slope at the top of which the old
home stood, we plunged into the river, and there was
more noise and shouting and excitement until the straining animals brought us safely out on the other side.
Gazing back, the low roof of the house was lost to
view before long, but the trees—the row of twenty-
five giant ombu-trees which gave the place its name—
were visible, blue in the distance, until we were many
miles on our way.

The undulating country had been left behind; before us and on both sides the land, far as one could
see, was absolutely flat, everywhere green with the winter grass, but flowerless at that season, and with the
gleam of water over the whole expanse. It had been
a season of great rains, and much of the flat country
had been turned into shallow lakes. That was all there
was to see, except the herds of cattle and horses and
an occasional horseman galloping over the plain, and
the sight at long distances of a grove or small plantation
of trees, marking the site of an estancia, or sheep and
cattle farm, these groves appearing like islands on the
sea-like flat country. At length this monotonous land-

scape faded and vanished quite away, and the lowing of cattle and tremulous bleating of sheep died out of hearing, so that the last leagues were a blank to me, and I only came back to my senses when it was dark and they lifted me down, so stiff with cold and drowsy that I could hardly stand on my feet.

Next morning I found myself in a new and strange world. The house to my childish eyes appeared of vast size: it consisted of a long range of rooms on the ground, built of brick, with brick floors and roof thatched with rushes. The rooms at one end, fronting the road, formed a store, where the people of the surrounding country came to buy and sell, and what they brought to sell was "the produce of the country"—hides and wool and tallow in bladders, horsehair in sacks, and native cheeses. In return they could purchase anything they wanted—knives, spurs, rings for horse-gear, clothing, yerba maté and sugar; tobacco, castor-oil, salt and pepper, and oil and vinegar, and such furniture as they required—iron pots, spits for roasting, cane-chairs, and coffins. A little distance from the house were the kitchen, bakery, dairy, huge barns for storing the produce, and wood-piles big as houses, the wood being nothing but stalks of the cardoon thistle or wild artichoke, which burns like paper, so that immense quantities had to be collected to supply fuel for a large establishment.

Two of the smallest of us were handed over to the care of a sharp little native boy, aged about nine or ten years, who was told to take us out of the way and keep us amused. The first place he took us to was the great barn, the door of which stood open; it was nearly empty just then, and was the biggest interior I had ever seen; how big it really was I don't know, but it seemed to me about as big as Olympia or the Agricultural Hall, or the Crystal Palace would be to any ordinary little London boy. No sooner were we in this vast place than we saw a strange and startling thing—a man, sitting or crouching on the floor, his hands before him, the wrists tied together, his body bound with thongs of raw hide to a big post which stood in the centre of the floor and supported the beam of the loft above. He was a young man, not more than twenty perhaps, with black hair and a smooth, pale, sallow face. His eyes were cast down, and he paid no attention to us, standing there staring at him, and he appeared to be suffering or ill. After a few moments I shrank away to the door and asked our conductor in a frightened whisper why he was tied up to a post there. Our native boy seemed to be quite pleased at the effect on us, and answered cheerfully that he was a murderer—he had committed a murder somewhere, and had been caught last evening, but as it was too late to take him to the lock-up at the village, which was a long distance away, they had brought him here as the most convenient place, and tied him in the barn to keep him safe. Later on they would come and take him away.

Murder was a common word in those days, but I had not at that time grasped its meaning; I had seen no murder done, nor any person killed in a fight; I only knew that it must be something wicked and horrible. Nevertheless, the shock I had received passed away in the course of that first morning in a new world; but what I had seen in the barn was not forgotten;

the image of that young man tied to the post, his bent head and downward gaze, and ghastly face shaded by lank black hair, is as plain to me now as if I had seen him but yesterday.

A little back from the buildings were gardens and several acres of plantation—both shade and fruit trees. Viewed from the outside, it all looked like an immense poplar grove, on account of the double rows of tall Lombardy poplar trees at the borders. The whole ground, including the buildings, was surrounded by an immense ditch or moat.

Up till now I had lived without trees, with the exception of those twenty-five I have spoken of, which formed a landmark for all the country round; so that this great number—hundreds and thousands—of trees was a marvel and delight. But the plantation and what it was to me will form the subject of a chapter by itself. It was a paradise of rats, as I very soon discovered. Our little native guide and instructor was full of the subject, and promised to let us see the rats with our own eyes as soon as the sun went down; that would finish the day of strange sights with the strangest of all.

Accordingly, when the time came he led us to a spot beyond the barns and wood-piles, where all the offal of slaughtered animals, bones, and unconsumed meats from the kitchen, and rubbish from a wasteful, disorderly establishment, were cast out each day. Here we all sat down in a row on a log among the dead weeds on the border of the evil-smelling place, and he told us to be very still and speak no word; for, said he, unless we move or make a sound the rats will not heed us; they will regard us as so many wooden images. And so it proved, for very soon after the sun had gone down we began to see rats stealing out of the wood-pile and from the dead weeds on every side, all con-verging to that one spot where a generous table was spread for them and for the brown carrion hawks that came by day. Big, old, grey rats with long, scaly tails, others smaller, and smaller still, the least of all being little bigger than mice, until the whole place swarmed with them, all busily hunting for food, feeding, squealing, fighting, and biting. I had not known that the whole world contained so many rats as I now saw congregated before me.

Suddenly our guide jumped up and loudly clapped his hands, which produced a curious effect—a short, sharp little shriek of terror from the busy multitude, followed by absolute stillness, every rat frozen to stone, which lasted for a second or two; then a swift scut-tling away in all directions, vanishing with a rustling sound through the dead grass and wood.

It had been a fine spectacle, and we enjoyed it amaz-ingly; it raised *Mus decumanus* to a beast of immense importance in my mind. Soon he became even more important in an unpleasant way when it was discov-ered that rats were abundant indoors as well as out. The various noises they made at night were terrify-ing; they would run over our beds and sometimes we would wake up to find that one had got in between the sheets and was trying frantically to get out. Then we would yell, and half the house would be roused and imagine some dreadful thing. But when they found out the cause, they would only laugh at and rebuke us for being such poor little cowards.

But what an astonishing place was this to which we had come! The great house and many buildings and the people in it, the foss, the trees that enchanted me, the dirt and disorder, vile rats and fleas and pests of all sorts! The place had been for some years in the hands of a Spanish or native family—indolent, careless, happy-go-lucky people. The husband and wife were never in harmony or agreement about anything for five minutes together, and by and by he would go away to the capital "on business," which would keep him from home for weeks, and even months, at a stretch. And she, with three light-headed, grown-up daughters, would be left to run the establishment with half-a-dozen hired men and women to assist her. I remember her well, as she stayed on a few days in order to hand over the place to us—an excessively fat, inactive woman, who sat most of the day in an easy-chair, surrounded by her pets—lap-dogs, Amazon parrots, and several shrieking parakeets.

Before many days she left, with all her noisy crowd of dogs and birds and daughters, and of the events of the succeeding days and weeks nothing remains in memory except one exceedingly vivid impression—my first sight of a beggar on horseback. It was by no means an uncommon sight in those days when, as the gauchos were accustomed to say, a man without a horse was a man without legs; but it was new to me when one morning I saw a tall man on a tall horse ride up to our gate, accompanied by a boy of nine or ten on a pony. I was struck with the man's singular appearance, sitting upright and stiff in his saddle, staring straight before him. He had long grey hair and beard, and wore a tall straw hat shaped like an inverted flower-pot, with a narrow brim—a form of hat which had lately gone out of fashion among the natives but was still used by a few. Over his clothes he wore a red cloak or poncho, and heavy iron spurs on his feet, which were cased in the *botas de potro,* or long stockings made of a colt's untanned hide.

Arrived at the gate he shouted *Ave Maria purissima* in a loud voice, then proceeded to give an account of himself, informing us that he was a blind man and obliged to subsist on the charity of his neighbours. They in their turn, he said, in providing him with all he required were only doing good to themselves, seeing that those who showed the greatest compassion towards their afflicted fellow-creatures were regarded with special favour by the Powers above.

After delivering himself of all this and much more as if preaching a sermon, he was assisted from his horse and led by the hand to the front door, after which the boy drew back and folding his arms across his breast stared haughtily at us children and the others who had congregated at the spot. Evidently he was proud of his position as page or squire or groom of the important person in the tall straw hat, red cloak, and iron spurs, who galloped about the land collecting tribute from the people and talking loftily about the Powers above.

Asked what he required at our hands the beggar

replied that he wanted yerba maté, sugar, bread, and some hard biscuits, also cut tobacco and paper for cigarettes and some leaf tobacco for cigars. When all these things had been given him, he was asked (not ironically) if there was anything else we could supply him with, and he replied, Yes, he was still in want of rice, flour, and farina, an onion or two, a head or two of garlic, also salt, pepper, and pimento, or red pepper. And when he had received all these comestibles and felt them safely packed in his saddle-bags, he returned thanks, bade good-bye in the most dignified manner, and was led back by the haughty little boy to his tall horse.

We had been settled some months in our new home, and I was just about half way through my sixth year, when one morning at breakfast we children were informed to our utter dismay that we could no longer be permitted to run absolutely wild; that a schoolmaster had been engaged who would live in the house and would have us in the schoolroom during the morning and part of the afternoon.

Our hearts were heavy in us that day, while we waited apprehensively for the appearance of the man who would exercise such a tremendous power over us and would stand between us and our parents, especially our mother, who had ever been our shield and refuge from all pains and troubles. Up till now they had acted on the principle that children were best left to themselves, that the more liberty they had the better it was for them. Now it almost looked as if they were turning against us: but we knew that it could not be so—

we knew that every slightest pain or grief that touched us was felt more keenly by our mother than by ourselves, and we were compelled to believe her when she told us that she, too, lamented the restraint that would be put upon us, but knew that it would be for our ultimate good.

And on that very afternoon the feared man arrived, Mr. Trigg by name, an Englishman, a short, stoutish, almost fat little man, with grey hair, clean-shaved sunburnt face, a crooked nose which had been broken or was born so, clever mobile mouth, and blue-grey eyes with a humorous twinkle in them and crow's-feet at the corners. Only to us youngsters, as we soon discovered, that humorous face and the twinkling eyes were capable of a terrible sternness. He was loved, I think, by adults generally, and regarded with feelings of an opposite nature by children. For he was a schoolmaster who hated and despised teaching as much as children in the wild hated to be taught. He followed teaching because all work was excessively irksome to him, yet he had to do something for a living, and this was the easiest thing he could find to do. How such a man ever came to be so far from home in a half-civilized country was a mystery, but there he was, a bachelor and homeless man after twenty or thirty years on the pampas, with little or no money in his pocket, and no belongings except his horse—he never owned more than one at a time—and its cumbrous native saddle, and the saddle-bags in which he kept his wardrobe and whatever he possessed besides. He didn't own a box. On his horse, with his saddle-bags behind him, he would journey about the land, visiting all the English, Scotch, and

Irish settlers, who were mostly sheep-farmers, but religiously avoiding the houses of the natives. With the natives he could not affiliate, and not properly knowing and incapable of understanding them he regarded them with secret dislike and suspicion. And by and by he would find a house where there were children old enough to be taught their letters, and Mr. Trigg would be hired by the month, like a shepherd or cowherd, to teach them, living with the family. He would go on very well for a time, his failings being condoned for the sake of the little ones; but by and by there would be a falling-out, and Mr. Trigg would saddle his horse, buckle on the saddle-bags, and ride forth over the wide plain in quest of a new home. With us he made an unusually long stay; he liked good living and comforts generally, and at the same time he was interested in the things of the mind, which had no place in the lives of the British settlers of that period; and now he found himself in a very comfortable house, where there were books to read and people to converse with who were not quite like the rude sheep- and cattle-farmers he had been accustomed to live with. He was on his best behaviour, and no doubt strove hard and not unsuccessfully to get the better of his weaknesses. He was looked on as a great acquisition, and made much of; in the school-room he was a tyrant, and having been forbidden to punish us by striking, he restrained himself when to thrash us would have been an immense relief to him. But pinching was not striking, and he would pinch our ears until they almost bled. It was a poor punishment and gave him little satisfaction, but it had to serve.

Out of school his temper would change as by magic. He was then the life of the house, a delightful talker with an inexhaustible fund of good stories, a good reader, mimic, and actor as well.

One afternoon we had a call from a quaint old Scotch dame, in a queer dress, sunbonnet, and spectacles, who introduced herself as the wife of Sandy Maclachlan, a sheep-farmer who lived about twenty-five miles away. It wasn't right, she said, that such near neighbours should not know one another, so she had ridden those few leagues to find out what we were like. Established at the tea-table, she poured out a torrent of talk in broadest Scotch, in her high-pitched cracked old-woman's voice, and gave us an intimate domestic history of all the British residents of the district. It was all about what delightful people they were, and how even their little weaknesses—their love of the bottle, their meannesses, their greed and low cunning—only served to make them more charming. Never was there such a funny old dame or one more given to gossip and scandal-mongering! Then she took herself off, and presently we children, still under her spell, stole out to watch her departure from the gate. But she was not there—she had vanished unaccountably; and by and by what was our astonishment and disgust to hear that the old Scotch body was none other than our own Mr. Trigg! That our needle-sharp eyes, concentrated for an hour on her face, had failed to detect the master who was so painfully familiar to us seemed like a miracle.

Mr. Trigg confessed that play-acting was one of the things he had done before quitting his country; but it was only one of a dozen or twenty vocations which he had taken up at various times, only to drop them again as soon as he made the discovery that they one and all entailed months and even years of hard work if he was ever to fulfil his ambitious desire of doing and being something great in the world. As a reader he certainly was great, and every evening, when the evenings were long, he would give a two hours' reading to the household. Dickens was then the most popular writer in the world, and he usually read Dickens, to the delight of his listeners. Here he could display his histrionic qualities to the full. He impersonated every character in the book, endowing him with voice, gestures, manner, and expression that fitted him perfectly. It was more like a play than a reading.

"What should we do without Mr. Trigg?" our elders were accustomed to say; but we little ones, remembering that it would not be the beneficent countenance of Mr. Pickwick that would look on us in the schoolroom on the following morning, only wished that Mr. Trigg was far, far away.

Perhaps they made too much of him: at all events he fell into the habit of going away every Saturday morning and not returning until the following Monday. His week-end visit was always to some English or Scotch neighbour, a sheep-farmer, ten or fifteen or twenty miles distant, where the bottle or demi-john of white Brazilian rum was always on the table. It was the British exile's only substitute for his dear lost whisky in that far country. At home there was only tea and coffee to drink. From these outings he would return on Monday morning, quite sober and almost too dignified in manner, but with inflamed eyes and (in the schoolroom) the temper of a devil. On one of these occasions, something—our stupidity perhaps, or an exceptionally bad headache—tried him beyond endurance, and taking down his *revenque,* or native horse-whip made of raw hide, from the wall, he began laying about him with such extraordinary fury that the room was quickly in an uproar. Then all at once my mother appeared on the scene, and the tempest was stilled, though the master, with the whip in his uplifted hand, still stood, glaring with rage at us. She stood silent a moment or two, her face very white, then spoke: "Children, you may go and play now. School is over;" then, lest the full purport of her words should not be understood, she added, "Your schoolmaster is going to leave us."

It was an unspeakable relief, a joyful moment; yet on that very day, and on the next before he rode away, I, even I who had been unjustly and cruelly struck with a horsewhip, felt my little heart heavy in me when I saw the change in his face—the dark, still, brooding look, and knew that the thought of his fall and the loss of his home was exceedingly bitter to him. Doubtless my mother noticed it, too, and shed a few compassionate tears for the poor man, once more homeless on the great plain. But he could not be kept after that insane outbreak. To strike their children was to my parents a crime; it changed their nature and degraded them, and Mr. Trigg could not be forgiven.

Mr. Trigg, as I have said before, was a long time

with us, and the happy deliverance I have related did not occur until I was near the end of my eighth year. At the present stage of my story I am not yet six, and the incident related in the following chapter, in which Mr. Trigg figures, occurred when I was within a couple of months of completing my sixth year.

CHAPTER III

Death of an Old Dog

The old dog Cæsar—His powerful personality—Last days and
end—The old dog's burial—The fact of death is brought
home to me—A child's mental anguish—My mother
comforts me—Limitations of the child's mind—Fear of
death—Witnessing the slaughter of cattle—A man in
the moat—Margarita, the nursery maid—Her beauty and
lovableness—Her death—I refuse to see her dead.

WHEN recalling the impressions and experiences of
that most eventful sixth year, the one incident which
looks biggest in memory, at all events in the last half
of that year, is the death of Cæsar. There is nothing
in the past I can remember so well: it was indeed the
most important event of my childhood—the first thing
in a young life which brought the eternal note of sadness in.

It was in the early spring, about the middle of August,
and I can even remember that it was windy weather and
bitterly cold for the time of year, when the old dog was
approaching his end.

Cæsar was an old valued dog, although of no superior breed : he was just an ordinary dog of the country,
short-haired, with long legs and a blunt muzzle. The
ordinary dog or native cur was about the size of a Scotch
collie; Cæsar was quite a third larger, and it was said

of him that he was as much above all other dogs of the house, numbering about twelve or fourteen, in intelligence and courage as in size. Naturally, he was the leader and master of the whole pack, and when he got up with an awful growl, baring his big teeth, and hurled himself on the others to chastise them for quarrelling or any other infringement of dog law, they took it lying down. He was a black dog, now in his old age sprinkled with white hairs all over his body, the face and legs having gone quite grey. Cæsar in a rage, or on guard at night, or when driving cattle in from the plains, was a terrible being; with us children he was mild-tempered and patient, allowing us to ride on his back, just like old Pechicho the sheep-dog, described in the first chapter. Now, in his decline, he grew irritable and surly, and ceased to be our playmate. The last two or three months of his life were very sad, and when it troubled us to see him so gaunt, with his big ribs protruding from his sides, to watch his twitchings when he dozed, groaning and wheezing the while, and marked, too, how painfully he struggled to get up on his feet, we wanted to know why it was so—why we could not give him something to make him well? For answer they would open his great mouth to show us his teeth—the big blunt canines and old molars worn down to stumps. Old age was what ailed him—he was thirteen years old, and that did verily seem to me a great age, for I was not half that, yet it seemed to me that I had been a very, very long time in the world.

No one dreamed of such a thing as putting an end to him—no hint of such a thing was ever spoken. It was not the custom in that country to shoot an old dog because he was past work. I remember his last day, and how often we came to look at him and tried to comfort him with warm rugs and the offer of food and drink where he was lying in a sheltered place, no longer able to stand up. And that night he died: we knew it as soon as we were up in the morning. Then, after breakfast, during which we had been very solemn and quiet, our schoolmaster said: "We must bury him to-day—at twelve o'clock, when I am free, will be the best time; the boys can come with me, and old John can bring his spade." This announcement greatly excited us, for we had never seen a dog buried, and had never even heard of such a thing having ever been done.

About noon that day old Cæsar, dead and stiff, was taken by one of the workmen to a green open spot among the old peach trees, where his grave had already been dug. We followed our schoolmaster and watched while the body was lowered and the red earth shovelled in. The grave was deep, and Mr. Trigg assisted in filling it, puffing very much over the task and stopping at intervals to mop his face with his coloured cotton handkerchief.

Then, when all was done, while we were still standing silently around, it came into Mr. Trigg's mind to improve the occasion. Assuming his schoolroom expression he looked round at us and said solemnly: "That's the end. Every dog has his day and so has every man; and the end is the same for both. We die like old Cæsar, and are put into the ground and have the earth shovelled over us."

Now these simple, common words affected me more than any other words I have heard in my life. They pierced me to the heart. I had heard something terrible—too terrible to think of, incredible—and yet—and yet if it was not so, why had he said it? Was it because he hated us, just because we were children and he had to teach us our lessons, and wanted to torture us? Alas! no, I could not believe that! Was this, then, the horrible fate that awaited us all? I had heard of death—I knew there was such a thing; I knew that all animals had to die, also that some men died. For how could any one, even a child in its sixth year, overlook such a fact, especially in the country of my birth—a land of battle, murder, and sudden death? I had not forgotten the young man tied to the post in the barn who had killed some one, and would perhaps, I had been told, be killed himself as a punishment. I knew, in fact, that there was good and evil in the world, good and bad men, and the bad men—murderers, thieves, and liars—would all have to die, just like animals; but that there was any life after death I did not know. All the others, myself and my own people included, were good and would never taste death. How it came about that I had got no further in my system or philosophy of life I cannot say; I can only suppose that my mother had not yet begun to give me instruction in such matters on account of my tender years, or else that she had done so and that I had understood it in my own way. Yet, as I discovered later, she was a religious woman, and from infancy I had been taught to kneel and say a little prayer each evening: "Now I lay me down to sleep,

I pray the Lord my soul to keep"; but who the Lord was or what my soul was I had no idea. It was just a pretty little way of saying in rhyme that I was going to bed. My world was a purely material one, and a most wonderful world it was, but how I came to be in it I didn't know; I only knew (or imagined) that I would be in it always, seeing new and strange things every day, and never, never get tired of it. In literature it is only in Vaughan, Traherne, and other mystics, that I find any adequate expression of that perpetual rapturous delight in nature and my own existence which I experienced at that period.

And now these never-to-be-forgotten words spoken over the grave of our old dog had come to awaken me from that beautiful dream of perpetual joy!

When I recall this event I am less astonished at my ignorance than at the intensity of the feeling I experienced, the terrible darkness it brought on so young a mind. The child's mind we think, and in fact know, is like that of the lower animals; or if higher than the animal mind, it is not so high as that of the simplest savage. He cannot concentrate his thought—he cannot think at all; his consciousness is in its dawn; he revels in colours, in odours, is thrilled by touch and taste and sound, and is like a well-nourished pup or kitten at play on a green turf in the sunshine. This being so, one would have thought that the pain of the revelation I had received would have quickly vanished—that the vivid impressions of external things would have blotted it out and restored the harmony. But it was not so; the pain continued and increased until it was no longer to be borne; then I sought my mother, first watching until she was alone in her room. Yet when with her I feared to speak lest with a word she should confirm the dreadful tidings. Looking down, she all at once became alarmed at the sight of my face, and began to question me. Then, struggling against my tears, I told her of the words which had been spoken at the old dog's burial, and asked her if it was true, if I—if she—if all of us had to die and be buried in the ground? She replied that it was not wholly true; it was only true in a way, since our bodies had to die and be buried in the earth, but we had an immortal part which could not die. It was true that old Cæsar had been a good, faithful dog, and felt and understood things almost like a human being, and most persons believed that when a dog died he died wholly and had no after-life. We could not know that; some very great, good men had thought differently; they believed that the animals, like us, would live again. That was also her belief—her strong hope; but we could not know for certain, because it had been hidden from us. For ourselves, we knew that we could not really die, because God Himself, who made us and all things, had told us so, and His promise of eternal life had been handed down to us in His Book—in the Bible.

To all this and much more I listened trembling, with a fearful interest, and when I had once grasped the idea that death when it came to me, as it must, would leave me alive after all—that, as she explained, the part of me that really mattered, the myself, the I am I, which knew and considered things, would never perish, I experienced a sudden immense relief. When I went out from her side again I wanted to run and jump for joy and cleave the air like a bird. For I had been in prison and had suffered torture, and was now free again —death would not destroy me!

There was another result of my having unburdened my heart to my mother. She had been startled at the poignancy of the feeling I had displayed, and, greatly blaming herself for having left me too long in that ignorant state, began to give me religious instruction. It was too early, since at that age it was not possible for me to rise to the conception of an immaterial world. That power, I imagine, comes later to the normal child at the age of ten or twelve. To tell him when he is five or six or seven that God is in all places at once and sees all things, only produces the idea of a wonderfully active and quick-sighted person, with eyes like a bird's, able to see what is going on all round. A short time ago I read an anecdote of a little girl who, on being put to bed by her mother, was told not to be afraid in the dark, since God would be there to watch and guard her while she slept. Then, taking the candle, the mother went downstairs; but presently her little girl came down too, in her nightdress, and, when questioned, replied, "I'm going to stay down here in the light, mummy, and you can go up to my room and sit with God." My own idea of God at that time was no higher. I would lie awake thinking of him there in the room, puzzling over the question as to how he could attend to all his numerous affairs and spend so much time looking after me. Lying with my eyes open, I could see nothing in the dark; still, I knew he was there, because I had been told so, and this troubled me. But no sooner would I close my eyes than his image would appear standing at a distance of three or four feet from the head of the bed, in the form of a column five feet high or so and about four feet in circumference. The colour was blue, but varied in depth and intensity; on some nights it was sky-blue, but usually of a deeper shade, a pure, soft, beautiful blue like that of the morning-glory or wild geranium.

It would not surprise me to find that many persons have some such material image or presentment of the spiritual entities they are taught to believe in at too tender an age. Recently, in comparing childish memories with a friend, he told me that he too always saw God as a blue object, but of no definite shape.

That blue column haunted me at night for many months; I don't think it quite vanished, ceasing to be anything but a memory, until I was seven—a date far ahead of where we are now.

To return to that second blissful revelation which came to me from my mother. Happy as it made me to know that death would not put an end to my existence, my state after the first joyful relief was not one of perfect happiness. All she said to comfort and make me brave had produced its effect—I knew now that death was but a change to an even greater bliss than I could have in this life. How could I, not yet six, think otherwise than as she had told me to think, or have a doubt? A mother is more to her child than any other being, human or divine, can ever be to him in his subsequent life. He is as dependent on her as any fledgling in the nest on its parent—even more, since she warms his callow mind or soul as well as body.

Notwithstanding all this, the fear of death came back to me in a little while, and for a long time disquieted me, especially when the fact of death was brought sharply before me. These reminders were only too frequent; there was seldom a day on which I did not see something killed. When the killing was instantaneous, as when a bird was shot and dropped dead like a stone, I was not disturbed; it was nothing but a strange, exciting spectacle, but failed to bring the fact of death home to me. It was chiefly when cattle were slaughtered that the terror returned in its full force. And no wonder! The native manner of killing a cow or bullock at that time was peculiarly painful. Occasionally it would be slaughtered out of sight on the plain, and the hide and flesh brought in by the men, but, as a rule, the beast would be driven up close to the house to save trouble. One of the two or three mounted men engaged in the operation would throw his lasso over the horns, and, galloping off, pull the rope taut; a second man would then drop from his horse, and running up to the animal behind, pluck out his big knife and with two lightning-quick blows sever the tendons of both hind legs. Instantly the beast would go down on his haunches, and the same man, knife in hand, would flit round to its front or side, and, watching his opportunity, presently thrust the long blade into its throat just above the chest, driving it in to the hilt and working it round; then when it was withdrawn a great torrent of blood would pour out from the tortured beast, still standing on his fore-legs, bellowing all the time with agony. At this point the slaughterer would often leap lightly on to its back, stick his spurs in its sides, and, using the flat of his long knife as a whip, pretend to be riding a race, yelling with fiendish glee. The bellowing would subside into deep, awful, sob-like sounds and chokings; then the rider, seeing the animal about to collapse, would fling himself nimbly off. The beast down, they would all run to it, and throwing themselves on its quivering side as on a couch, begin making and lighting their cigarettes.

Slaughtering a cow was grand sport for them, and the more active and dangerous the animal, the more prolonged the fight, the better they liked it; they were as joyfully excited as at a fight with knives or an ostrich hunt. To me it was an awful object-lesson, and held me fascinated with horror. For this was death! The crimson torrents of blood, the deep, human-like cries, made the beast appear like some huge, powerful man caught in a snare by small, weak, but cunning adversaries, who tortured him for their delight and mocked him in his agony.

There were other occurrences about that time to keep the thoughts and fear of death alive. One day a traveller came to the gate, and, after unsaddling his horse, went about sixty or seventy yards away to a shady spot, where he sat down on the green slope of the foss to cool himself. He had been riding many hours in a burning sun, and wanted cooling. He attracted everybody's attention on his arrival by his appearance: middle-aged, with good features and curly brown hair and beard, but huge—one of the biggest men I had ever seen; his weight could not have been under about seventeen stone. Sitting or reclining on the grass, he fell asleep, and rolling down the slope fell with a tremendous splash into the water, which was about six feet deep. So loud was the splash that it was heard by some of the men at work in the barn, and running out to ascertain the cause, they found out what had happened. The man had gone under and did not rise; with a good deal of trouble he was raised up and drawn with ropes to the top of the bank.

I gazed on him lying motionless, to all appearances stone dead—the huge, ox-like man I had seen less than an hour ago, when he had excited our wonder at his great size and strength, and now still in death— dead as old Cæsar under the ground with the grass growing over him! Meanwhile the men who had hauled him out were busy with him, turning him over and rubbing his body, and after about twelve or fifteen minutes there was a gasp and signs of returning life, and by and by he opened his eyes. The dead man was alive again; yet the shock to me was just as great and the effect as lasting as if he had been truly dead.

Another instance which will bring me down to the end of my sixth year and the conclusion of this sad chapter. At this time we had a girl in the house, whose sweet face is one of a little group of half a dozen which I remember most vividly. She was a niece of our shepherd's wife, an Argentine woman married to an Englishman, and came to us to look after the smaller children. She was nineteen years old, a pale, slim, pretty girl, with large dark eyes and abundant black hair. Margarita had the sweetest smile imaginable, the softest voice and gentlest manner, and was so much loved by everybody in the house that she was like one of the family. Unhappily she was consumptive, and after a few months had to be sent back to her aunt. Their little place was only half a mile or so from the house, and every day my mother visited her, doing all that was possible with such skill and remedies as she possessed to give her ease, and providing her with delicacies. The girl did not want a priest to visit her and prepare her for death; she worshipped her mistress, and wished to be of the same faith, and in the end she died a pervert or convert, according to this or that person's point of view.

The day after her death we children were taken to see our beloved Margarita for the last time; but when we arrived at the door, and the others following my mother went in, I alone hung back. They came out and tried to persuade me to enter, even to pull me in, and described her appearance to excite my curiosity. She was lying all in white, with her black hair combed out and loose, on her white bed, with our flowers on her breast and at her sides, and looked very, very beautiful. It was all in vain. To look on Margarita dead was more than I could bear. I was told that only her body of clay was dead— the beautiful body we had come to say good bye to; that her soul—she herself, our loved Margarita—was alive and happy, far, far happier than any person could ever be on this earth; that when her end was near she had smiled very sweetly, and assured them that all fear of death had left her—that God was taking her to Himself. Even this was not enough to **make** me face the awful sight of Margarita dead; the **very** thought of it was an intolerable weight on my heart; but it was not grief that gave me this sensation, much **as** I grieved; it was solely my fear of death.

CHAPTER IV

The Plantation

Living with trees—Winter violets—The house is made
habitable—Red willow—Scissor-tail and carrion-hawk
—Lombardy poplars—Black acacia—Other trees—The
foss or moat—Rats—A trial of strength with an armadillo
—Opossums living with a snake—Alfalfa field and butterflies—Cane brake—Weeds and fennel—Peach trees
in blossom—Paroquets—Singing of a field finch—Concert-singing in birds—Old John—Cow-birds' singing—
Arrival of summer migrants.

I REMEMBER—better than any orchard, grove, or wood
I have ever entered or seen, do I remember that shady
oasis of trees at my new home on the illimitable grassy
plain.   Up till now I had never lived with trees excepting those twenty-five I have told about and that
other one which was called *el arbol* because it was the
only tree of its kind in all the land.   Here there were
hundreds, thousands of trees, and to my childish unaccustomed eyes it was like a great unexplored forest.
There were no pines, firs, nor eucalyptus (unknown in
the country then), nor evergreens of any kind; the
trees being all deciduous were leafless now in mid-
winter, but even so it was to me a wonderful experience to be among them, to feel and smell their rough
moist bark stained green with moss, and to look up at

45

the blue sky through the network of interlacing twigs. And spring with foliage and blossom would be with us by and by, in a month or two; even now in midwinter there was a foretaste of it, and it came to us first as a delicious fragrance in the air at one spot beside a row of old Lombardy poplars—an odour that to the child is like wine that maketh the heart glad to the adult. Here at the roots of the poplars there was a bed or carpet of round leaves which we knew well, and putting the clusters apart with our hands, lo! there were the violets already open—the dim, purple-blue, hidden violets, the earliest, sweetest, of all flowers the most loved by children in that land, and doubtless in many other lands.

There was more than time enough for us small children to feast on violets and run wild in our forest; since for several weeks we were encouraged to live out of doors as far away as we could keep from the house where we were not wanted. For just then great altera-tions were being made to render it habitable: new rooms were being added on to the old building, wooden flooring laid over the old bricks and tiles, and the half-rotten thatch, a haunt of rats and the home of centipedes and of many other hybernating creeping things, was being stripped off to be replaced by a clean healthy wooden roof. For me it was no hardship to be sent away to make my playground in that wooded wonderland. The trees, both fruit and shade, were of many kinds, and belonged to two widely-separated periods. The first were the old trees planted by some tree-loving owner a century or more before our time, and the second the others which had been put in a generation or two later to fill up some gaps and vacant places and for the sake of a greater variety.

The biggest of the old trees, which I shall describe first, was a red willow growing by itself within forty yards of the house. This is a native tree, and derives its specific name *rubra,* as well as its vernacular name, from the reddish colour of the rough bark. It grows to a great size, like the black poplar, but has long narrow leaves like those of the weeping willow. In summer I was never tired of watching this tree, since high up in one of the branches, which in those days seemed to me "so close against the sky," a scissor-tail tyrant-bird always had its nest, and this high open exposed nest was a constant attraction to the common brown carrion-hawk, called *chimango*—a hawk with the carrion-crow's habit of perpetually loitering about in search of eggs and fledglings.

The scissor-tail is one of the most courageous of that hawk-hating, violent-tempered tyrant-bird family, and every time a *chimango* appeared, which was about forty times a day, he would sally out to attack him in mid-air with amazing fury. The marauder driven off, he would return to the tree to utter his triumphant rattling castanet-like notes and (no doubt) to receive the congratulations of his mate; then to settle down again to watch the sky for the appearance of the next *chimango.*

A second red willow was the next largest tree in the plantation, but of this willow I shall have more to say in a later chapter.

The tall Lombardy poplars were the most numerous

of the older trees, and grew in double rows, forming walks or avenues, on three sides of the entire enclosed ground. There was also a cross-row of poplars dividing the gardens and buildings from the plantation, and these were the favourite nesting-trees of two of our best-loved birds—the beautiful little goldfinch or Argentine siskin, and the bird called firewood-gatherer by the natives on account of the enormous collection of sticks which formed the nest.

Between the border poplar walk and the foss outside, there grew a single row of trees of a very different kind—the black acacia, a rare and singular tree, and of all our trees this one made the strongest and sharpest impression on my mind as well as flesh, pricking its image in me, so to speak. It had probably been planted originally by the early first planter, and, I imagine, experimentally, as a possible improvement on the wide-spreading disorderly aloe, a favourite with the first settlers; but it is a wild lawless plant and had refused to make a proper hedge. Some of these acacias had remained small and were like old scraggy bushes, some were dwarfish trees, while others had sprung up like the fabled bean-stalk and were as tall as the poplars that grew side by side with them. These tall specimens had slender boles and threw out their slender horizontal branches of great length on all sides, from the roots to the crown, the branches and the bole itself being armed with thorns two to four inches long, hard as iron, black or chocolate-brown, polished and sharp as needles; and to make itself more formidable every long thorn had two smaller thorns growing out of it near the base, so that it was in shape like a round tapering dagger with a cross-guard to the handle. It was a terrible tree to climb, yet, when a little older, I had to climb it a thousand times, since there were certain birds which would make their nests in it, often as high up as they could, and some of these were birds that laid beautiful eggs, such as those of the Guira cuckoo, the size of pullets' eggs, of the purest turquoise blue flecked with snowy white.

Among our old or ancient trees the peach was the favourite of the whole house on account of the fruit it gave us in February and March, also later, in April and May, when what we called our winter peach ripened. Peach, quince, and cherry were the three favourite fruit-trees in the colonial times, and all three were found in some of the quintas or orchards of the old estancia houses. We had a score of quince trees, with thick gnarled trunks and old twisted branches like rams' horns, but the peach trees numbered about four to five hundred and grew well apart from one another, and were certainly the largest I have ever seen. Their size was equal to that of the oldest and largest cherry trees one sees in certain favoured spots in Southern England, where they grow not in close formation but wide apart with ample room for the branches to spread on all sides.

The trees planted by a later generation, both shade and fruit, were more varied. The most abundant was the mulberry, of which there were many hundreds, mostly in rows, forming walks, and albeit of the same species as our English mulberry they differed from it in the great size and roughness of the leaves and in producing fruit of a much smaller size. The taste of the fruit was also less luscious and it was rarely eaten by our elders. We small children feasted on it, but it was mostly for the birds. The mulberry was looked on as a shade, not a fruit tree, and the other two most important shade trees, in number, were the *acacia blanca*, or false acacia, and the paradise tree or pride of China. Besides these there was a row of eight or ten ailanthus trees, or tree of heaven as it is sometimes called, with tall white smooth trunk crowned with a cluster of palm-like foliage. There was also a modern orchard, containing pear, apple, plum, and cherry trees.

The entire plantation, the buildings included, comprising an area of eight or nine acres, was surrounded by an immense ditch or foss about twelve feet deep and twenty to thirty feet wide. It was undoubtedly very old and had grown in width owing to the crumbling away of the earth at the sides. This in time would have filled and almost obliterated it, but at intervals of two or three years, at a time when it was dry, quantities of earth were dug up from the bottom and thrown on the mound inside. It was in appearance something like a prehistoric earthwork. In winter as a rule it became full of water and was a favourite haunt, especially at night, of flocks of teal, also duck of a few other kinds—widgeon, pintail, and shoveller. In summer it gradually dried up, but a few pools of muddy water usually remained through all the hot season and were haunted by the solitary or summer snipe, one of the many species of sandpiper and birds of that family which bred in the northern hemisphere and wintered with us when it was our summer. Once the water had gone down in the moat, long grass and herbage would spring up and flourish on its sloping sides, and the rats and other small beasties would return and riddle it with innumerable burrows.

The rats were killed down from time to time with the "smoking machine," which pumped the fumes of sulphur, bad tobacco, and other deadly substances into their holes and suffocated them; and I recall two curious incidents during these crusades. One day I was standing on the mound at the side of the moat or foss some forty yards from where the men were at work, when an armadillo bolted from his earth and running to the very spot where I was standing began vigorously digging to escape by burying himself in the soil. Neither men nor dogs had seen him, and I at once determined to capture him unaided by any one and imagined it would prove a very easy task. Accordingly I laid hold of his black bone-cased tail with both hands and began tugging to get him off the ground, but couldn't move him. He went on digging furiously, getting deeper and deeper into the earth, and I soon found that instead of my pulling him out he was pulling me in after him. It hurt my small-boy pride to think that an animal no bigger than a cat was going to beat me in a trial of strength, and this made me hold on more tenaciously than ever and tug and strain more violently, until not to lose him I had to go flat down on the ground. But it was all for nothing: first my hands, then my aching arms were carried down into the earth, and I was forced to release my hold and get up to rid myself of the mould he had been throwing up into my face and all over my head, neck, and shoulders.

In the other case, one of my older brothers seeing the dogs sniffing and scratching at a large burrow, took a spade and dug a couple of feet into the soil and found an adult black-and-white opossum with eight or nine half-grown young lying together in a nest of dry grass, and, wonderful to tell, a large venomous snake coiled up amongst them.   The snake was the dreaded *vivora de la cruz,* as the gauchos call it, a pit-viper of the same family as the fer-de-lance, the bush-master, and the rattlesnake.   It was about three feet long, very thick in proportion, and with broad head and blunt tail.   It came forth hissing and striking blindly right and left when the dogs pulled the opossums out, but was killed with a blow of the spade without injuring the dogs.

This was the first *serpent with a cross* I had seen, and the sight of the thick blunt body of a greenish-grey colour blotched with dull black, and the broad flat head with its stony-white lidless eyes, gave me a thrill of horror.   In after years I became familiar with it and could even venture to pick it up without harm to myself, just as now in England I pick up the less dangerous adder when I come upon one.   The wonder to us was that this extremely irascible and venomous serpent should be living in a nest with a large family of opossums, for it must be borne in mind that the opossum is a rapacious and an exceedingly savage-tempered beast.

This then was the world in which I moved and had my being, within the limits of the old rat-haunted foss among the enchanted trees. But it was not the trees only that made it so fascinating, it had open spaces and other forms of vegetation which were exceedingly attractive too.

There was a field of alfalfa about half an acre in size, which flowered three times a year, and during the flowering time it drew the butterflies from all the surrounding plain with its luscious bean-like fragrance, until the field was full of them, red, black, yellow, and white butterflies, fluttering in flocks round every blue spike.

Canes, too, in a large patch or "brake" as we called it, grew at another spot; a graceful plant about twenty-five feet high, in appearance unlike the bamboo, as the long pointed leaves were of a glaucous blue-green colour. The canes were valuable to us as they served as fishing-rods when we were old enough for that sport, and were also used as lances when we rode forth to engage in mimic battles on the plain. But they also had an economic value, as they were used by the natives when making their thatched roofs as a substitute for the bamboo cane, which cost much more as it had to be imported from other countries. Accordingly at the end of the summer, after the cane had flowered, they were all cut down, stripped of their leaves, and taken away in bundles, and we were then deprived till the following season of the pleasure of hunting for the tallest and straightest canes to cut them down and strip off leaves and bark to make beautiful green polished rods for our sports.

There were other open spaces covered with a vegetation almost as interesting as the canes and the trees: this was where what were called "weeds" were allowed to flourish. Here were the thorn-apple, chenopodium, sow-thistle, wild mustard, redweed, viper's bugloss, and others, both native and introduced, in dense thickets five or six feet high. It was difficult to push one's way through these thickets, and one was always in dread of treading on a snake. At another spot fennel flourished by itself, as if it had some mysterious power, perhaps its peculiar smell, of keeping other plants at a proper distance. It formed quite a thicket, and grew to a height of ten or twelve feet. This spot was a favourite haunt of mine, as it was in a waste place at the furthest point from the house, a wild solitary spot where I could spend long hours by myself watching the birds. But I also loved the fennel for itself, its beautiful green feathery foliage and the smell of it, also the taste, so that whenever I visited that secluded spot I would rub the crushed leaves in my palms and chew the small twigs for their peculiar fennel flavour.

Winter made a great change in the plantation, since it not only stripped the trees of their leaves but swept away all that rank herbage, the fennel included, allowing the grass to grow again. The large luxuriantly-growing annuals also disappeared from the garden and all about the house, the big four-o'clock bushes with deep red stems and wealth of crimson blossoms, and the morning-glory convolvulus with its great blue trumpets, climbing over and covering every available place with its hop-like mass of leaves and abundant blooms. My life in the plantation in winter was a constant watching for spring. May, June, and July were the leafless months, but not wholly songless. On any genial and windless day of sunshine in winter a few swallows would reappear, nobody could guess from where, to spend the bright hours wheeling like house-martins about the house, revisiting their old breeding-holes under the eaves, and uttering their lively little rippling songs, as of water running in a pebbly stream. When the sun declined they would vanish, to be seen no more until we had another perfect spring-like day.

On such days in July and on any mild misty morning, standing on the mound within the moat I would listen to the sounds from the wide open plain, and they were sounds of spring—the constant drumming and rhythmic cries of the spur-wing lapwings engaged in their social meetings and "dances," and the song of the pipit soaring high up and pouring out its thick prolonged strains as it slowly floated downwards to the earth.

In August the peach blossomed. The great old trees standing wide apart on their grassy carpet, barely touching each other with the tips of their widest branches, were like great mound-shaped clouds of exquisite rosy-pink blossoms. There was then nothing in the universe which could compare in loveliness to that spectacle. I was a worshipper of trees at this season, and I remember my shocked and indignant feeling when one day a flock of green paroquets came screaming down and alighted on one of the trees near me. This paroquet never bred in our plantation; they were occasional visitors from their home in an old grove about nine miles away, and their visits were always a great pleasure to us. On this occasion I was particularly glad, because the birds had elected to settle on a tree close to where I was standing. But the blossoms thickly covering every twig annoyed the parrots, as they could not find space enough to grasp a twig without grasping its flower as well; so what did the birds do in their impatience but begin stripping the blossoms off the branches on which they were perched with their sharp beaks, so rapidly that the flowers came down in a pink shower, and in this way in half a minute every bird made a twig bare where he could sit perched at ease. There were millions of blossoms; only one here and there would ever be a peach, yet it vexed me to see the parrots cut them off in that heedless way: it was a desecration, a crime even in a bird.

Even now when I recall the sight of those old flowering peach trees, with trunks as thick as a man's body, and the huge mounds or clouds of myriads of roseate blossoms seen against the blue ethereal sky, I am not sure that I have seen anything in my life more perfectly beautiful. Yet this great beauty was but half the charm I found in these trees: the other half was in the bird-music that issued from them. It was the music of but one kind of bird, a small greenish yellow field finch, in size like the linnet though with a longer and slimmer body, and resembling a linnet too in its general habits. Thus, in autumn it unites in immense flocks, which keep together during the winter months and sing in concert and do not break up until the return of the breeding season. In a country where there were no bird-catchers or human persecutors of small birds, the flocks of this finch, called *Misto* by the natives, were far larger than any linnet flocks ever seen in England. The flock we used to have about our plantation numbered many thousands, and you would see them like a cloud wheeling about in the air, then suddenly dropping and vanishing from sight in the grass, where they fed on small seeds and tender leaves and buds. On going to the spot they would rise with a loud humming sound of innumerable wings, and begin rushing and whirling about again, chasing each other in play and chirping, and presently all would drop to the ground again.

In August, when the spring begins to infect their blood, they repair to the trees at intervals during the day, where they sit perched and motionless for an hour or longer, all singing together. This singing time was when the peach trees were in blossom, and it was invariably in the peach trees they settled and could be seen, the little yellow birds in thousands amid the millions of pink blossoms, pouring out their wonderful music.

One of the most delightful bird sounds or noises to be heard in England is the concert-singing of a flock of several hundreds, and sometimes of a thousand or more linnets in September and October, and even later in the year, before these great congregations have been broken up or have migrated. The effect produced by the small field finch of the pampas was quite different. The linnet has a little twittering song with breaks in it and small chirping sounds, and when a great multitude of birds sing together the sound at a distance of fifty or sixty yards is as of a high wind among the trees, but on a nearer approach the mass of sound resolves itself into a tangle of thousands of individual sounds, resembling that of a great concourse of starlings at roosting time, but more musical in character. It is as if hundreds of fairy minstrels were all playing on stringed and wind instruments of various forms, every one intent on his own performance without regard to the others.

The field finch does not twitter or chirp and has no break or sudden change in his song, which is composed of a series of long-drawn notes, the first somewhat throaty but growing clearer and brighter towards the end, so that when thousands sing together it is as if they sang in perfect unison, the effect on the hearing being like that on the sight of flowing water or of rain when the multitudinous falling drops appear as silvery-grey lines on the vision. It is an exceedingly beautiful effect, and so far as I know unique among birds that have the habit of singing in large companies.

I remember that we had a carpenter in those days, an Englishman named John, a native of Cumberland, who used to make us laugh at his slow heavy way when, after asking him some simple question, we had to wait until he put down his tools and stared at us for about twenty seconds before replying. One of my elder brothers had dubbed him the "Cumberland boor." I remember one day on going to listen to the choir of finches in the blossoming orchard, I was surprised to see John standing near the trees doing nothing, and as I came up to him he turned towards me with a look which astonished me on his dull old face—that look which perhaps one of my readers has by chance seen on the face of a religious mystic in a moment of exaltation. "Those little birds! I never heard anything like it!" he exclaimed, then trudged off to his work. Like most Englishmen, he had, no doubt, a vein of poetic feeling hidden away somewhere in his soul.

We also had the other kind of concert-singing by another species in the plantation. This was the common purple cow-bird, one of the Troupial family, exclusively American, but supposed to have affinities with the starlings of the Old World. This cow-bird is parasitical (like the European cuckoo) in its breeding habits, and having no domestic affairs of its own to attend to it lives in flocks all the year round, leading an idle vagabond life. The male is of a uniform deep purple-black, the female a drab or mouse-colour. The cow-birds were excessively numerous among the trees in summer, perpetually hunting for nests in which to deposit their eggs: they fed on the ground out on the plain and were often in such big flocks as to look like a huge black carpet spread out on the green sward. On a rainy day they did not feed: they congregated on the trees in thousands and sang by the hour. Their favourite gathering-place at such times was behind the house, where the trees grew pretty thick and were sheltered on two sides by the black acacias and double rows of Lombardy poplars, succeeded by double rows of large mulberry trees, forming walks, and these by pear, apple and cherry trees. From whichever side the wind blew it was calm here, and during the heaviest rain the birds would sit here in their thousands, pouring out a continuous torrent of song, which resembled the noise produced by thousands of starlings at roosting-time, but was louder and differed somewhat in character owing to the peculiar song of the cow-bird, which begins with hollow guttural sounds, followed by a burst of loud clear ringing notes.

These concert-singers, the little green and yellow field finch and the purple cow-bird, were with us all the year round, with many others which it would take a whole chapter to tell of. When, in July and August, I watched for the coming spring, it was the migrants, the birds that came annually to us from the far north, that chiefly attracted me. Before their arrival the bloom was gone from the peach trees, and the choir of countless little finches broken up and scattered all over the plain. Then the opening leaves were watched, and after the willows the first and best-loved were the poplars. During all the time they were opening, when they were still a yellowish-green in colour, the air was full of the fragrance, but not satisfied with that I would crush and rub the new small leaves in my hands and on my face to get the delicious balsamic smell in fuller measure. And of all the trees, after the peach, the poplars appeared to feel the new season with the greatest intensity, for it seemed to me that they felt the sunshine even as I did, and they expressed it in their fragrance just as the peach and other trees did in their flowers. And it was also expressed in the new sound they gave out to the wind. The change was really wonderful when the rows on rows of immensely tall trees which for months had talked and cried in that strange sibilant language, rising to shrieks when a gale was blowing, now gave out a larger volume of sound, more continuous, softer, deeper, and like the wash of the sea on a wide shore.

The other trees would follow, and by and by all would be in full foliage once more, and ready to receive their strange beautiful guests from the tropical forests in the distant north.

The most striking of the newcomers was the small scarlet tyrant-bird, which is about the size of our spotted flycatcher; all a shining scarlet except the black wings and tail. This bird had a delicate bell-like voice, but it was the scarlet colour shining amid the green foliage which made me delight in it above all other birds. Yet the humming-bird, which arrived at the same time, was wonderfully beautiful too, especially when he flew close to your face and remained suspended motionless on mist-like wings for a few moments, his feathers looking and glittering like minute emerald scales.

Then came other tyrant-birds and the loved swallows —the house-swallow, which resembles the English house-martin, the large purple martin, the *Golodrina domestica,* and the brown tree-martin. Then, too, came the yellow-billed cuckoo—the *kowe-kowe* as it is called from its cry. Year after year I listened for its deep mysterious call, which sounded like *gow-gow-gow-gow-gow,* in late September, even as the small English boy listens for the call of *his* cuckoo in April; and the human-like character of the sound, together with the startlingly impressive way in which it was enunciated, always produced the idea that it was something more than a mere bird call. Later, in October when the weather was hot, I would hunt for the nest, a frail platform made of a few sticks with four or five oval eggs like those of the turtledove in size and of a pale green colour.

There were other summer visitors, but I must not speak of them as this chapter contains too much on that subject. My feathered friends were so much to me that I am constantly tempted to make this sketch of my first years a book about birds and little else. There remains, too, much more to say about the plantation, the trees and their effect on my mind, also some adventures I met with, some with birds and others with snakes, which will occupy two or three or more chapters later on.

CHAPTER V
Aspects of the Plain

Appearance of a green level land—Cardoon and giant thistles
—Villages of the Vizcacha, a large burrowing rodent—
Groves and plantations seen like islands on the wide
level plains—Trees planted by the early colonists—
Decline of the colonists from an agricultural to a pastoral
people—Houses as part of the landscape—Flesh diet
of the gauchos—Summer change in the aspect of the
plain—The water-like mirage—The giant thistle and a
"thistle year"—Fear of fires—An incident at a fire—
The *pampero*, or south-west wind, and the fall of the
thistles—Thistle-down and thistle-seed as food for
animals—A great pampero storm—Big hailstones—
Damage caused by hail—Zango, an old horse, killed—
Zango and his master.

As a small boy of six but well able to ride bare-backed
at a fast gallop without falling off, I invite the reader,
mounted too, albeit on nothing but an imaginary animal,
to follow me a league or so from the gate to some spot
where the land rises to a couple or three or four feet
above the surrounding level. There, sitting on our
horses, we shall command a wider horizon than even the
tallest man would have standing on his own legs, and in
this way get a better idea of the district in which ten
of the most impressionable years of my life, from five
to fifteen, were spent.

We see all round us a flat land, its horizon a perfect ring of misty blue colour where the crystal-blue dome of the sky rests on the level green world. Green in late autumn, winter, and spring, or say from April to November, but not all like a green lawn or field: there were smooth areas where sheep had pastured, but the surface varied greatly and was mostly more or less rough. In places the land as far as one could see was covered with a dense growth of cardoon thistles, or wild artichoke, of a bluish or grey-green colour, while in other places the giant thistle flourished, a plant with big variegated green and white leaves, and standing when in flower six to ten feet high.

There were other breaks and roughnesses on that flat green expanse caused by the *vizcachas,* a big rodent the size of a hare, a mighty burrower in the earth. *Vizcachas* swarmed in all that district where they have now practically been exterminated, and lived in villages, called *vizcacheras,* composed of thirty or forty huge burrows—about the size of half a dozen badgers' earths grouped together. The earth thrown out of these diggings formed a mound, and being bare of vegetation it appeared in the landscape as a clay-coloured spot on the green surface. Sitting on a horse one could count a score to fifty or sixty of these mounds or *vizcacheras* on the surrounding plain.

On all this visible earth there were no fences, and no trees excepting those which had been planted at the old estancia houses, and these being far apart the groves and plantations looked like small islands of trees, or mounds, blue in the distance, on the great plain or pampa. They were mostly shade trees, the commonest being the Lombardy poplar, which of all trees is the easiest one to grow in that land. And these trees at the estancias or cattle-ranches were, at the time I am writing about, almost invariably aged and in many instances in an advanced state of decay. It is interesting to know how these old groves and plantations ever came into existence in a land where at that time there was practically no tree-planting.

The first colonists who made their homes in this vast vacant space, called the pampas, came from a land where the people are accustomed to sit in the shade of trees, where corn and wine and oil are supposed to be necessaries, and where there is salad in the garden. Naturally they made gardens and planted trees, both for shade and fruit, wherever they built themselves a house on the pampas, and no doubt for two or three generations they tried to live as people live in Spain, in the rural districts. But now the main business of their lives was cattle-raising, and as the cattle roamed at will over the vast plains and were more like wild than domestic animals, it was a life on horseback. They could no longer dig or plough the earth or protect their crops from insects and birds and their own animals. They gave up their oil and wine and bread and lived on flesh alone. They sat in the shade and ate the fruit of trees planted by their fathers or their great-grandfathers until the trees died of old age, or were blown down or killed by the cattle, and there was no more shade and fruit.

It thus came about that the Spanish colonists on the pampas declined from the state of an agricultural people to that of an exclusively pastoral and hunting one; and later, when the Spanish yoke, as it was called, was shaken off, the incessant throat-cutting wars of the various factions, which were like the wars of "crows and pies," except that knives were used instead of beaks, confirmed and sunk them deeper in their wild and barbarous manner of life.

Thus, too, the tree-clumps on the pampas were mostly remains of a vanished past. To these clumps or plantations we shall return later on when I come to describe the home life of some of our nearest neighbours; here the houses only, with or without trees growing about them, need be mentioned as parts of the landscape. The houses were always low and scarcely visible at a distance of a mile and a half: one always had to stoop on entering a door. They were built of burnt or unburnt brick, more often clay and brushwood, and thatched with sedges or bulrushes. At some of the better houses there would be a small garden, a few yards of soil protected in some way from the poultry and animals, in which a few flowers and herbs were grown, especially parsley, rue, sage, tansy, and horehound. But there was no other cultivation attempted, and no vegetables were eaten except onions and garlic, which were bought at the stores, with bread, rice, maté tea, oil, vinegar, raisins, cinnamon, pepper, cummin seed, and whatever else they could afford to season their meat-pies or give a flavour to the monotonous diet of cow's flesh and mutton and pig. Almost the only game eaten was ostrich, armadillo, and tinamou (the partridge of the country), which the boys could catch by snaring or running them down. Wild duck, plover, and such birds they rarely or never tasted, as they could not shoot; and as to the big rodent, the vizcacha, which swarmed everywhere, no gaucho would touch its flesh, although to my taste it was better than rabbit.

The summer change in the aspect of the plain would begin in November: the dead dry grass would take on a yellowish-brown colour, the giant thistle a dark rust brown, and at this season, from November to February, the grove or plantation at the estancia house, with its deep fresh unchanging verdure and shade, was a veritable refuge on the vast flat yellow earth. It was then, when the water-courses were gradually drying up and the thirsty days coming to flocks and herds, that the mocking illusion of the mirage was constantly about us. Quite early in spring, on any warm cloudless day, this water-mirage was visible, and was like the appearance on a hot summer's day of the atmosphere in England when the air near the surface becomes visible, when one sees it dancing before one's eyes, like thin wavering and ascending tongues of flame—crystal-clear flames mixed with flames of a faint pearly or silver grey. On the level and hotter pampas this appearance is intensified, and the faintly visible wavering flames change to an appearance of lakelets or sheets of water looking as if ruffled by the wind and shining like molten silver in the sun. The resemblance to water is increased when there are groves and buildings on the horizon, which look like dark blue islands or banks in the distance, while the cattle and horses feeding not far from the spectator appear to be wading knee or belly deep in the brilliant water.

The aspect of the plain was different in what was

called a "thistle year," when the giant thistles, which usually occupied definite areas or grew in isolated patches, suddenly sprang up everywhere, and for a season covered most of the land. In these luxuriant years the plants grew as thick as sedges and bulrushes in their beds, and were taller than usual, attaining a height of about ten feet. The wonder was to see a plant which throws out leaves as large as those of the rhubarb, with its stems so close together as to be almost touching. Standing among the thistles in the growing season one could in a sense *hear* them growing, as the huge leaves freed themselves with a jerk from a cramped position, producing a crackling sound. It was like the crackling sound of the furze seed-vessels which one hears in June in England, only much louder.

To the gaucho who lives half his day on his horse and loves his freedom as much as a wild bird, a thistle year was a hateful period of restraint. His small, low-roofed, mud house was then too like a cage to him, as the tall thistles hemmed it in and shut out the view on all sides. On his horse he was compelled to keep to the narrow cattle track and to draw in or draw up his legs to keep them from the long pricking spines. In those distant primitive days the gaucho if a poor man was usually shod with nothing but a pair of iron spurs.

By the end of November the thistles would be dead, and their huge hollow stalks as dry and light as the shaft of a bird's feather—a feather-shaft twice as big round as a broomstick and six to eight feet long. The roots were not only dead but turned to dust in the ground, so that one could push a stalk from its place with one finger, but it would not fall since it was held up by scores of other sticks all round it, and these by hundreds more, and the hundreds by thousands and millions. The thistle dead was just as great a nuisance as the thistle living, and in this dead dry condition they would sometimes stand all through December and January when the days were hottest and the danger of fire was ever present to people's minds. At any moment a careless spark from a cigarette might kindle a dangerous blaze. At such times the sight of smoke in the distance would cause every man who saw it to mount his horse and fly to the danger-spot, where an attempt would be made to stop the fire by making a broad path in the thistles some fifty to a hundred yards ahead of it. One way to make the path was to lasso and kill a few sheep from the nearest flock and drag them up and down at a gallop through the dense thistles until a broad space was clear where the flames could be stamped and beaten out with horse-rugs. But sheep to be used in this way were not always to be found on the spot, and even when a broad space could be made, if a hot north wind was blowing it would carry showers of sparks and burning sticks to the other side and the fire would travel on.

I remember going to one of these big fires when I was about twelve years old. It broke out a few miles from home and was travelling in our direction; I saw my father mount and dash off, but it took me half an hour or more to catch a horse for myself, so that I arrived late on the scene. A fresh fire had broken out a quarter of a mile in advance of the main one, where most of the men were fighting the flames; and to this spot I went first, and found some half a dozen neighbours who had just arrived on the scene. Before we started operations about twenty men from the main fire came galloping up to us. They had made their path, but seeing this new fire so far ahead, had left it in despair after an hour's hard hot work, and had flown to the new danger spot. As they came up I looked in wonder at one who rode ahead, a tall black man in his shirt sleeves who was a stranger to me. "Who is this black fellow, I wonder?" said I to myself, and just then he shouted to me in English, "Hullo, my boy, what are you doing here?" It was my father; an hour's fighting with the flames in a cloud of black ashes in that burning sun and wind had made him look like a pure-blooded negro!

During December and January when this desert world of thistles dead and dry as tinder continued standing, a menace and danger, the one desire and hope of every one was for the *pampero*—the south-west wind, which in hot weather is apt to come with startling suddenness, and to blow with extraordinary violence. And it would come at last, usually in the afternoon of a close hot day, after the north wind had been blowing persistently for days with a breath as from a furnace. At last the hateful wind would drop and a strange gloom that was not from any cloud would cover the sky; and by and by a cloud would rise, a dull dark cloud as of a mountain becoming visible on the plain at an enormous distance. In a little while it would cover half the sky, and there would be thunder and lightning and a torrent of rain, and at the same moment the wind would strike and

roar in the bent-down trees and shake the house.
And in an hour or two it would perhaps be all over,
and next morning the detested thistles would be gone,
or at all events levelled to the ground.

After such a storm the sense of relief to the horseman, now able to mount and gallop forth in any direction over the wide plain and see the earth once more
spread out for miles before him, was like that of a
prisoner released from his cell, or of the sick man, when
he at length repairs his vigour lost and breathes and
walks again.

To this day it gives me a thrill, or perhaps it would
be safer to say the ghost of a vanished thrill, when
I remember the relief it was in my case, albeit I was
never so tied to a horse, so parasitical, as the gaucho,
after one of these great thistle-levelling *pampero* winds.
It was a rare pleasure to ride out and gallop my horse
over wide brown stretches of level land, to hear his
hard hoofs crushing the hollow desiccated stalks covering the earth in millions like the bones of a countless
host of perished foes. It was a queer kind of joy, a
mixed feeling with a dash of gratified revenge to give
it a sharp savour.

After all this abuse of the giant thistle, the *Cardo
asnal* of the natives and *Carduus mariana* of the
botanists, it may sound odd to say that a "thistle
year" was a blessing in some ways. It was an
anxious year on account of the fear of fire, and a
season of great apprehension too when reports of
robberies and other crimes were abroad in the land,
especially for the poor women who were left so much
alone in their low-roofed hovels, shut in by the dense

prickly growth. But a thistle year was called a fat year, since the animals—cattle, horses, sheep, and even pigs—browsed freely on the huge leaves and soft sweet-ish-tasting stems, and were in excellent condition. The only drawbacks were that the riding-horses lost strength as they gained in fat, and cow's milk didn't taste nice.

The best and fattest time would come when the hardening plant was no longer fit to eat and the flowers began to shed their seed. Each flower, in size like a small coffee-cup, would open out in a white mass and shed its scores of silvery balls, and these when freed of heavy seed would float aloft in the wind, and the whole air as far as one could see would be filled with millions and myriads of floating balls. The fallen seed was so abundant as to cover the ground under the dead but still standing plants. It is a long, slender seed, about the size of a grain of Carolina rice, of a greenish or bluish-grey colour, spotted with black. The sheep feasted on it, using their mobile and extensible upper lips like a crumb-brush to gather it into their mouths. Horses gathered it in the same way, but the cattle were out of it, either because they could not learn the trick, or because their lips and tongues cannot be used to gather a crumb-like food. Pigs, however, flourished on it, and to birds, domestic and wild, it was even more than to the mammals.

In conclusion of this chapter I will return for a page or two to the subject of the *pampero,* the south-west wind of the Argentine pampas, to describe the greatest of all the great *pampero* storms I have witnessed. This was when I was in my seventh year.

The wind blowing from this quarter is not like the south-west wind of the North Atlantic and Britain, a warm wind laden with moisture from hot tropical seas —that great wind which Joseph Conrad in his *Mirror of the Sea* has personified in one of the sublimest passages in recent literature. It is an excessively violent wind, as all mariners know who have encountered it on the South Atlantic off the River Plate, but it is cool and dry, although it frequently comes with great thunder-clouds and torrents of rain and hail. The rain may last half-an-hour to half-a-day, but when over the sky is without a vapour and a spell of fine weather ensues.

It was in sultry summer weather, and towards evening all of us boys and girls went out for a ramble on the plain, and were about a quarter of a mile from home when a blackness appeared in the south-west, and began to cover the sky in that quarter so rapidly that, taking alarm, we started homewards as fast as we could run. But the stupendous slaty-black darkness, mixed with yellow clouds of dust, gained on us, and before we got to the gate the terrified screams of wild birds reached our ears, and glancing back we saw multitudes of gulls and plover flying madly before the storm, trying to keep ahead of it. Then a swarm of big dragon-flies came like a cloud over us, and was gone in an instant, and just as we reached the gate the first big drops splashed down in the form of liquid mud. We had hardly got indoors before the tempest broke in its full fury, a blackness as of night, a blended uproar of thunder and wind, blinding flashes of lightning, and torrents of rain. Then as the first thick darkness began to pass away, we saw that the air was white with falling hailstones of an extraordinary size and appearance. They were big as fowls' eggs, but not egg-shaped: they were flat, and about half-an-inch thick, and being white, looked like little blocks or bricklets made of compressed snow. The hail continued falling until the earth was white with them, and in spite of their great size they were driven by the furious wind into drifts two or three feet deep against the walls of the buildings.

It was evening and growing dark when the storm ended, but the light next morning revealed the damage we had suffered. Pumpkins, gourds, and water-melons were cut to pieces, and most of the vegetables, including the Indian corn, were destroyed. The fruit trees, too, had suffered greatly. Forty or fifty sheep had been killed outright, and hundreds more were so much hurt that for days they went limping about or appeared stupefied from blows on the head. Three of our heifers were dead, and one horse—an old loved riding-horse with a history, old Zango—the whole house was in grief at his death! He belonged originally to a cavalry officer who had an extraordinary affection for him—a rare thing in a land where horseflesh was too cheap, and men as a rule careless of their animals and even cruel. The officer had spent years in the Banda Oriental, in guerilla warfare, and had ridden Zango in every fight in which he had been engaged. Coming back to Buenos Ayres he brought the old horse home with him. Two or three years later he came to my father, whom he had come to know very well, and said he had been ordered to the upper provinces and was in great trouble about his horse. He was twenty years old, he said, and no longer fit to be ridden in a fight; and of all the people he knew there was but one man in whose care he wished to leave his horse. I know, he said, that if you will take him and promise to care for him until his old life ends, he will be safe; and I should be happy about him—as happy as I can be without the horse I have loved more than any other being on earth. My father consented, and had kept the old horse for over nine years when he was killed by the hail. He was a well-shaped dark brown animal, with long mane and tail, but, as I knew him, always lean and old-looking, and the chief use he was put to was for the children to take their first riding-lessons on his back.

My parents had already experienced one great sadness on account of Zango before his strange death. For years they had looked for a letter, a message, from the absent officer, and had often pictured his return and joy at finding alive still and embracing his beloved old friend again. But he never returned, and no message came and no news could be heard of him, and it was at last concluded that he had lost his life in that distant part of the country, where there had been much fighting.

To return to the hailstones. The greatest destruction had fallen on the wild birds. Before the storm immense numbers of golden plover had appeared and were in large flocks on the plain. One of our native boys rode in and offered to get a sackful of plover for the table, and getting the sack he took me up on his horse behind him. A mile or so from home we came upon scores of dead plover lying together where they had been in close flocks, but my companion would not pick up a dead bird. There were others running about with one wing broken, and these he went after, leaving me to hold his horse, and catching them would wring their necks and drop them in the sack. When he had collected two or three dozen he remounted and we rode back.

Later that morning we heard of one human being, a boy of six, in one of our poor neighbours' houses, who had lost his life in a curious way. He was standing in the middle of the room, gazing out at the falling hail, when a hailstone, cutting through the thatched roof, struck him on the head and killed him instantly.

CHAPTER VI

Some Bird Adventures

Visit to a river on the pampas—A first long walk—Water-
fowl—My first sight of flamingoes—A great dove visi-
tation—Strange tameness of the birds—Vain attempts
at putting salt on their tails—An ethical question:
When is a lie not a lie?—The carancho, a vulture-eagle
—Our pair of caranchos—Their nest in a peach tree—
I am ambitious to take their eggs—The birds' crimes—
I am driven off by the birds—The nest pulled down.

JUST before my riding days began in real earnest, when
I was not yet quite confident enough to gallop off alone
for miles to see the world for myself, I had my first
long walk on the plain. One of my elder brothers
invited me to accompany him to a water-course, one of
the slow-flowing shallow marshy rivers of the pampas
which was but two miles from home. The thought of
the half-wild cattle we would meet terrified me, but he
was anxious for my company that day and assured me
that he could see no herd in that direction and he would
be careful to give a wide berth to anything with horns
we might come upon. Then I joyfully consented and
we set out, three of us, to survey the wonders of a
great stream of running water, where bulrushes grew
and large wild birds, never seen by us at home, would

be found. I had had a glimpse of the river before, as, when driving to visit a neighbour, we had crossed it at one of the fords and I had wished to get down and run on its moist green low banks, and now that desire would be gratified. It was for me a tremendously long walk, as we had to take many a turn to avoid the patches of cardoon and giant thistles, and by and by we came to low ground where the grass was almost waist-high and full of flowers. It was all like an English meadow in June, when every grass and every herb is in flower, beautiful and fragrant, but tiring to a boy six years old to walk through. At last we came out to a smooth grass turf, and in a little while were by the stream, which had overflowed its banks owing to recent heavy rains and was now about fifty yards wide. An astonishing number of birds were visible—chiefly wild duck, a few swans, and many waders—ibises, herons, spoonbills, and others, but the most wonderful of all were three immensely tall white-and-rose-coloured birds, wading solemnly in a row a yard or so apart from one another some twenty yards out from the bank. I was amazed and enchanted at the sight, and my delight was intensified when the leading bird stood still and, raising his head and long neck aloft, opened and shook his wings. For the wings when open were of a glorious crimson colour, and the bird was to me the most angel-like creature on earth.

What were these wonderful birds? I asked of my brothers, but they could not tell me. They said they had never seen birds like them before, and later I found that the flamingo was not known in our neighbourhood as the water-courses were not large enough for it, but that it could be seen in flocks at a lake less than a day's journey from our home.

It was not for several years that I had an opportunity of seeing the bird again; later I have seen it scores and hundreds of times, at rest or flying, at all times of the day and in all states of the atmosphere, in all its most beautiful aspects, as when at sunset or in the early morning it stands motionless in the still water with its clear image reflected below; or when seen flying in flocks—seen from some high bank beneath one—moving low over the blue water in a long crimson line or half moon, the birds at equal distances apart, their wingtips all but touching; but the delight in these spectacles has never equalled in degree that which I experienced on this occasion when I was six years old.

The next little bird adventure to be told exhibits me more in the character of an innocent and exceedingly credulous baby of three than of a field naturalist of six with a considerable experience of wild birds.

One spring day an immense number of doves appeared and settled in the plantation. It was a species common in the country and bred in our trees, and in fact in every grove or orchard in the land—a pretty dove-coloured bird with a pretty sorrowful song, about a third less in size than the domestic pigeon, and belongs to the American genus *Zenaida*. This dove was a resident with us all the year round, but occasionally in spring and autumn they were to be seen travelling in immense flocks, and these were evidently strangers in the land and came from some sub-tropical country in the north where they had no fear of the human form. At all events, on going out into the plantation I

found them all about on the ground, diligently searching for seeds, and so tame and heedless of my
presence that I actually attempted to capture them
with my hands. But they wouldn't be caught: the
bird when I stooped and put out my hands slipped
away, and flying a yard or two would settle down
in front of me and go on looking for and picking up
invisible seeds.

My attempts failing I rushed back to the house,
wildly excited, to look for an old gentleman who lived
with us and took an interest in me and my passion for
birds, and finding him I told him the whole place was
swarming with doves and they were perfectly tame but
wouldn't let me catch them—could he tell me how to
catch them? He laughed and said I must be a little
fool not to know how to catch a bird. The only way
was to put salt on their tails. There would be no difficulty in doing that, I thought, and how delighted I
was to know that birds could be caught so easily! Off
I ran to the salt-barrel and filled my pockets and hands
with coarse salt used to make brine in which to dip
the hides; for I wanted to catch a great many doves—
armfuls of doves.

In a few minutes I was out again in the plantation,
with doves in hundreds moving over the ground all
about me and taking no notice of me. It was a joyful
and exciting moment when I started operations, but I
soon found that when I tossed a handful of salt at the
bird's tail it never fell on its tail—it fell on the ground
two or three or four inches short of the tail. If, I
thought, the bird would only keep still a moment longer!
But then it wouldn't, and I think I spent quite two

hours in these vain attempts to make the salt fall on the right place. At last I went back to my mentor to confess that I had failed and to ask for fresh instructions, but all he would say was that I was on the right track, that the plan I had adopted was the proper one, and all that was wanted was a little more practice to enable me to drop the salt on the right spot. Thus encouraged I filled my pockets again and started afresh, and then finding that by following the proper plan I made no progress I adopted a new one, which was to take a handful of salt and hurl it at the bird's tail. Still I couldn't touch the tail; my violent action only frightened the bird and caused it to fly away, a dozen yards or so, before dropping down again to resume its seed-searching business.

By-and-by I was told by somebody that birds could not be caught by putting salt on their tails; that I was being made a fool of, and this was a great shock to me, since I had been taught to believe that it was wicked to tell a lie. Now for the first time I discovered that there were lies and lies, or untruths that were not lies, which one could tell innocently although they were invented and deliberately told to deceive. This angered me at first, and I wanted to know how I was to distinguish between real lies and lies that were not lies, and the only answer I got was that I could distinguish them by not being a fool!

In the next adventure to be told we pass from the love (or tameness) of the turtle to the rage of the vulture. It may be remarked in passing that the vernacular name of the dove I have described is *Torcasa,* which I take it is a corruption of *Tortola,* the name first given to it by the early colonists on account of its slight resemblance to the turtle-dove of Europe.

Then, as to the vulture, it was not a true vulture nor a strictly true eagle, but a carrion-hawk, a bird the size of a small eagle, blackish brown in colour with a white neck and breast suffused with brown and spotted with black; also it had a very big eagle-shaped beak, and claws not so strong as an eagle's nor so weak as a vulture's. In its habits it was both eagle and vulture, as it fed on dead flesh, and was also a hunter and killer of animals and birds, especially of the weakly and young. A somewhat destructive creature to poultry and young sucking lambs and pigs. Its feeding habits were, in fact, very like those of the raven, and its voice, too, was raven-like, or rather like that of the carrion-crow at his loudest and harshest. Considering the character of this big rapacious bird, the *Polyborus tharus* of naturalists and the *carancho* of the natives, it may seem strange that a pair were allowed to nest and live for years in our plantation, but in those days people were singularly tolerant not only of injurious birds and beasts but even of beings of their own species of predaceous habits.

On the outskirts of our old peach orchard, described in a former chapter, there was a solitary tree of a somewhat singular shape, standing about forty yards from the others on the edge of a piece of waste weedy land. It was a big old tree like the others, and had a smooth round trunk standing about fourteen feet high and throwing out branches all round, so that its upper part had the shape of an open inverted umbrella. And

in the convenient hollow formed by the circle of
branches the *caranchos* had built their huge nest, composed of sticks, lumps of turf, dry bones of sheep and
other animals, pieces of rope and raw hide, and any
other object they could carry. The nest was their
home; they roosted in it by night and visited it at
odd times during the day, usually bringing a bleached
bone or thistle-stalk or some such object to add to
the pile.

Our birds never attacked the fowls, and were not
offensive or obtrusive, but kept to their own end of
the plantation furthest away from the buildings. They
only came when an animal was killed for meat, and
would then hang about, keeping a sharp eye on the
proceedings and watching their chance. This would
come when the carcass was dressed and lights and
other portions thrown to the dogs; then the *carancho*
would swoop down like a kite, and snatching up the
meat with his beak would rise to a height of twenty
or thirty yards in the air, and dropping his prize would
deftly catch it again in his claws and soar away to feed
on it at leisure. I was never tired of admiring this
feat of the *carancho,* which is, I believe, unique in
birds of prey.

The big nest in the old inverted-umbrella-shaped
peach tree had a great attraction for me; I used often
to visit it and wonder if I would ever have the power
of getting up to it. Oh, what a delight it would be
to get up there, above the nest, and look down into
the great basin-like hollow lined with sheep's wool and
see the eggs, bigger than turkey's eggs, all marbled
with deep red, or creamy white splashed with blood-

red! For I had seen *carancho* eggs brought in by a gaucho, and I was ambitious to take a clutch from a nest with my own hands. It was true I had been told by my mother that if I wanted wild birds' eggs I was never to take more than one from a nest, unless it was of some injurious species. And injurious the *carancho* certainly was, in spite of his good behaviour when at home. On one of my early rides on my pony I had seen a pair of them, and I think they were our own birds, furiously attacking a weak and sickly ewe; she had refused to lie down to be killed, and they were on her neck, beating and tearing at her face and trying to pull her down. Also I had seen a litter of little pigs a sow had brought forth on the plain attacked by six or seven *caranchos,* and found on approaching the spot that they had killed half of them (about six, I think), and were devouring them at some distance from the old pig and the survivors of the litter. But how could I climb the tree and get over the rim of the huge nest? And I was afraid of the birds, they looked so unspeakably savage and formidable whenever I went near them. But my desire to get the eggs was over-mastering, and when it was spring and I had reason to think that eggs were being laid, I went oftener than ever to watch and wait for an opportunity. And one evening just after sunset I could not see the birds anywhere about and thought my chance had now come. I managed to swarm up the smooth trunk to the branches, and then with wildly beating heart began the task of trying to get through the close branches and to work my way over the huge rim of the nest. Just then I heard the harsh grating cry of the bird, and peering through the leaves in the direction it came from I caught sight of the two birds flying furiously towards me, screaming again as they came nearer. Then terror seized me, and down I went through the branches, and catching hold of the lowest one managed to swing myself clear and dropped to the ground. It was a good long drop, but I fell on a soft turf, and springing to my feet fled to the shelter of the orchard and then on towards the house, without ever looking back to see if they were following.

That was my only attempt to raid the nest, and from that time the birds continued in peaceful possession of it, until it came into some person's mind that this huge nest was detrimental to the tree, and was the cause of its producing so little fruit compared with any other tree, and the nest was accordingly pulled down, and the birds forsook the place.

In the description in a former chapter of our old peach trees in their blossoming time I mentioned the paroquets which occasionally visited us but had their breeding-place some distance away. This bird was one of the two common parrots of the district, the other larger species being the Patagonian parrot, *Conarus patagonus,* the *Loro barranquero* or Cliff Parrot of the natives. In my early years this bird was common on the treeless pampas extending for hundreds of miles south of Buenos Ayres as well as in Patagonia, and bred in holes it excavated in cliffs and steep banks at the side of lakes and rivers. These breeding-sites were far south of my home, and I did not visit them until my boyhood's days were over.

In winter these birds had a partial migration to the

north: at that season we were visited by flocks, and as a child it was a joy to me when the resounding screams of the travelling parrots, heard in the silence long before the birds became visible in the sky, announced their approach. Then, when they appeared flying at a moderate height, how strange and beautiful they looked, with long pointed wings and long graduated tails, in their sombre green plumage touched with yellow, blue, and crimson colour! How I longed for a nearer acquaintance with these winter visitors and hoped they would settle on our trees! Sometimes they did settle to rest, perhaps to spend half a day or longer in the plantation; and sometimes, to my great happiness, a flock would elect to remain with us for whole days and weeks, feeding on the surrounding plain, coming at intervals to the trees during the day, and at night to roost. I used to go out on my pony to follow and watch the flock at feed, and wondered at their partiality for the bitter-tasting seeds of the wild pumpkin. This plant, which was abundant with us, produced an egg-shaped fruit about half the size of an ostrich's egg, with a hard shell-like rind, but the birds with their sharp iron-hard beaks would quickly break up the dry shell and feast on the pips, scattering the seed-shells about till the ground was whitened with them. When I approached the feeding flock on my pony the birds would rise up and, flying to and at me, hover in a compact crowd just above my head, almost deafening me with their angry screams.

The smaller bird, the paroquet, which was about the size of a turtle-dove, had a uniform rich green colour above and ashy-grey beneath, and, like most

parrots, it nested in trees.   It is one of the most social
birds I know; it lives all the year round in communi-
ties and builds huge nests of sticks near together as in
a rookery, each nest having accommodation for two or
three to half-a-dozen pairs.   Each pair has an entrance
and nest cavity of its own in the big structure.

The only breeding-place in our neighbourhood was
in a grove or remains of an ancient ruined plantation
at an estancia house, about nine miles from us, owned
by an Englishman named Ramsdale.   Here there was
a colony of about a couple of hundred birds, and the
dozen or more trees they had built on were laden with
their great nests, each one containing as much material
as would have filled a cart.

Mr. Ramsdale was not our nearest English neighbour—the one to be described in another chapter; nor
was he a man we cared much about, and his meagre
establishment was not attractive, as his old slatternly
native housekeeper and the other servants were allowed
to do just what they liked.   But he was English and
a neighbour, and my parents made it a point of paying
him an occasional visit, and I always managed to go
with them—certainly not to see Mr. Ramsdale, who
had nothing to say to a shy little boy and whose hard
red face looked the face of a hard drinker.   *My* visits
were to the paroquets exclusively.   Oh, why, thought
I many and many a time, did not these dear green
people come over to us and have their happy village
in our trees!   Yet when I visited them they didn't
like it; no sooner would I run out to the grove where
the nests were than the place would be in an uproar.
Out and up they would rush, to unite in a flock and

hover shrieking over my head, and the commotion would last until I left them.

On our return late one afternoon in early spring from one of our rare visits to Mr. Ramsdale, we witnessed a strange thing. The plain at that place was covered with a dense growth of cardoon-thistle or wild artichoke, and leaving the estancia house in our trap, we followed the cattle tracks as there was no road on that side. About half-way home we saw a troop of seven or eight deer in an open green space among the big grey thistle-bushes, but instead of uttering their whistling alarm-cry and making off at our approach they remained at the same spot, although we passed within forty yards of them. The troop was composed of two bucks engaged in a furious fight, and five or six does walking round and round the two fighters. The bucks kept their heads so low down that their noses were almost touching the ground, while with their horns locked together they pushed violently, and from time to time one would succeed in forcing the other ten or twenty feet back. Then a pause, then another violent push, then with horns still together they would move sideways, round and round, and so on until we left them behind and lost sight of them.

This spectacle greatly excited us at the time and was vividly recalled several months afterwards when one of our gaucho neighbours told us of a curious thing he had just seen. He had been out on that cardoon-covered spot where we had seen the fighting deer, and at that very spot in the little green space he had come upon the skeletons of two deer with their horns interlocked.

Tragedies of this kind in the wild animal world have often been recorded, but they are exceedingly rare on the pampas, as the smooth few-pronged antlers of the native deer, *corvus campestris,* are not so liable to get hopelessly locked as in many other species.

Deer were common in our district in those days, and were partial to land overgrown with cardoon thistle, which in the absence of trees and thickets afforded them some sort of cover. I seldom rode to that side without getting a sight of a group of deer, often looking exceedingly conspicuous in their bright fawn colour as they stood gazing at the intruder amidst the wide waste of grey cardoon bushes.

These rough plains were also the haunt of the rhea, our ostrich, and it was here that I first had a close sight of this greatest and most unbird-like bird of our continent. I was eight years old then, when one afternoon in late summer I was just setting off for a ride on my pony, when I was told to go out on the east side till I came to the cardoon-covered land about a mile beyond the shepherd's ranch. The shepherd was wanted in the plantation and could not go to the flock just yet, and I was told to look for the flock and turn it towards home.

I found the flock just where I had been told to look for it, the sheep very widely scattered, and some groups of a dozen or two to a hundred were just visible at a distance among the rough bushes. Just where these furthest sheep were grazing there was a scattered troop of seventy or eighty horses grazing too, and when I rode to that spot I all at once found myself among a lot of rheas, feeding too among the sheep and horses.

Their grey plumage being so much like the cardoon
bushes in colour had prevented me from seeing them
before I was right among them.

The strange thing was that they paid not the slightest
attention to me, and pulling up my pony I sat staring
in astonishment at them, particularly at one, a very
big one and nearest to me, engaged in leisurely pecking
at the clover plants growing among the big prickly
thistle leaves, and as it seemed carefully selecting the
best sprays.

What a great noble-looking bird it was and how beautiful in its loose grey-and-white plumage, hanging like
a picturesquely-worn mantle about its body! Why
were they so tame? I wondered. The sight of a
mounted gaucho, even at a great distance, will invariably set them off at their topmost speed; yet here
I was within a dozen yards of one of them, with
several others about me, all occupied in examining the
herbage and selecting the nicest-looking leaves to pluck,
just as if I was not there at all! I suppose it was
because I was only a small boy on a small horse
and was not associated in the ostrich brain with the
wild-looking gaucho on his big animal charging upon
him with a deadly purpose. Presently I went straight
at the one near me, and he then raised his head
and neck and moved carelessly away to a distance
of a few yards, then began cropping the clover once
more. I rode at him again, putting my pony to a
trot, and when within two yards of him he all at
once swung his body round in a quaint way towards
me, and breaking into a sort of dancing trot brushed
past me.

Pulling up again and looking back I found he was ten or twelve yards behind me, once more quietly engaged in cropping clover leaves!

Again and again this bird, and one of the others I rode at, practised the same pretty trick, first appearing perfectly unconcerned at my presence and then, when I made a charge at them, with just one little careless movement placing themselves a dozen yards behind me.

But this same trick of the rhea is wonderful to see when the hunted bird is spent with running and is finally overtaken by one of the hunters who has perhaps lost the bolas with which he captures his quarry, and who endeavours to place himself side by side with it so as to reach it with his knife. It seems an easy thing to do: the bird is plainly exhausted, panting, his wings hanging, as he lopes on, yet no sooner is the man within striking distance than the sudden motion comes into play, and the bird as by a miracle is now behind instead of at the side of the horse. And before the horse going at top speed can be reined in and turned round, the rhea has had time to recover his wind and get a hundred yards away or more. It is on account of this tricky instinct of the rhea that the gauchos say, "El avestruz es el mas *gaucho* de los animales," which means that the ostrich, in its resourcefulness and the tricks it practises to save itself when hard pressed, is as clever as the gaucho knows himself to be.

CHAPTER VII

My First Visit to Buenos Ayres

Happiest time—First visit to the Capital—Old and New
Buenos Ayres—Vivid impressions—Solitary walk—
How I learnt to go alone—Lost—The house we stayed
at and the sea-like river—Rough and narrow streets—
Rows of posts—Carts and noise—A great church festival
—Young men in black and scarlet—River scenes—
Washerwomen and their language—Their word-fights
with young fashionables—Night watchmen—A young
gentleman's pastime—A fishing dog—A fine gentleman
seen stoning little birds—A glimpse of Don Eusebio,
the Dictator's fool.

THE happiest time of my boyhood was at that early
period, a little past the age of six, when I had my
own pony to ride on, and was allowed to stay on his
back just as long and go as far from home as I liked.
I was like the young bird when on first quitting the
nest it suddenly becomes conscious of its power to
fly. My early flying days were, however, soon inter-
rupted, when my mother took me on my first visit to
Buenos Ayres; that is to say, the first I remember,
as I must have been taken there once before as an
infant in arms, since we lived too far from town for
any missionary-clergyman to travel all that distance
just to baptize a little baby. Buenos Ayres is now
the wealthiest, most populous, Europeanized city in

South America: what it was like at that time these glimpses into a far past will serve to show. Coming as a small boy of an exceptionally impressionable mind, from that green plain where people lived the simple pastoral life, everything I saw in the city impressed me deeply, and the sights which impressed me the most are as vivid in my mind to-day as they ever were. I was a solitary little boy in my rambles about the streets, for though I had a younger brother who was my only playmate, he was not yet five, and too small to keep me company in my walks. Nor did I mind having no one with me. Very, very early in my boyhood I had acquired the habit of going about alone to amuse myself in my own way, and it was only after years, when my age was about twelve, that my mother told me how anxious this singularity in me used to make her. She would miss me when looking out to see what the children were doing, and I would be called and searched for, to be found hidden away somewhere in the plantation. Then she began to keep an eye on me, and when I was observed stealing off she would secretly follow and watch me, standing motionless among the tall weeds or under the trees by the half-hour, staring at vacancy. This distressed her very much; then to her great relief and joy she discovered that I was there with a motive which she could understand and appreciate: that I was watching some living thing, an insect perhaps, but oftener a bird—a pair of little scarlet flycatchers building a nest of lichen on a peach tree, or some such beautiful thing. And as she loved all living things herself she was quite satisfied that I was not going queer in my head, for that was what she had been fearing.

The strangeness of the streets was a little too much for me at the start, and I remember that on first venturing out by myself a little distance from home I got lost. In despair of ever finding my way back I began to cry, hiding my face against a post at a street corner, and was there soon surrounded by quite a number of passers-by; then a policeman came up, with brass buttons on his blue coat and a sword at his side, and taking me by the arm he asked me in a commanding voice where I lived—the name of the street and the number of the house. I couldn't tell him; then I began to get frightened on account of his sword and big black moustache and loud rasping voice, and suddenly ran away, and after running for about six or eight minutes found myself back at home, to my surprise and joy.

The house where we stayed with English friends was near the front, or what was then the front, that part of the city which faced the Plata river, a river which was like the sea, with no visible shore beyond; and like the sea it was tidal, and differed only in its colour, which was a muddy red instead of blue or green. The house was roomy, and like most of the houses at that date had a large courtyard paved with red tiles and planted with small lemon trees and flowering shrubs of various kinds. The streets were straight and narrow, paved with round boulder stones the size of a football, the pavements with brick or flagstones, and so narrow they would hardly admit of more than two persons walking abreast. Along the pavements on each side of the street were rows of posts placed at a distance of ten yards apart. These strange-looking rows of posts, which foreigners laughed to see, were no doubt the remains of yet ruder times, when ropes of hide were stretched along the side of the pavements to protect the foot-passengers from runaway horses, wild cattle driven by wild men from the plains, and other dangers of the narrow streets. As they were then paved the streets must have been the noisiest in the world, on account of the immense numbers of big springless carts in them. Imagine the thunderous racket made by a long procession of these carts, when they were returning empty, and the drivers, as was often the case, urged their horses to a gallop, and they bumped and thundered over the big round stones!

Just opposite the house we stayed at there was a large church, one of the largest of the numerous churches of the city, and one of my most vivid memories relates to a great annual festival at the church—that of the patron saint's day. It had been open to worshippers all day, but the chief service was held about three o'clock in the afternoon; at all events it was at that hour when a great attendance of fashionable people took place. I watched them as they came in couples, families and small groups, in every case the ladies, beautifully dressed, attended by their cavaliers. At the door of the church the gentleman would make his bow and withdraw to the street before the building, where a sort of outdoor gathering was formed of all those who had come as escorts to the ladies, and where they would remain until the service was over. The crowd in the street grew and grew until there were about four or five hundred gentlemen, mostly young, in the gathering, all standing in small groups, conversing in an animated way, so that the street was filled with the loud humming sound of their blended voices. These men were all natives, all of the good or upper class of the native society, and all dressed exactly alike in the fashion of that time. It was their dress and the uniform appearance of so large a number of persons, most of them with young, handsome, animated faces, that fascinated me and kept me on the spot gazing at them until the big bells began to thunder at the conclusion of the service and the immense concourse of gaily-dressed ladies swarmed out, and immediately the meeting broke up, the gentlemen hurrying back to meet them.

They all wore silk hats and the glossiest black broadcloth, not even a pair of trousers of any other shade was seen; and all wore the scarlet silk or fine cloth waistcoat which, at that period, was considered the right thing for every citizen of the republic to wear; also, in lieu of buttonhole, a scarlet ribbon pinned to the lapel of the coat. It was a pretty sight, and the concourse reminded me of a flock of military starlings, a black or dark-plumaged bird with a scarlet breast, one of my feathered favourites.

My rambles were almost always on the front, since I could walk there a mile or two from home, north or south, without getting lost, always with the vast expanse of water on one hand, with many big ships looking dim in the distance, and numerous lighters or belanders coming from them with cargoes of merchandise which they unloaded into carts, these going out a quarter of a mile in the shallow water to meet them. Then there were the water-carts going and coming in scores and hundreds, for at that period there was no water supply to the houses, and every house-holder had to buy muddy water by the bucket at his own door from the watermen.

One of the most attractive spots to me was the congregating place of the *lavanderas,* south of my street. Here on the broad beach under the cliff one saw a whiteness like a white cloud, covering the ground for a space of about a third of a mile; and the cloud, as one drew near, resolved itself into innumerable garments, sheets and quilts, and other linen pieces, fluttering from long lines, and covering the low rocks washed clean by the tide and the stretches of green turf between. It was the spot where the washerwomen were allowed to wash all the dirty linen of Buenos Ayres in public. All over the ground the women, mostly negresses, were seen on their knees, beside the pools among the rocks, furiously scrubbing and pound-ing away at their work, and like all negresses they were exceedingly vociferous, and their loud gabble, mingled with yells and shrieks of laughter, reminded me of the hubbub made by a great concourse of gulls, ibises, god-wits, geese, and other noisy water-fowl on some marshy lake. It was a wonderfully animated scene, and drew me to it again and again: I found, however, that it was necessary to go warily among these women, as they looked with suspicion at idling boys, and sometimes, when I picked my way among the spread garments, I was sharply ordered off. Then, too, they often quarrelled over their right to certain places and spaces among themselves; then very suddenly their hilarious gabble would change to wild cries of anger and torrents of abuse. By and by I discovered that their greatest rages and worst language were when certain young gentlemen of the upper classes visited the spot to amuse themselves by baiting the *lavanderas*. The young gentleman would saunter about in an absent-minded manner and presently walk right on to a beautifully embroidered and belaced nightdress or other dainty garment spread out to dry on the sward or rock, and, standing on it, calmly proceed to take out and light a cigarette. Instantly the black virago would be on her feet confronting him and pouring out a torrent of her foulest expressions and deadliest curses. He, in a pretended rage, would reply in even worse language. That would put her on her mettle; for now all her friends and foes scattered about the ground would suspend their work to listen with all their ears; and the contest of words growing louder and fiercer would last until the combatants were both exhausted and unable to invent any more new and horrible expressions of opprobrium to hurl at each other. Then the insulted young gentleman would kick the garment away in a fury and hurling the unfinished cigarette in his adversary's face would walk off with his nose in the air.

I laugh to recall these unseemly word-battles on the beach, but they were shocking to me when I first heard them as a small, innocent-minded boy, and it only made the case worse when I was assured that the young gentleman was only acting a part, that the extreme anger he exhibited, which might have served as an excuse for using such language, was all pretence.

Another favourite pastime of these same idle, rich young gentlemen offended me as much as the one I have related. The night-watchmen, called *Serenos,* of that time interested me in an extraordinary way. When night came it appeared that the fierce policemen, with their swords and brass buttons, were no longer needed to safeguard the people, and their place in the streets was taken by a quaint, frowsy-looking body of men, mostly old, some almost decrepit, wearing big cloaks and carrying staffs and heavy iron lanterns with a tallow candle alight inside. But what a pleasure it was to lie awake at night and listen to their voices calling the hours! The calls began at the stroke of eleven, and then from beneath the window would come the wonderful long drawling call of *Las ón—ce han dá—do y se —ré—no,* which means eleven of the clock and all serene, but if clouded the concluding word would be *nu— blá—do,* and so on, according to the weather. From all the streets, from all over the town, the long-drawn calls would float to my listening ears, with infinite variety in the voices—the high and shrill, the falsetto, the harsh, raucous note like the caw of the carrion crow, the solemn, booming bass, and then some fine, rich, pure voice that soared heavenwards above all the others and was like the pealing notes of an organ.

I loved the poor night-watchmen and their cries, and it grieved my little soft heart to hear that it was considered fine sport by the rich young gentlemen to sally forth at night and do battle with them, and to deprive them of their staffs and lanterns, which they took home and kept as trophies.

Another human phenomenon which annoyed and shocked my tender mind, like that of the contests on the beach between young gentlemen and washerwomen, was the multitude of beggars which infested the town. These were not like our dignified beggar on horseback, with his red poncho, spurs and tall staw hat, who rode to your gate, and having received his tribute, blessed you and rode away to the next estancia. These city beggars on the pavement were the most brutal, even fiendish, looking men I had ever seen. Most of them were old soldiers, who, having served their ten, fifteen, or twenty years, according to the nature of the crime for which they had been condemned to the army, had been discharged or thrown out to live like carrion-hawks on what they could pick up. Twenty times a day at least you would hear the iron gate opening from the courtyard into the street swung open, followed by the call or shout of the beggar demanding charity in the name of God. Outside you could not walk far without being confronted by one of these men, who would boldly square himself in front of you on the narrow pavement and beg for alms. If you had no change and said, *"Perdon, por Dios,"* he would scowl and let you pass; but if you looked annoyed or disgusted, or ordered him out of the way, or pushed by without a word, he would glare at you with a concentrated rage which seemed to say, "Oh, to have you down at my mercy, bound hand and foot, a sharp knife in my hand!" And this would be followed by a blast of the most horrible language.

One day I witnessed a very strange thing, the action of a dog, by the waterside. It was evening and the beach was forsaken; cartmen, fishermen, boatmen all gone, and I was the only idler left on the rocks; but the tide was coming in, rolling quite big waves on to the rocks, and the novel sight of the waves, the freshness, the joy of it, kept me at that spot, standing on one of the outermost rocks not yet washed over by the water. By and by a gentleman, followed by a big dog, came down on to the beach and stood at a distance of forty or fifty yards from me, while the dog bounded forward over the flat, slippery rocks and through pools of water until he came to my side, and sitting on the edge of the rock began gazing intently down at the water. He was a big, shaggy, round-headed animal, with a greyish coat with some patches of light reddish colour on it; what his breed was I cannot say, but he looked somewhat like a sheep-dog or an otter-hound. Suddenly he plunged in, quite disappearing from sight, but quickly reappeared with a big shad of about three and a half or four pounds' weight in his jaws. Climbing on to the rock he dropped the fish, which he did not appear to have injured much, as it began floundering about in an exceedingly lively manner. I was astonished and looked back at the dog's master; but there he stood in the same place, smoking and paying no attention to what his animal was doing. Again the dog plunged in and brought out a second big fish and dropped it on the flat rock, and again and again he dived, until there were five big shads all floundering about on the wet rock and likely soon to be washed back into the water.

The shad is a common fish in the Plata and the best to eat of all its fishes, resembling the salmon in its rich flavour, and is eagerly watched for when it comes up from the sea by the Buenos Ayres fishermen, just as our fishermen watch for mackerel on our coasts. But on this evening the beach was deserted by every one, watchers included, and the fish came and swarmed along the rocks, and there was no one to catch them— not even some poor hungry idler to pounce upon and carry off the five fishes the dog had captured. One by one I saw them washed back into the water, and presently the dog, hearing his master whistling to him, bounded away.

For many years after this incident I failed to find any one who had even seen or heard of a dog catching fish. Eventually, in reading I met with an account of fishing-dogs in Newfoundland and other countries.

One other strange adventure met with on the front remains to be told. It was about eleven o'clock in the morning and I was on the parade, walking north, pausing from time to time to look over the sea-wall to watch the flocks of small birds that came to feed on the beach below. Presently my attention was drawn to a young man walking on before me, pausing and peering too from time to time over the wall, and when he did so throwing something at the small birds. I ran on and overtook him, and was rather taken aback at his wonderfully fine appearance. He was like one of the gentlemen of the gathering before the church, described a few pages back, and wore a silk hat and fashionable black coat and trousers and scarlet silk waistcoat; he was also a remarkably handsome young gentleman, with a golden-brown curly beard and moustache and dark liquid eyes that studied my face with a half-amused curiosity when I looked up at him. In one hand he carried a washleather bag by its handle, and holding a pebble in his right hand he watched the birds, the small parties of crested song sparrows, yellow house sparrows, siskins, field finches, and other kinds, and from time to time he would hurl a pebble at the bird he had singled out forty yards down below us on the rocks. I did not see him actually hit a bird, but his precision was amazing, for almost invariably the missile, thrown from such a distance at so minute an object, appeared to graze the feathers and to miss killing by but a fraction of an inch.

I followed him for some distance, my wonder and curiosity growing every minute to see such a superior-looking person engaged in such a pastime. For it is a fact that the natives do not persecute small birds. On the contrary, they despise the aliens in the land who shoot and trap them. Besides, if he wanted small birds for any purpose, why did he try to get them by throwing pebbles at them? As he did not order me off, but looked in a kindly way at me every little while, with a slight smile on his face, I at length ventured to tell him that he would never get a bird that way—that it would be impossible at that distance to hit one with a small pebble. "Oh, no, not impossible," he returned, smiling and walking on, still with an eye on the rocks. "Well, you haven't hit one yet," I was bold enough to say, and at that he stopped, and putting his finger and thumb in his waistcoat pocket he pulled out a dead male siskin and put it in my hands.

This was the bird called "goldfinch" by the English resident in La Plata, and to the Spanish it is also goldfinch; it is, however, a siskin, *Chrysomitris magellanica,* and has a velvet-black head, the rest of its plumage being black, green, and shining yellow. It was one of my best-loved birds, but I had never had one in my hand, dead or alive, before, and now its wonderful unimagined loveliness, its graceful form, and the exquisitely pure flower-like yellow hue affected me with a delight so keen that I could hardly keep from tears.

After gloating a few moments over it, touching it with my finger-tips and opening the little black and gold wings, I looked up pleadingly and begged him to let me keep it. He smiled and shook his head: he would not waste his breath talking; all his energy was to be spent in hurling pebbles at other lovely little birds.

"Oh, señor, will you not give it to me?" I pleaded still; and then, with sudden hope, "Are you going to sell it?"

He laughed, and taking it from my hand put it back in his waistcoat pocket; then, with a pleasant smile and a nod to say that the interview was now over, he went on his way.

Standing on the spot where he left me, and still bitterly regretting that I had failed to get the bird, I watched him until he disappeared from sight in the distance, walking towards the suburb of Palermo; and a mystery he remains to this day, the one and only Argentine gentleman, a citizen of the Athens of South America, amusing himself by killing little birds with pebbles. But I do not know that it was an amusement. He had perhaps in some wild moment made a vow to kill so many siskins in that way, or a bet to prove his skill in throwing a pebble; or he might have been practising a cure for some mysterious deadly malady, prescribed by some wandering physician from Bagdad or Ispaham; or, more probable still, some heartless, soulless woman he was in love with had imposed this fantastical task on him.

Perhaps the most wonderful thing I saw during that first eventful visit to the capital was the famed Don Eusebio, the court jester or fool of the President or Dictator Rosas, the "Nero of South America," who lived in his palace at Palermo, just outside the city. I had been sent with my sisters and little brother to spend the day at the house of an Anglo-Argentine family in another part of the town, and we were in the large courtyard playing with the children of the house when some one opened a window above us and called out, "Don Eusebio!" That conveyed nothing to me, but the little boys of the house knew what it meant; it meant that if we went quickly out to the street we might catch a glimpse of the great man in all his glory. At all events, they jumped up, flinging their toys away, and rushed to the street door, and we after them. Coming out we found quite a crowd of lookers-on, and then down the street, in his general's dress—for it was one of the Dictator's little jokes to make his fool a general—all scarlet, with a big scarlet three-cornered hat surmounted by an immense aigrette of scarlet plumes, came Don Eusebio. He marched along with tremendous dignity, his sword at his side, and twelve soldiers, also in scarlet, his bodyguard, walking six on each side of him with drawn swords in their hands.

We gazed with joyful excitement at this splendid spectacle, and it made it all the more thrilling when one of the boys whispered in my ear that if any person in the crowd laughed or made any insulting or rude remark, he would be instantly cut to pieces by the guard. And they looked truculent enough for anything.

The great Rosas himself I did not see, but it was something to have had this momentary sight of General Eusebio, his fool, on the eve of his fall after a reign of over twenty years, during which he proved himself one of the bloodiest as well as the most original-minded of the Caudillos and Dictators, and altogether, perhaps, the greatest of those who have climbed into power in this continent of republics and revolutions.

CHAPTER VIII
The Tyrant's Fall and What Followed

The portraits in our drawing-room—The Dictator Rosas
who was like an Englishman—The strange face of his
wife, Encarnacion—The traitor Urquiza—The Minister of War, his peacocks, and his son—Home again
from the city—The War deprives us of our playmate—
Natalia, our shepherd's wife—Her son, Medardo—The
Alcalde our grand old man—Battle of Monte Caseros—
The defeated army—Demands for fresh horses—In peril
—My father's shining defects—His pleasure in a thunder storm—A childlike trust in his fellow-men—Soldiers
turn upon their officer—A refugee given up and murdered
—Our Alcalde again—On cutting throats—Ferocity and
cynicism—Native blood-lust and its effect on a boy's
mind—Feeling about Rosas—A bird poem or tale—Vain
search for lost poem and story of its authorship—
The Dictator's daughter—Time, the old god.

At the end of the last chapter, when describing my
one sight of the famous jester, Don Eusebio, in his
glory, attended by a body-guard with drawn swords
who were ready to cut down any one of the spectators
who failed to remove his hat or laughed at the show,
I said it was on the eve of the fall of the President of
the Republic, or Dictator, "the Tyrant," as he was
called by his adversaries when they didn't call him the

"Nero of South America" or the "Tiger of Palermo" —this being the name of a park on the north side of Buenos Ayres where Rosas lived in a white stuccoed house called his palace.

At that time the portrait, in colours, of the great man occupied the post of honour above the mantelpiece in our *sala,* or drawing-room—the picture of a man with fine clear-cut regular features, light reddish-brown hair and side-whiskers, and blue eyes; he was sometimes called "Englishman" on account of his regular features and blonde complexion. That picture of a stern handsome face, with flags and cannon and olive-branch— the arms of the republic—in its heavy gold frame, was one of the principal ornaments of the room, and my father was proud of it, since he was, for reasons to be stated by and by, a great admirer of Rosas, an out-and-out Rosista, as the loyal ones were called. This portrait was flanked by two others: one of Doña Encarnacion, the wife, long dead, of Rosas; a handsome, proud-looking young woman with a vast amount of black hair piled up on her head in a fantastic fashion, surmounted by a large tortoiseshell comb. I remember that as small children we used to look with a queer, almost uncanny sort of feeling at this face under its pile of black hair, because it was handsome but not sweet nor gentle, and because she was dead and had died long ago; yet it was like the picture of one alive when we looked at it, and those black unloving eyes gazed straight back into ours. Why did those eyes, unless they moved, which they didn't, always look back into ours no matter in what part of the room we stood?—a perpetual puzzle to our childish uninformed brains.

On the other side was the repellent, truculent countenance of the Captain-General Urquiza, who was the Dictator's right-hand man, a ferocious cut-throat if ever there was one, who had upheld his authority for many years in the rebellious upper provinces, but who had just now raised the standard of revolt against him and in a little while, with the aid of a Brazilian army, would succeed in overthrowing him.

The central portrait inspired us with a kind of awe and reverential feeling, since even as small children we were made to know that he was the greatest man in the republic, that he had unlimited power over all men's lives and fortunes and was terrible in his anger against evil-doers, especially those who rebelled against his authority.

Two more portraits of the famous men of the republic of that date adorned the same wall. Next to Urquiza was General Oribe, commander of the army sent by Rosas against Montevideo, which maintained the siege of that city for the space of ten years. On the other side, next to Doña Encarnacion, was the portrait of the Minister of War, a face which had no attraction for us children, as it was not coloured like that of the Dictator, nor had any romance or mystery in it like that of his dead wife; yet it served to bring all these pictured people into our actual world —to make us realize that they were the counterfeit presentments of real men and women. For it happened that this same Minister of War was in a way a neighbour of ours, as he owned an estancia, which he sometimes visited, about three leagues from us, on that part of the plain to the east of our place which I have described in a former chapter as being covered with a dense growth of the bluish-grey wild artichoke, the *cardo de Castilla*, as it is called in the vernacular. Like most of the estancia houses of that day it was a long low building of brick with thatched roof, surrounded by an enclosed *quinta*, or plantation, with rows of century-old Lombardy poplars conspicuous at a great distance, and many old acacia, peach, quince, and cherry trees. It was a cattle and horse-breeding establishment, but the beasts were of less account to the owner than his peacocks, a fowl for which he had so great a predilection that he could not have too many of them; he was always buying more peacocks to send out to the estate, and they multiplied until the whole place swarmed with them. And he wanted them all for himself, so that it was forbidden to sell or give even an egg away. The place was in the charge of a major-domo, a good-natured fellow, and when he discovered that we liked peacocks' feathers for decorative purposes in the house, he made it a custom to send us each year at the moulting-time large bundles, whole armfuls, of feathers.

Another curious thing in the estancia was a large room set apart for the display of trophies sent from Buenos Ayres by the Minister's eldest son. I have already given an account of a favourite pastime of the young gentlemen of the capital—that of giving battle to the night-watchmen and wresting their staffs and lanterns from them. Our Minister's heir was a leader in this sport, and from time to time sent consignments of his trophies to the country place, where the walls of the room were covered with staffs and festoons of lanterns.

Once or twice as a small boy I had the privilege of meeting this young gentleman and looked at him with an intense curiosity which has served to keep his image in my mind till now. His figure was slender and graceful, his features good, and he had a rather long Spanish face; his eyes were grey-blue, and his hair and moustache a reddish golden-brown. It was a handsome face, but with a curiously repelling, impatient, reckless, almost devilish expression.

I was at home again, back in the plantation among my beloved birds, glad to escape from the noisy dusty city into the sweet green silences, with the great green plain glittering with the false water of the mirage spreading around our shady oasis, and the fact that war, which for the short period of my own little life and for many long years before I was born, had not visited our province, thanks to Rosas the Tyrant, the man of blood and iron, had now come to us did not make the sunshine less sweet and pleasant to behold. Our elders, it is true, showed anxious faces, but they were often anxious about matters which did not affect us children, and therefore didn't **matter**. But by and by even we little ones were made to realize that there was a trouble in the land which touched us too, since it deprived us of the companionship of the native boy who was our particular friend and guardian during our early horseback rambles on the plain. This boy, Medardo, or Dardo, was the fifteen-years-old son— illegitimate of course—of the native woman our English shepherd had made his wife. Why he had done so was a perpetual mystery and marvel to every one on account of her person and temper. The very thought of this poor Natalia, or Doña Nata as she was called, long dead and turned to dust in that far pampa, troubles my spirit even now and gives me the uncomfortable feeling that in putting her portrait on this paper I am doing a mean thing.

She was an excessively lean creature, careless, and even dirty in her person, with slippers but no stockings on her feet, an old dirty gown of a coarse blue cotton stuff and a large coloured cotton handkerchief or piece of calico wound turban-wise about her head. She was of a yellowish parchment colour, the skin tight-drawn over the small bony aquiline features, and it would have seemed like the face of a corpse or mummy but for the deeply-sunken jet-black eyes burning with a troubled fire in their sockets. There was a tremor and strangely pathetic note in her thin high-pitched voice, as of a woman speaking with effort between half-suppressed sobs, or like the mournful cry of some wild bird of the marshes. Voice and face were true indications of her anxious mind. She was in a perpetual state of worry over some trifling matter, and when a real trouble came, as when our flock "got mixed" with a neighbour's flock and four or five thousand sheep had to be parted, sheep by sheep, according to their ear-marks, or when her husband came home drunk and tumbled off his horse at the door instead of dismounting in the usual manner, she would be almost out of her mind and wring her hands and shriek and cry out that such conduct would not be endured by his long-suffering master, and they would no longer have a roof over their heads!

Poor anxious-minded ˙Nata, who moved us both to pity and repulsion, it was impossible not to admire her efforts to keep her stolid inarticulate husband in the right path and her intense wild animal-like love of her children—the three dirty-faced English-looking off-spring of her strange marriage, and Dardo, her first-born, the son of the wind. He, too, was an interesting person; small or short for his years, he was thick and had a curiously solid mature appearance, with a round head, wide open, startlingly bright eyes, and aquiline features which gave him a resemblance to a sparrow-hawk. He was mature in mind, too, and had all the horse lore of the seasoned gaucho, and at the same time he was like a child in his love of fun and play, and wanted nothing better than to serve us as a per-petual playmate. But he had his work, which was to look after the flock when the shepherd's services were required elsewhere; an easy task for him on his horse, especially in summer when for long hours the sheep would stand motionless on the plain. Dardo, who was teaching us to swim, would then invite us to go to the river—to one of two streams within half an hour's ride from home, where there were good bathing-pools! but always before starting he would have to go and ask his mother's consent. Mounting my pony I would follow him to the *puesto* or shepherd's ranche, only to be denied permission: "No, you are not to go to-day: you must not think of such a thing. I forbid you to take the boys to the river this day!"

Then Dardo, turning his horse's head, would

exclaim, "Oh, caram-bam-bam-ba!" And she, seeing
him going, would rush out after us, shrieking, "Don't
caram-bam-bam-ba me! You are not to go to the
river this day—I forbid it! I know if you go to the
river this day there will be a terrible calamity! Listen
to me, Dardo, rebel, devil that you are, you shall not
go bathing to-day!" And the cries would continue
until, breaking into a gallop, we would quickly be out
of earshot. Then Dardo would say, "Now we'll go
back to the house for the others and go to the river.
You see, she made me kneel before the crucifix and
promise never to take you to bathe without asking her
consent. And that's all I've got to do; I never
promised to obey her commands, so it's all right."

These pleasant adventures with Dardo on the plain
were suddenly put a stop to by the war. One morning a number of persons on foot and on horseback
were seen coming to us over the green plain from the
shepherd's ranche, and as they drew nearer we recognized our old Alcalde on his horse as the leader of the
procession, and behind him walked Doña Nata, holding
her son by the hand; then followed others on foot,
and behind them all rode four old gauchos, the Alcalde's
henchmen, wearing their swords.

What matter of tremendous importance had brought
this crowd to our house? The Alcalde, Don Amáro
Avalos, was not only the representative of the "authorities" in our parts—police officer, petty magistrate
of sorts, and several other things besides—but a grand
old man in himself, and he looms large in memory
among the old gaucho patriarchs in our neighbourhood.
He was a big man, about six feet high, exceedingly

dignified in manner, his long hair and beard of a silvery whiteness; he wore the gaucho costume with a great profusion of silver ornaments, including ponderous silver spurs weighing about four pounds, and heavy silver whip-handle. As a rule he rode on a big black horse which admirably suited his figure and the scarlet colour and silver of his costume.

On arrival Don Amáro was conducted to the drawing-room, followed by all the others; and when all were seated, including the four old gauchos wearing swords, the Alcalde addressed my parents and informed them of the object of the visit. He had received an imperative order from his superiors, he said, to take at once and send to headquarters twelve more young men as recruits for the army from his small section of the district. Now most of the young men had already been taken, or had disappeared from the neighbourhood in order to avoid service, and to make up this last twelve he had even to take boys of the age of this one, and Medardo would have to go. But this woman would not have her boy taken, and after spending many words in trying to convince her that she must submit he had at last, to satisfy her, consented to accompany her to her master's house to discuss the matter again in her master and mistress's presence.

It was a long speech, pronounced with great dignity; then, almost before it finished, the distracted mother jumped up and threw herself on her knees before my parents, and in her wild tremulous voice began crying to them, imploring them to have compassion on her and help her to save her boy from such a dreadful destiny. What would he be, she cried, a boy of his tender years dragged from his home, from his mother's care, and thrown among a crowd of old hardened soldiers, and of evil-minded men—murderers, robbers, and criminals of all descriptions drawn from all the prisons of the land to serve in the army!

It was dreadful to see her on her knees wringing her hands, and to listen to her wild lamentable cries; and again and again while the matter was being discussed between the old Alcalde and my parents, she would break out and plead with such passion and despair in her voice and words, that all the people in the room were affected to tears. She was like some wild animal trying to save her offspring from the hunters. Never, exclaimed my mother, when the struggle was over, had she passed so painful, so terrible, an hour! And the struggle had all been in vain, and Dardo was taken from us.

One morning, some weeks later, the dull roar from distant big guns came to our ears, and we were told that a great battle was being fought, that Rosas himself was at the head of his army—a poor little force of 25,000 men got together in hot haste to oppose a mixed Argentine and Brazilian force of about 40,000 men commanded by the traitor Urquiza. During several hours of that anxious day the dull, heavy sound of firing continued and was like distant thunder: then in the evening came the tidings of the overthrow of the defending army, and of the march of the enemy on Buenos Ayres city! On the following day, from dawn to dark, we were in the midst of an incessant

stream of the defeated men, flying to the south, in
small parties of two or three to half a dozen men,
with some larger bands, all in their scarlet uniforms
and armed with lances and carbines and broadswords,
many of the bands driving large numbers of horses
before them.

My father was warned by the neighbours that we
were in great danger, since these men were now
lawless and would not hesitate to plunder and kill in
their retreat, and that all riding-horses would certainly
be seized by them. As a precaution he had the horses
driven in and concealed in the plantation, and that
was all he would do. "Oh no," he said, with a laugh,
"they won't hurt us," and so we were all out and
about all day with the front gate and all doors and
windows standing open. From time to time a band
on tired horses rode to the gate and, without dismounting, shouted a demand for fresh horses. In every case
he went out and talked to them, always with a smiling,
pleasant face, and after assuring them that he had no
horses for them they slowly and reluctantly took their
departure.

About three o'clock in the afternoon, the hottest
hour of the day, a troop of ten men rode up at
a gallop, raising a great cloud of dust, and coming in
at the gate drew rein before the verandah. My father
as usual went out to meet them, whereupon they
demanded fresh horses in loud menacing voices.

Indoors we were all gathered in the large sitting-
room, waiting the upshot in a state of intense anxiety,
for no preparations had been made and no means of
defence existed in the event of a sudden attack on

the house. We watched the proceedings from the interior, which was too much in shadow for our dangerous visitors to see that they were only women and children there and one man, a visitor, who had withdrawn to the further end of the room and sat leaning back in an easy chair, trembling and white as a corpse, with a naked sword in his hand. He explained to us afterwards, when the danger was all over, that fortunately he was an excellent swordsman, and that having found the weapon in the room, he had resolved to give a good account of the ten ruffians if they had made a rush to get in.

My father replied to these men as he had done to the others, assuring them that he had no horses to give them. Meanwhile we who were indoors all noticed that one of the ten men was an officer, a beardless young man of about twenty-one or two, with a singularly engaging face. He took no part in the proceedings, but sat silent on his horse, watching the others with a peculiar expression, half contemptuous and half anxious, on his countenance. And he alone was unarmed, a circumstance which struck us as very strange. The others were all old veterans, middle-aged and oldish men with grizzled beards, all in scarlet jacket and scarlet *chiripá* and a scarlet cap of the quaint form then worn, shaped like a boat turned upside down, with a horn-like peak in front, and beneath the peak a brass plate on which was the number of the regiment.

The men appeared surprised at the refusal of horses, and stated plainly that they would not accept it; at which my father shook his head and smiled. One of the men then asked for water to quench his thirst. Some one in the house then took out a large jug of cold water, and my father taking it handed it up to the man; he drank, then passed the jug on to the other thirsty ones, and after going its rounds the jug was handed back and the demand for fresh horses renewed in menacing tones. There was some water left in the jug, and my father began pouring it out in a thin stream, making little circles and figures on the dry dusty ground, then once more shook his head and smiled very pleasantly on them. Then one of the men, fixing his eyes on my father's face, bent forward and suddenly struck his hand violently on the hilt of his broadsword and, rattling the weapon, half drew it from its sheath. This nerve-trying experiment was a complete failure, its only effect being to make my father smile up at the man even more pleasantly than before, as if the little practical joke had greatly amused him.

The strange thing was that my father was not playing a part—that it was his nature to act in just that way. It is a curious thing to say of any person that his highest or most shining qualities were nothing but defects, since, apart from these same singular qualities, he was just an ordinary person with nothing to distinguish him from his neighbours, excepting perhaps that he was not anxious to get rich and was more neighbourly or more brotherly towards his fellows than most men. The sense of danger, the instinct of self-preservation supposed to be universal, was not in him, and there were occasions when this extraordinary defect produced the keenest distress in my mother. In hot summers we were subject to thunderstorms of an amazing violence, and at such times, when thunder and lightning were nearest together and most terrifying to everybody else, he would stand out of doors gazing calmly up at the sky as if the blinding flashes and world-shaking thunder-crashes had some soothing effect, like music, on his mind. One day, just before noon, it was reported by one of the men that the saddle-horses could not be found, and my father, with his spy-glass in his hand, went out and ran up the wooden stairs to the *mirador* or look-out constructed at the top of the big barn-like building used for storing wool. The *mirador* was so high that standing on it one was able to see even over the tops of the tall plantation trees, and to protect the looker-out there was a high wooden railing round it, and against this the tall flag-staff was fastened. When my father went up to the look-out a terribly violent thunderstorm was just bursting on us. The dazzling, almost continuous lightning appeared to be not only in the black cloud over the house but all round us, and crash quickly followed crash, making the doors and windows rattle in their frames, while there high above us in the very midst of the awful tumult stood my father calm as ever. Not satisfied that he was high enough on the floor of the look-out he had got up on the topmost rail, and standing on it, with his back against the tall pole, he surveyed the open plain all round through his spy-glass in search of the lost horses. I remember that indoors my mother with white terror-stricken face stood gazing out at him, and that the whole house was in a state of terror, expecting every moment to see him struck by lightning and hurled down to the earth below.

A second and in its results a more disastrous shining quality was a childlike trust in the absolute good faith of every person with whom he came into business relations. Things being what they are this inevitably led to his ruin.

To return to our unwelcome visitors. On this occasion my father's perfectly cool smiling demeanour, resulting from his foolhardiness, served him and the house well: it deceived them, for they could not believe that he would have acted in that way if they had not been watched by men with rifles in their hands from the interior who would open fire on the least hostile movement on their part.

Suddenly the scowling spokesman of the troop, with a shouted "Vamos!" turned his horse's head and, followed by all the others, rode out and broke into a gallop. We too then hurried out, and from the screen of poplar and black acacia trees growing at the side of the moat, watched their movements, and saw, when they had got away a few hundred yards from the gate, the young unarmed officer break away from them and start off at the greatest speed he could get out of his horse. The others quickly gave chase and at length disappeared from sight in the direction of the Alcalde's or local petty magistrate's house, about a mile and a half away. It was a long low thatched ranch without trees, and could not be seen from our house as it stood behind a marshy lake overgrown with all bulrushes.

While we were straining our eyes to see the result of the chase, and after the hunted man and his pursuers had vanished from sight among the herds of cattle and horses grazing on the plain, the tragedy was being carried out in exceedingly painful circumstances. The young officer, whose home was more than a day's journey from our district, had visited the neighbourhood on a former occasion and remembered that he had relations in it; and when he broke away from the men, divining that it was their intention to murder him, he made for the old Alcalde's house. He succeeded in keeping ahead of his pursuers until he arrived at the gate, and throwing himself from his horse and rushing into the house, and finding the old Alcalde surrounded by the women of the house, addressed him as uncle and claimed his protection. The Alcalde was not, strictly speaking, his uncle but was his mother's first cousin. It was an awful moment: the nine armed ruffians were already standing outside, shouting to the owner of the place to give them up their prisoner, and threatening to burn down the house and kill all the inmates if he refused. The old Alcalde stood in the middle of the room, surrounded by a crowd of women and children, his own two handsome daughters, aged about twenty and twenty-two respectively, among them, fainting with terror and crying for him to save them, while the young officer on his knees implored him for the sake of his mother's memory, and of the Mother of God and of all he held sacred, to refuse to give him up to be slaughtered.

The old man was not equal to the situation: he trembled and sobbed with anguish, and at last faltered out that he could not protect him—that he must save his own daughters and the wives and children of his neighbours who had sought refuge in his house. The men outside, hearing how the argument was going, came to the door, and finally seizing the young man by the arm led him out and made him mount his horse again and ride with them. They rode back the way they had gone for half a mile towards our house, then pulled him off his horse and cut his throat.

On the following day a mulatto boy who looked after the flock and went on errands for the Alcalde, came to me and said that if I would mount my pony and go with him he would show me something. It was not seldom this same little fellow came to me to offer to show me something, and it usually turned out to be a bird's nest, an object which keenly interested us both. I gladly mounted my pony and followed. The broken army had ceased passing our way by now, and it was peaceful and safe once more on the great plain. We rode about a mile, and he then pulled up his horse and pointed to the turf at our feet, where I saw a great stain of blood on the short dry grass. Here, he told me, was where they had cut the young officer's throat: the body had been taken by the Alcalde to his house, where it had been lying since the evening before, and it would be taken for burial next day to our nearest village, about eight miles distant.

The murder was the talk of the place for some days, chiefly on account of the painful facts of the case— that the old Alcalde, who was respected and even loved by every one, should have failed in so pitiful a way to make any attempt at saving his young relation. But the mere fact that the soldiers had cut the throat of their officer surprised no one; it was a common thing in the case of a defeat in those days for the men to turn upon and murder their officers. Nor was throat-cutting a mere custom or convention: to the old soldier it was the only satisfactory way of finishing off your adversary, or prisoner of war, or your officer who had been your tyrant, on the day of defeat. Their feeling was similar to that of the man who is inspired by the hunting instinct in its primitive form, as described by Richard Jefferies. To kill the creatures with bullets at a distance was no satisfaction to him: he must with his own hands drive the shaft into the quivering flesh—he must feel its quivering and see the blood gush up beneath his hand. One smiles at a vision of the gentle Richard Jefferies slaughtering wild cattle in the palæolithic way, but that feeling and desire which he describes with such passion in his *Story of My Heart*, that survival of the past, is not uncommon in the hearts of hunters, and if we were ever to drop out of our civilization I fancy we should return rather joy-fully to the primitive method. And so in those dark times in the Argentine Republic when, during half a century of civil strife which followed on casting off the Spanish "yoke," as it was called, the people of the plains had developed an amazing ferocity, they loved to kill a man not with a bullet but in a manner to make them know and feel that they were really and truly killing.

As a child those dreadful deeds did not impress me, since I did not witness them myself, and after looking at that stain of blood on the grass the subject faded

out of my mind.   But as time went on and I heard
more about this painful subject I began to realize what
it meant.   The full horror of it came only a few years
later, when I was big enough to go about to the native
houses and among the gauchos in their gatherings, at
cattle-partings and brandings, races, and on other occasions.   I listened to the conversation of groups of men
whose lives had been mostly spent in the army, as a
rule in guerilla warfare, and the talk turned with surprising frequency to the subject of cutting throats.
Not to waste powder on prisoners was an unwritten
law of the Argentine army at that period, and the
veteran gaucho clever with the knife took delight in
obeying it.   It always came as a relief, I heard them
say, to have as victim a young man with a good neck
after an experience of tough, scraggy old throats: with
a person of that sort they were in no hurry to finish
the business; it was performed in a leisurely, loving
way.   Darwin, writing in praise of the gaucho in his
Voyage of a Naturalist, says that if a gaucho cuts your
throat he does it like a gentleman: even as a small
boy I knew better—that he did his business rather like
a hellish creature revelling in his cruelty.   He would
listen to all his captive could say to soften his heart—
all his heartrending prayers and pleadings; and would
reply: "Ah, friend,"—or little friend, or brother—
"your words pierce me to the heart and I would gladly
spare you for the sake of that poor mother of yours
who fed you with her milk, and for your own sake
too, since in this short time I have conceived a great
friendship towards you; but your beautiful neck is
your undoing, for how could I possibly deny myself

the pleasure of cutting such a throat—so shapely, so smooth and soft and so white! Think of the sight of warm red blood gushing from that white column!" And so on, with wavings of the steel blade before the captive's eyes, until the end.

When I heard them relate such things—and I am quoting their very words, remembered all these years only too well—laughingly, gloating over such memories, such a loathing and hatred possessed me that ever afterwards the very sight of these men was enough to produce a sensation of nausea, just as when in the dog days one inadvertently rides too near the putrid carcass of some large beast on the plain.

As I have said, all this feeling about throat-cutting and the power to realize and visualize it, came to me by degrees long after the sight of a blood-stain on the turf near our home; and in like manner the significance of the tyrant's fall and the mighty changes it brought about in the land only came to me long after the event. People were in perpetual conflict about the character of the great man. He was abhorred by many, perhaps by most; others were on his side even for years after he had vanished from their ken, and among these were most of the English residents of the country, my father among them. Quite naturally I followed my father and came to believe that all the bloodshed during a quarter of a century, all the crimes and cruelties practised by Rosas, were not like the crimes committed by a private person, but were all for the good of the country, with the result that in Buenos Ayres and throughout our province there had been a long period of peace and prosperity, and that all this ended with his fall and was succeeded by years of fresh revolutionary outbreaks and bloodshed and anarchy. Another thing about Rosas which made me ready to fall in with my father's high opinion of him was the number of stories about him which appealed to my childish imagination. Many of these related to his adventures when he would disguise himself as a person of humble status and prowl about the city by night, especially in the squalid quarters, where he would make the acquaintance of the very poor in their hovels. Most of these stories were probably inventions and need not be told here; but there was one which I must say something about because it is a bird story and greatly excited my boyish interest.

I was often asked by our gaucho neighbours when I talked with them about birds—and they all knew that that subject interested me above all others—if I had ever heard *el canto,* or *el cuento del Bien-te-veo.* That is to say, the ballad or tale of the *Bien-te-veo*—a species of tyrant-bird quite common in the country, with a brown back and sulphur-yellow under parts, a crest on its head, and face barred with black and white. It is a little larger than our butcher-bird and, like it, is partly rapacious in its habits. The barred face and long kingfisher-like beak give it a peculiarly knowing or cunning look, and the effect is heightened by the long trisyllabic call constantly uttered by the bird, from which it derives its name of Bien-te-veo, which means I-can-see-you. He is always letting you know that he is there, that he has got his eye on you, so that you had better be careful about your actions.

The Bien-te-veo, I need hardly say, was one of my

feathered favourites, and I begged my gaucho friends to tell me this *cuento,* but although I met scores of men who had heard it, not one remembered it: they could only say that it was very long—very few persons could remember such a long story; and I further gathered that it was a sort of history of the bird's life and his adventures among the other birds; that the Bien-te-veo was always doing clever naughty things and getting into trouble, but invariably escaping the penalty. From all I could hear it was a tale of the Reynard the Fox order, or like the tales told by the gauchos of the armadillo and how that quaint little beast always managed to fool his fellow-animals, especially the fox, who regarded himself as the cleverest of all the beasts and who looked on his honest, dull-witted neighbour the armadillo as a born fool. Old gauchos used to tell me that twenty or more years ago one often met with a reciter of ballads who could relate the whole story of the Bien-te-veo. Good reciters were common enough in my time: at dances it was always possible to find one or two to amuse the company with long poems and ballads in the intervals of dancing, and first and last I questioned many who had this talent, but failed to find one who knew the famous bird-ballad, and in the end I gave up the quest.

The story invariably told was that a man convicted of some serious crime and condemned to suffer the last penalty, and left, as the custom then was, for long months in the gaol in Buenos Ayres, amused himself by composing the story of the Bien-te-veo, and thinking well of it he made a present of the manuscript to the gaoler in acknowledgment of some kindness he had received from that person. The condemned man had no money and no friends to interest themselves on his behalf; but it was not the custom at that time to execute a criminal as soon as he was condemned. The prison authorities preferred to wait until there were a dozen or so to execute; these would then be taken out, ranged against a wall of the prison, opposite a file of soldiers with muskets in their hands, and shot, the soldiers after the first discharge reloading their weapons and going up to the fallen men to finish off those who were still kicking. This was the prospect our prisoner had to look forward to. Meanwhile his ballad was being circulated and read with immense delight by various persons in authority, and one of these who was privileged to approach the Dictator, thinking it would afford him a little amusement, took the ballad and read it to him. Rosas was so pleased with it that he pardoned the condemned man and ordered his liberation.

All this, I conjectured, must have happened at least twenty years before I was born. I also concluded that the ballad had never been printed, otherwise I would most probably have found it; but some copies in writing had evidently been made and it had become a favourite composition with the reciters at festive gatherings, but had now gone out and was hopelessly lost.

These, as I have already intimated, were but the little things that touched a child's fancy; there was another romantic circumstance in the life of Rosas which appealed to everybody, adult as well as child.

He was the father of Doña Manuela, known by the affectionate diminutive, Manuelita, throughout the land, and loved and admired by all, even by her father's enemies, for her compassionate disposition. Perhaps she was the one being in the world for whom he, a widower and lonely man, cherished a great tenderness. It is certain that her power over him was very great and that many lives that would have been taken for State reasons were saved by her interposition. It was a beautiful and fearful part that she, a girl, was called on to play on that dreadful stage; and very naturally it was said that she, who was the very spirit of mercy incarnate, could not have acted as the loving, devoted daughter to one who was the monster of cruelty his enemies proclaimed him to be.

Here, in conclusion to this chapter, I had intended to introduce a few sober reflections on the character of Rosas—certainly the greatest and most interesting of all the South America Caudillos, or leaders, who rose to absolute power during the long stormy period that followed on the war of independence—reflections which came to me later, in my teens, when I began to think for myself and form my own judgments. This I now perceive would be a mistake, if not an impertinence, since I have not the temper of mind for such exercises and should give too much importance to certain singular acts on the Dictator's part which others would perhaps regard as political errors, or due to sudden fits of passion or petulance rather than as crimes. And some of his acts are inexplicable, as for instance the public execution in the interests of religion and morality of a charming young lady of good family and her lover, the handsome young priest who had captivated the town with his eloquence. Why he did it will remain a puzzle for ever. There were many other acts which to foreigners and to those born in later times might seem the result of insanity, but which were really the outcome of a peculiar, sardonic, and somewhat primitive sense of humour on his part which appeals powerfully to the men of the plains, the gauchos, among whom Rosas lived from boyhood, when he ran away from his father's house, and by whose aid he eventually rose to supreme power.

All these things do not much affect the question of Rosas as a ruler and his place in history. Time, the old god, says the poet, invests all things with honour, and makes them white. The poet-prophet is not to be taken literally, but his words so undoubtedly contain a tremendous truth. And here, then, one may let the question rest. If after half a century, and more, the old god is still sitting, chin on hand, revolving this question, it would be as well to give him, say, another fifty years to make up his mind and pronounce a final judgment.

CHAPTER IX

Our Neighbours at the Poplars

Homes on the great green plain —Making the acquaintance
of our neighbours—The attraction of birds—Los Alamos
and the old lady of the house—Her treatment of St.
Anthony—The strange Barboza family—The man of
blood—Great fighters—Barboza as a singer—A great
quarrel but no fight—A cattle-marking—Doña Lucia
del Ombu—A feast—Barboza sings and is insulted by
El Rengo—Refuses to fight—The two kinds of fighters—
A poor little angel on horseback—My feeling for Anjelita—Boys unable to express sympathy—A quarrel
with a friend—Enduring image of a little girl.

In a former chapter on the aspects of the plain I
described the groves and plantations, which marked the
sites of the estancia houses, as appearing like banks or
islands of trees, blue in the distance, on the vast flat
sea-like plain. Some of these were many miles away
and were but faintly visible on the horizon, others nearer,
and the nearest of all was but two miles from us, on the
hither side of that shallow river to which my first long
walk was taken, where I was amazed and enchanted
with my first sight of flamingoes. This place was
called Los Alamos, or The Poplars, a name which
would have suited a large majority of the estancia
houses with trees growing about them, seeing that the

tall Lombardy poplar was almost always there in long rows towering high above all other trees and a landmark in the district. It is about the people dwelling at Los Alamos I have now to write.

When I first started on my riding rambles about the plain I began to make the acquaintance of some of our nearest neighbours, but at first it was a slow process. As a child I was excessively shy of strangers, and I also greatly feared the big savage house-dogs that would rush out to attack any one approaching the gate. But a house with a grove or plantation fascinated me, for where there were trees there were birds, and I had soon made the discovery that you could sometimes meet with birds of a new kind in a plantation quite near to your own. Little by little I found out that the people were invariably friendly towards a small boy, even the child of an alien and heretic race; also that the dogs in spite of all their noise and fury never really tried to pull me off my horse and tear me to pieces. In this way, thinking of and looking only for the birds, I became acquainted with some of the people individually, and as I grew to know them better from year to year I sometimes became interested in them too, and in this and three or four succeeding chapters I will describe those I knew best or that interested me the most. Not only as I first knew or began to know them in my seventh year, but in several instances I shall be able to trace their lives and fortunes for some years further on.

When out riding I went oftenest in the direction of Los Alamos, which was west of us, or as the gauchos would say, "on the side where the sun sets." For just behind the plantation, enclosed in its rows of tall old poplars, was that bird-haunted stream which was an irresistible attraction. The sight of running water, too, was a never-failing joy, also the odours which greeted me in that moist green place—odours earthy, herby, fishy, flowery, and even birdy, particularly that peculiar musky odour given out on hot days by large flocks of the glossy ibis.

The person—owner or tenant, I forget which—who lived in the house was an old woman named Doña Pascuala, whom I never saw without a cigar in her mouth. Her hair was white, and her thousand-wrinkled face was as brown as the cigar, and she had fun-loving eyes, a loud authoritative voice and a masterful manner, and she was esteemed by her neighbours as a wise and good woman. I was shy of her and avoided the house while anxious to get peeps into the plantation to watch the birds and look for nests, as whenever she caught sight of me she would not let me off without a sharp cross-examination as to my motives and doings. She would also have a hundred questions besides about the family, how they were, what they were all doing, and whether it was really true that we drank coffee every morning for breakfast; also if it was true that all of us children, even the girls, when big enough were going to be taught to read the almanac.

I remember once when we had been having a long spell of wet weather, and the low-lying plain about Los Alamos was getting flooded, she came to visit my mother and told her reassuringly that the rain would not last much longer. St. Anthony was the saint she was devoted to, and she had taken his image from its place in her bedroom and tied a string round its legs and let it down the well and left it there with its head in the water. He was her own saint, she said, and after all her devotion to him, and all the candles and flowers, this was how he treated her! It was all very well, she told her saint, to amuse himself by causing the rain to fall for days and weeks just to find out whether men would be drowned or turn themselves into frogs to save themselves: now she, Doña Pascuala, was going to find out how *he* liked it. There, with his head in the water, he would have to hang in the well until the weather changed.

Four years later, in my tenth year, Doña Pascuala moved away and was succeeded at Los Alamos by a family named Barboza: strange people! Half a dozen brothers and sisters, one or two married, and one, the head and leader of the tribe, or family, a big man aged about forty with fierce eagle-like eyes under bushy black eyebrows that looked like tufts of feathers. But his chief glory was an immense crow-black beard, of which he appeared to be excessively proud and was usually seen stroking it in a slow deliberate manner, now with one hand, then with both, pulling it out, dividing it, then spreading it over his chest to display its full magnificence. He wore at his waist, in front, a knife or *facon*, with a sword-shaped hilt and a long curved blade about two-thirds the length of a sword.

He was a great fighter: at all events he came to our neighbourhood with that reputation, and I at that time, at the age of nine, like my elder brothers had come to take a keen interest in the fighting gaucho. A duel between two men with knives, their ponchas wrapped round their left arms and used as shields, was a thrilling spectacle to us; I had already witnessed several encounters of this kind; but these were fights of ordinary or small men and were very small affairs compared with the encounters of the famous fighters, about which we had news from time to time. Now that we had one of the genuine big ones among us it would perhaps be our great good fortune to witness a real big fight; for sooner or later some champion duellist from a distance would appear to challenge our man, or else some one of our own neighbours would rise up one day to dispute his claim to be cock of the walk. But nothing of the kind happened, although on two occasions I thought the wished moment had come.

The first occasion was at a big gathering of gauchos when Barboza was asked and graciously consented to sing a *decima*—a song or ballad consisting of four ten-line stanzas. Now Barboza was a singer but not a player on the guitar, so that an accompanist had to be called for. A stranger at the meeting quickly responded to the call. Yes, he could play to any man's singing—any tune he liked to call. He was a big, loud-voiced, talkative man, not known to any person present; he was a passer-by, and seeing a crowd at a rancho had ridden up and joined them, ready to take a hand in whatever work or games might be going on. Taking the guitar he settled down by Barboza's side and began tuning the instrument and discussing the question of the air to be played. And this was soon settled.

Here I must pause to remark that Barboza, although

almost as famous for his *decimas* as for his sanguinary duels, was not what one would call a musical person. His singing voice was inexpressibly harsh, like that, for example, of the carrion crow when that bird is most vocal in its love season and makes the woods resound with its prolonged grating metallic calls. The interesting point was that his songs were his own composition and were recitals of his strange adventures, mixed with his thoughts and feelings about things in general—his philosophy of life. Probably if I had these compositions before me now in manuscript they would strike me as dreadfully crude stuff; nevertheless I am sorry I did not write some of them down and that I can only recall a few lines.

The *decima* he now started to sing related to his early experiences, and swaying his body from side to side and bending forward until his beard was all over his knees he began in his raucous voice:

> En el año mil ochocientos y quarenta,
> Quando citaron todos los enrolados,

which, roughly translated, means:

> Eighteen hundred and forty was the year
> When all the enrolled were cited to appear.

Thus far he had got when the guitarist, smiting angrily on the strings with his palm, leaped to his feet, shouting, "No, no—no more of that! What! do you sing to me of 1840—that cursed year! I refuse to play to you! Nor will I listen to you, nor will I allow any person to sing of that year and that event in my presence."

Naturally every one was astonished, and the first thought was, What will happen now? Blood would assuredly flow, and I was there to see—and how my elder brothers would envy me!

Barboza rose scowling from his seat, and dropping his hand on the hilt of his *facon* said: "Who is this who forbids me, Basilio Barboza, to sing of 1840?"

"I forbid you!" shouted the stranger in a rage and smiting his breast. "Do you know what it is to me to hear that date—that fatal year? It is like the stab of a knife. I, a boy, was of that year; and when the fifteen years of my slavery and misery were over there was no longer a roof to shelter me, nor father nor mother nor land nor cattle!"

Every one instantly understood the case of this poor man, half crazed at the sudden recollection of his wasted and ruined life, and it did not seem right that he should bleed and perhaps die for such a cause, and all at once there was a rush and the crowd thrust itself between him and his antagonist and hustled him a dozen yards away. Then one in the crowd, an old man, shouted: "Do you think, friend, that you are the only one in this gathering who lost his liberty and all he possessed on earth in that fatal year? I, too, suffered as you have suffered——"

"And I!" "And I!" shouted others, and while this noisy demonstration was going on some of those who were pressing close to the stranger began to ask him if he knew who the man was he had forbidden to sing of 1840? Had he never heard of Barboza, the celebrated fighter who had killed so many men in fights?

Perhaps he had heard and did not wish to die just yet: at all events a change came over his spirit; he became more rational and even apologetic, and Barboza graciously accepted the assurance that he had no desire to provoke a quarrel.

And so there was no fight after all!

The second occasion was about two years later—a long period, during which there had been a good many duels with knives in our neighbourhood; but Barboza was not in any of them, no person had come forward to challenge his supremacy. It is commonly said among the gauchos that when a man has proved his prowess by killing a few of his opponents, he is thereafter permitted to live in peace.

One day I attended a cattle-marking at a small native estancia a few miles from home, owned by an old woman whom I used to think the oldest person in the world as she hobbled about supporting herself with two sticks, bent nearly double, with her half-blind, colourless eyes always fixed on the ground. But she had granddaughters living with her who were not bad-looking: the eldest, Antonia, a big loud-voiced young woman, known as the "white mare" on account of the whiteness of her skin and large size, and three others. It was not strange that cattle-branding at this estancia brought all the men and youths for leagues around to do a service to the venerable Doña Lucia del Ombú. That was what she was called, because there was a solitary grand old ombú tree growing about a hundred yards from the house—a well-known landmark in the district. There were also half a dozen weeping willows close to the house, but no plantation, no garden, and no ditch or enclosure of any kind. The old mud-built rancho, thatched with rushes, stood on the level naked plain; it was one of the old decayed establishments, and the cattle were not many, so that by midday the work was done and the men, numbering about forty or fifty, trooped to the house to be entertained at dinner.

As the day was hot and the indoor accommodation insufficient, the tables were in the shade of the willows, and there we had our feast of roast and boiled meat, with bread and wine and big dishes of *aros con leche*— rice boiled in milk with sugar and cinnamon. Next to cummin-seed cinnamon is the spice best loved of the gaucho: he will ride long leagues to get it.

The dinner over and tables cleared, the men and youths disposed themselves on the benches and chairs and on their spread ponchos on the ground, and started smoking and conversing. A guitar was produced, and Barboza being present, surrounded as usual by a crowd of his particular friends or parasites, all eagerly listening to his talk and applauding his sallies with bursts of laughter, he was naturally first asked to sing. The accompanist in this case was Goyo Montes, a little thick-set gaucho with round staring blue eyes set in a round pinky-brown face, and the tune agreed on was one known as *La Lechera*— the Milkmaid.

Then, while the instrument was being tuned and Barboza began to sway his body about, and talking ceased, a gaucho named Marcos but usually called *El Rengo* on account of his lameness, pushed himself into the crowd surrounding the great man and seated himself on a table and put his foot of his lame leg on the bench below.

El Rengo was a strange being, a man with remarkably fine aquiline features, piercing black eyes, and long black hair. As a youth he had distinguished himself among his fellow-gauchos by his daring feats of horsemanship, mad adventures, and fights; then he met with the accident which lamed him for life and at the same time saved him from the army; when, at a cattle-parting, he was thrown from his horse and gored by a furious bull, the animal's horn having been driven deep into his thigh. From that time Marcos was a man of peace and was liked and respected by every one as a good neighbour and a good fellow. He was also admired for the peculiarly amusing way of talking he had, when in the proper mood, which was usually when he was a little exhilarated by drink. His eyes would sparkle and his face light up, and he would set his listeners laughing at the queer way in which he would play with his subject; but there was always some mockery and bitterness in it which served to show that something of the dangerous spirit of his youth still survived in him.

On this occasion he was in one of his most wilful, mocking, reckless moods, and was no sooner seated than he began smilingly, in his quiet conversational tone, to discuss the question of the singer and the tune. Yes, he said, the Milkmaid was a good tune, but another name to it would have suited the subject better. Oh, the subject! Any one might guess what that would be. The words mattered more than the air. For here we had before us not a small sweet singer, a goldfinch in a cage, but a cock—a fighting cock with well-trimmed comb and tail and a pair of sharp spurs to its feet. Listen, friends, he is now about to flap his wings and crow.

I was leaning against the table on which he sat and began to think it was a dangerous place for me, since I was certain that every word was distinctly heard by Barboza; yet he made no sign, but went on swaying from side to side as if no mocking word had reached him, then launched out in one of his most atrocious *decimas,* autobiographical and philosophical. In the first stanza he mentions that he had slain eleven men, but using a poet's license he states the fact in a roundabout way, saying that he slew six men, and then five more, making eleven in all:

> Seis muertes é hecho y cinco son once.

which may be paraphrased thus:

> Six men had I sent to hades or heaven,
> Then added five more to make them eleven.

The stanza ended, Marcos resumed his comments. What I desire to know, said he, is, why eleven? It is not the proper number in this case. One more is wanted to make the full dozen. He who rests at eleven has not completed his task and should not boast of what he has done. Here am I at his service: here is a life worth nothing to any one waiting to be taken if he is willing and has the power to take it.

This was a challenge direct enough, yet strange to say no sudden furious action followed, no flashing of steel and blood splashed on table and benches; nor was there the faintest sign of emotion in the singer's face, or any tremor or change in his voice when he resumed his singing. And so it went on to the end—boastful stanza and insulting remarks from Marcos; and by the time the *decima* ended a dozen or twenty men had forced themselves in between the two so that there could be no fight on this occasion.

Among those present was an old gaucho who took a peculiar interest in me on account of my bird lore and who used to talk and expound gaucho philosophy to me in a fatherly way. Meeting him a day or two later I remarked I did not think Barboza deserving of his fame as a fighter. I thought him a coward. No, he said, he was not a coward. He could have killed Marcos, but he considered that it would be a mistake, since it would add nothing to his reputation and would probably make him disliked in the district. That was all very well, I replied, but how could any one who was not a poltroon endure to be publicly insulted and challenged without flying into a rage and going for his enemy?

He smiled and answered that I was an ignorant boy and would understand these things better some day, after knowing a good many fighters. There were some, he said, who were men of fiery temper, who would fly at and kill any one for the slightest cause—an idle or imprudent word perhaps. There were others of a cool temper whose ambition it was to be great fighters, who fought and killed people not because they hated or were in a rage with them, but for the sake of the fame it would give them. Barboza was one of this cool kind, who when he fought killed, and he was not to be drawn into a fight by any ordinary person or any fool who thought proper to challenge him.

Thus spoke my mentor and did not wholly remove my doubts. But I must now go back to the earlier date, when this strange family were newly come to our neighbourhood.

All of the family appeared proud of their strangeness and of the reputation of their fighting brother, their protector and chief. No doubt he was an unspeakable ruffian, and although I was accustomed to ruffians even as a child and did not find that they differed much from other men, this one with his fierce piercing eyes and cloud of black beard and hair, somehow made me uncomfortable, and I accordingly avoided Los Alamos. I disliked the whole tribe, except a little girl of about eight, a child, it was said, of one of the unmarried sisters. I never discovered which of her aunts, as she called all these tall, white-faced heavy-browed women, was her mother. I used to see her almost every day, for though a child she was out on horseback early and late, riding barebacked and boy fashion, flying about the plain, now to drive in the horses, now to turn back the flock when it was getting too far afield, then the cattle, and finally to ride on errands to neighbours' houses or to buy groceries at the store. I can see her now at full gallop on the plain, bare-footed and bare-legged, in her thin old cotton frock, her raven-black hair flying loose behind. The strangest thing in her was her whiteness: her beautifully chiselled face was like alabaster, without a freckle or trace of colour in spite of the burning hot sun and wind she was constantly exposed to. She was also extremely lean, and strangely serious for a little girl: she never laughed and rarely smiled. Her name was Angela, and she was called Anjelita, the affectionate diminutive, but I doubt that much affection was ever bestowed on her.

To my small-boy's eyes she was a beautiful being with a cloud on her, and I wished it had been in my power to say something to make her laugh and forget, though but for a minute, the many cares and anxieties which made her so unnaturally grave for a little girl. Nothing proper to say ever came to me, and if it had come it would no doubt have remained unspoken. Boys are always inarticulate where their deepest feelings are concerned; however much they may desire it they cannot express kind and sympathetic feelings. In a halting way they may sometimes say a word of that nature to another boy, or pal, but before a girl, however much she may move their compassion, they remain dumb. I remember, when my age was about nine, the case of a quarrel about some trivial matter I once had with my closest friend, a boy of my own age who, with his people, used to come yearly on a month's visit to us from Buenos Ayres. For three whole days we spoke not a word and took no notice of each other, whereas before we had been inseparable. Then he all at once came up to me and holding out his hand said, "Let's be friends." I seized the proffered hand, and was more grateful to him than I have ever felt towards any one since, just because by approaching me first I was spared the agony of having to say those three words to him. Now that boy—that is to say, the material part of him—is but a handful of grey ashes, long, long ago at rest; but I can believe that if the other still living part should by chance be in this room now, peeping over my shoulder to see what I am writing, he would burst into as hearty a laugh as a ghost is capable of at this ancient memory, and say to himself that it took him all his courage to speak those three simple words.

And so it came about that I said no gentle word to white-faced Anjelita, and in due time she vanished out of my life with all that queer tribe of hers, the bloody uncle included, to leave an enduring image in my mind which has never quite lost a certain disturbing effect.

CHAPTER X

Our Nearest English Neighbour

Casa Antigua, our nearest English neighbour's house—
Old Lombardy poplars—Cardoon thistle or wild artichoke—Mr. Royd, an English sheep-farmer—Making
sheep's-milk cheeses under difficulties—Mr. Royd's
native wife—The negro servants—The two daughters:
a striking contrast—The white blue-eyed child and her
dusky playmate—A happy family—Our visits to Casa
Antigua—Gorgeous dinners—Estanislao and his love
of wild life—The Royds' return visits—A home-made
carriage—The gaucho's primitive conveyance—The
happy home broken up.

ONE of the most important estancias in our neighbourhood, at all events to us, was called Casa Antigua, and
that it was an ancient dwelling-place in that district
appeared likely enough, since the trees were the largest
and had an appearance of extreme age. It must, however, be remembered that in speaking of ancient things
on the pampas we mean things a century or two old,
not many hundreds or thousands of years as in Europe.
Three centuries in that part of South America takes us
back to prehistoric times. These Lombardy poplars,
planted in long rows, were the largest I had seen: they
were very tall; many of them appeared to be dying of
old age, and all had enormous rough-barked buttressed

trunks. The other shade-trees were also old and gnarled, some of them dying. The house itself did not look ancient, and was built of unburnt bricks and thatched, and had a broad corridor supported by wooden posts or pillars.

The Casa Antigua was situated about six miles from our house, but looked no more than three on account of the great height of the trees, which made it appear large and conspicuous on that wide level plain. The land for miles round it was covered with a dense growth of cardoon thistles. Now the cardoon is the European artichoke run wild and its character somewhat altered in a different soil and climate. The large deep-cut leaves are of a palish grey-green colour, the stalks covered with a whitish-grey down, and the leaves and stems thickly set with long yellow spines. It grows in thick bushes, and the bushes grow close together to the exclusion of grasses and most other plant-life, and produces purple blossoms big as a small boy's head, on stems four or five feet high. The stalks, which are about as thick as a man's wrist, were used when dead and dry as firewood; and this indeed was the only fuel obtainable at that time in the country, except "cow chips," from the grazing lands and "peat" from the sheepfold. At the end of summer, in February, the firewood-gatherers would set to work gathering the cardoon-stalks, their hands and arms protected with sheep-skin gloves, and at that season our carters would bring in huge loads, to be stacked up in piles high as a house for the year's use.

The land where the cardoon grows so abundantly is not good for sheep, and at Casa Antigua all the land was of this character. The tenant was an Englishman, a Mr. George Royd, and it was thought by his neighbours that he had made a serious mistake which would perhaps lead to disastrous consequences, when investing his capital in the expensive fine-wool breeds to put them on such land. All this I heard years afterwards. At that time I only knew that he was our nearest English neighbour, and more to us on that account than any other. We certainly had other English neighbours —those who lived half a day's journey on horseback from us were our neighbours there—English, Welsh, Irish, Scotch, but they were not like Mr. Royd. These others, however prosperous (and some were the owners of large estates), came mostly from the working or lower middle class in their own country and were interested solely in their own affairs. Mr. Royd was of a different order. He was about forty-five when my years were seven, a handsome clean-shaved man with bright blue humorous eyes and brown hair. He was an educated man, and loved to meet with others of like mind with himself, with whom he could converse in his own language. There was no English in his house. He had a bright genial disposition, a love of fun, and a hearty ringing laugh it was a pleasure to hear. He was an enthusiast about his sheep-farming, always full of fine projects, always dreaming of the things he intended doing and of the great results which would follow. One of his pet notions was that cheeses made with sheep's milk would be worth any price he liked to put on them, and he accordingly began to make them under very great difficulties, since the sheep had to be broken to it and they yielded but a small quantity compared with the sheep of certain districts in France and other countries where they have been milked for many generations and have enlarged their udders. Worst of all, his native servants considered it a degradation to have to stoop to milk such creatures as sheep. "Why not milk the cats?" they scornfully demanded. However, he succeeded in making cheeses, and very nice they were, far nicer in fact than any native cheeses made from cows' milk we had ever tasted. But the difficulties were too great for him to produce them in sufficient quantity for the market, and eventually the sheep-milking came to an end.

Unfortunately Mr. Royd had no one to help him in his schemes, or to advise and infuse a little more practicality into him. His family could never have been anything but a burden and drag on him in his struggle, and his disaster probably resulted from his romantic and over-sanguine temper, which made him the husband of his wife and caused him to dream of a fortune built on cheeses made from sheep's milk.

His wife was a native; in other words, a lady of Spanish blood, of a good family, city born and bred. They had met in Buenos Ayres when in their bloom, at the most emotional period of life, and in spite of opposition from her people and of the tremendous difficulties in the way of a union between one of the Faith and a heretic in those religious days, they were eventually made man and wife. As a girl she had been beautiful; now, aged about forty, she was only fat— a large fat woman, with an extremely white skin, raven-black hair and eyebrows, and velvet-black eyes. That was Doña Mercedes as I knew her. She did no work in the house, and never went for a walk or a ride on horseback: she spent her time in an easy-chair, always well dressed, and in warm weather always with a fan in her hand. I can hear the rattle of that fan now as she played with it, producing a succession of graceful waving motions and rhythmic sounds as an accompaniment to the endless torrent of small talk which she poured out; for she was an exceedingly voluble person, and to assist in making the conversation more lively there were always two or three screaming parrots on their perches near her. She also liked to be surrounded by all the other females in the house, her two daughters and the indoor servants, four or five in number, all full-blooded negresses, black but comely, fat, pleasant-looking, laughing young and middle-aged women, all as a rule dressed in white. They were unmarried, but two or three of them were the mothers of certain small darkies to be seen playing about and rolling in the dust near the servants' quarters at the far end of the long low house.

The eldest daughter, Eulodia, was about fifteen as I first remember her, a tall slim handsome girl with blue-black hair, black eyes, coral-red lips, and a remarkably white skin without a trace of red colour in it. She was no doubt just like what her mother had been when the dashing impressionable young George Royd had first met her and lost his heart—and soul. The younger sister, about eight at that time, was a perfect contrast to Eulodia: she had taken after her father, and in colour and appearance generally was a perfect little English girl of the usual angel type, with long shining golden hair, worn in curls, eyes of the purest turquoise blue, and a complexion like the petals of a wild rose. Adelina was her pretty name, and to us Adelina was the most beautiful human being in the world, especially when seen with her dusky little playmate Liberata, who was of the same age and height and was the child of one of the black servants. These two had grown fond of each other from the cradle, and so Liberata had been promoted to be Adelina's constant companion in the house and to wear pretty dresses. Being a *mulatita* she was dark or dusky skinned, with a reddish tinge in the duskiness, purple-red lips, and liquid black eyes with orange-brown reflections in them—the eyes called tortoiseshell in America. Her crisp cast-iron coloured hair was worn like a fleece round her small head, and her features were so refined one could only suppose that her father had been a singularly handsome as well as a white man. Adelina and Liberata were insepar-able, except at meal-times, when the dusky little girl had to go back among her own tribe on the mother's side; and they formed an exquisite picture as one often saw them, standing by the Señora's chair with their arms round each other's necks—the pretty dark-skinned child and the beautiful white child with shining hair and blue forget-me-not eyes.

Adelina was her father's favourite, but he was fond of all his people, the black servants included, and they of him, and the life at Casa Antigua appeared to be an exceedingly happy and harmonious one.

Looking back at this distance of time it strikes me when I come to think of it, that it was a most extra-ordinary *ménage,* a collection of the most incongruous beings it would be possible to bring together—a sort of Happy Family in the zoological sense. It did not seem so at the time, when in any house on the wide pampas one would meet with people whose lives and characters would be regarded in civilized countries as exceedingly odd and almost incredible.

It was a red-letter day to us children when, about once a month, we were packed into a trap and driven with our parents to spend a day at Casa Antigua. The dinner at noon was the most gorgeous affair of the kind we knew. One of Mr. Royd's enthusiasms was cookery—the making of rare and delicate dishes—and the servants had been taught so well that we used to be amazed at the richness and profusion of the repast. These dinners were to us like the "collations" and feasts so minutely and lovingly described in the *Arabian Nights,* especially that dinner of many courses given by the Barmecide to his hungry guest which followed the first tantalizing imaginary one. The wonder was that any man in the position of a sheep-farmer in a semi-barbarous land, far from any town, could provide such dinners for his visitors.

After dinner my best time would come, when I would steal off to look for Estanislao, the young native horseman, who was only too enthusiastic about wild life and spent more time hunting rheas than in attending to his duties. "When I see an ostrich," he would say, "I leave the flock and drop my work no matter what it is. I would rather lose my place on the estancia than not chase it." But he never lost his place, since it appeared that no one could do anything wrong on the estancia and not be forgiven by its master.

Then Estanislao, a big fellow in gaucho dress, wearing a red handkerchief tied round his head in place of hat, and a mass or cloud of blackish crinkled hair on his neck and shoulders, would take me round the plantation to show me any nests he had found and any rare birds that happened to be about.

Towards evening we would be bundled back into the trap and driven home. Then, when the day came round for the return visit, Mr. Royd would bundle his family into their "carriage," which he, without being a carriage-builder or even a carpenter, had made with his own hands. It had four solid wooden wheels about a yard in diameter, and upright wooden sides about four or five feet high. It was springless and without seats, and had a long pole to which two horses were fastened, and Estanislao, mounted on one, would thrash them into a gallop and carry the thing bounding over the roadless plain. The fat lady and other passengers were saved from being bumped to death by several mattresses, pillows, and cushions heaped inside. It was the strangest, most primitive conveyance I ever saw, except the one commonly used by a gaucho to take his wife on a visit to a neighbour's house when she was in a delicate condition or too timid to ride on a horse or not well enough off to own a side-saddle. This was a well-stretched, dried horse-hide, with a lasso attached at one end to the head or fore-part of the hide and the other end to the gaucho's horse, as a rule to the surcingle. A stool or cushion was placed in the centre of the big hide for the lady to sit on, and when she had established herself on it the man would whip up his horse and away he would gallop, dragging the strange conveyance after him—a sight which filled the foreigner with amazement.

Our intimate happy relations with the Royd family continued till about my twelfth year, then came rather suddenly to an end. Mr. Royd, who had always seemed one of the brightest, happiest men we knew, all at once fell into a state of profound melancholy. No one could guess the cause, as he was quite well and appeared to be prosperous. He was at length persuaded by his friends to go to Buenos Ayres to consult a doctor, and went alone and stayed in the house of an Anglo-Argentine family who were also friends of ours. By-and-by the dreadful news came that he had committed suicide by cutting his throat with a razor. His wife and daughters then left the Casa Antigua, and not long afterwards Doña Mercedes wrote to my mother that they were left penniless; that their flocks and other possessions at the estancia were to be sold for the benefit of their creditors, and that she and her daughters were living on the charity of some of her relations who were not well off. Her only hope was that her two daughters, being good-looking girls, would find husbands and be in a position to keep her from want. Her one word about her dead husband, the lovable, easy-going George Royd, the bright handsome English boy who had wooed and won her so many years before, was that she looked upon her meeting with him in girlhood as the great calamity of her life, that in killing himself and leaving his wife and daughters to poverty and suffering, he had committed an unpardonable crime.

So ends the story of our nearest English neighbour.

CHAPTER XI

A Breeder of Piebalds

La Tapera, a native estancia—Don Gregorio Gandara—
His grotesque appearance and strange laugh—Gandara's
wife and her habits and pets—My dislike of hairless
dogs—Gandara's daughters—A pet ostrich—In the
peach orchard—Gandara's herds of piebald brood mares
—His masterful temper—His own saddle-horses—
Creating a sensation at gaucho gatherings—The younger
daughter's lovers—Her marriage at our house—The
priest and the wedding breakfast—Demetria forsaken
by her husband.

WHEN, standing by the front gate of our home, we
looked out to the north over the level plain and let
our eyes rove west from the tall Lombardy poplars of
Casa Antigua, they presently rested on another pile or
island of trees, blue in the distance, marking the site
of another estancia house. This was the estancia
called La Tapera, with whose owner we also had
friendly relations during all the years we lived in that
district. The owner was Don Gregorio Gandara, a
native, and like our nearest English neighbour, Mr.
Royd, an enthusiast, and was also like him in being
the husband of a fat indolent wife who kept parrots
and other pet animals, and the father of two daughters.
In this case, too, there were no sons. There, however,

all resemblance ceased, since two men more unlike in their appearance, character, and fortune it would not be easy to find. Don Gregorio was an extraordinary person to look at; he had a round or barrel-shaped body, short bow legs, and a big round head, which resembled a ball fashioned out of a block of dark-coloured wood with a coarse human face and huge ears rudely carved on it. He had a curly head, the crisp dark hair growing as knobs, which gave his round skull the appearance of being embossed like the head of a curly retriever. The large brown eyes were extremely prominent, with a tremendous staring power in them, and the whole expression was one of toad-like gravity. But he could laugh on occasion, and his laugh to us children was the most grotesque and consequently the most delightful thing about him. Whenever we saw him ride up and dismount, and after fastening his magnificently caparisoned horse to the outer gate come in to make a call on our parents, we children would abandon our sports or whatever we were doing and joyfully run to the house; then distributing ourselves about the room on chairs and stools, sit, silent and meek, listening and watching for Don Gregorio's laugh. He talked in a startlingly emphatic way, almost making one jump when he assented to what was being said with his loud sudden *si-si-si-si-si,* and when he spoke bringing out his sentences two or three words at a time, sounding like angry barks. And by and by something would be said to touch his risible faculties, which would send him off in a sort of fit; and throwing himself back in his chair, closing his eyes and opening wide his big mouth he would draw his breath in with a prolonged wailing or sibilant sound until his lungs were too full to hold any more, and it would then be discharged with a rush, accompanied by a sort of wild animal scream, something like the scream of a fox. Then instantly, almost before the scream was over, his countenance would recover its preternatural gravity and intense staring attention.

Our keen delight in this performance made it actually painful since the feeling could not be expressed—since we knew that our father knew that we were only too liable to explode in the presence of an honoured guest, and nothing vexed him more. While in the room we dared not change glances or even smile; but after seeing and hearing the wonderful laugh a few times we would steal off and going to some quiet spot sit in a circle and start imitating it, finding it a very delightful pastime.

After I had learnt to ride I used sometimes to go with my mother and sisters for an afternoon's visit to La Tapera. The wife was the biggest and fattest woman in our neighbourhood and stood a head and shoulders taller than her barrel-shaped husband. She was not, like Doña Mercedes, a lady by birth, nor an educated person, but resembled her in her habits and tastes. She sat always in a large cane easy-chair, outdoors or in, invariably with four hairless dogs in her company, one on her broad lap, another on a lambskin rug at her feet, and one on rugs at each side. The three on the floor were ever patiently waiting for their respective turns to occupy the broad warm lap when the time came to remove the last-favoured one from that position. I had an invincible dislike to these dogs with their shiny blue-black naked skins, like the bald head of an old negro, and their long white scattered whiskers. These white stiff hairs on their faces and their dim blinking eyes gave them a certain resemblance to very old ugly men with black blood in them, and made them all the more repulsive.

The two daughters, both grown to womanhood, were named Marcelina and Demetria; the first big, brown, jolly, and fat like her mother, the other with better features, a pale olive skin, dark melancholy eyes, and a gentle pensive voice and air which made her seem like one of a different family and race. The daughters would serve maté to us, a beverage which as a small boy I did not like, but there was no chocolate or tea in that house for visitors, and in fruit-time I was always glad to get away to the orchard. As at our own home the old peach trees grew in the middle part of the plantation, the other parts being planted with rows of Lombardy poplars and other large shade trees. A tame ostrich, or rhea, was kept at the house, and as long as we remained indoors or seated in the verandah he would hang about close by, but would follow us as soon as we started off to the orchard. He was like a pet dog and could not endure to be left alone or in the uncongenial company of other domestic creatures—dogs, cats, fowls, turkeys, and geese. He regarded men and women as the only suitable associates for an ostrich, but was not allowed in the rooms on account of his inconvenient habit of swallowing metal objects such as scissors, spoons, thimbles, bodkins, copper coins, and anything of the kind he could snatch up when no one was looking. In the orchard when he saw us eating peaches he would do the same, and if he couldn't reach high enough to pluck them for himself he would beg of us. It was great fun to give him half a dozen or more at a time, then, when they had been quickly gobbled up, watch their progress as the long row of big round lumps slowly travelled down his neck and disappeared one by one as the peaches passed into his crop.

Gandara's great business was horse-breeding, and as a rule he kept about a thousand brood mares, so that the herds usually numbered about three thousand head. Strange to say, they were nearly all piebalds. The gaucho, from the poorest worker on horseback to the largest owner of lands and cattle, has, or had in those days, a fancy for having all his riding-horses of one colour. Every man as a rule had his *tropilla*—his own half a dozen or a dozen or more saddle-horses, and he would have them all as nearly alike as possible, so that one man had chestnuts, another browns, bays, silver- or iron-greys, duns, fawns, cream-noses, or blacks, or whites, or piebalds. On some estancias the cattle, too, were all of one colour, and I remember one estate where the cattle, numbering about six thousand, were all black. Our neighbour's fancy was for piebald horses, and so strong was it that he wished not to have any one-coloured animals in his herd, despite the fact that he bred horses for sale and that piebalds were not so popular as horses of a more normal colouring. He would have done better if, sticking to one colour, he had bred iron-greys, cream-noses, chestnuts, or fawns or duns— all favourite colours; or better still if he had not confined himself to any one colour. The stallions were all piebalds, but many of the brood mares were white, as he had discovered that he could get as good if not better results from keeping white as well as piebald mares. Nobody quarrelled with Gandara on account of his taste in horses; on the contrary, he and his vast parti-coloured herds were greatly admired, but his ambition to have a monopoly in piebalds was sometimes a cause of offence. He sold two-year-old geldings only, but never a mare unless for slaughter, for in those days the half-wild horses of the pampas were annually slaughtered in vast numbers just for the hides and grease. If he found a white or piebald mare in a neighbour's herd he would not rest until he got possession of it, and by giving double its value in money or horses he seldom found any difficulty in getting what he wanted. But occasionally some poor gaucho with only a few animals would refuse to part with a piebald mare, either out of pride, or "cussedness" as an American would say, or because he was attached to it, and this would stir Gandara's soul to its deepest depth and bring up all the blackness in him to the surface. "What do you want, then?" he would shout, sitting on his horse and making violent gestures with his right hand and arm, barking out his words. "Have I not offered you enough? Listen! What is a white mare to you—to you, a poor man—more than a mare of any other colour? If your riding-horses must be of one colour, tell me the colour you want. Black or brown or bay or chestnut, or what? Look! you shall have two young unbroken geldings of two years in exchange for the mare. Could you make a better exchange? Were you ever treated more generously? If you refuse it will be out of spite, and I shall know how to treat you. When you lose your animals and are broken, when your children are sick with fever, when your wife is starving, you shall not come to me for a horse to ride on, nor for money, nor meat, nor medicine, since you will have me for an enemy instead of a friend."

That, they say, was how he raged and bullied when he met with a repulse from a poor neighbour. So fond was Don Gregorio of his piebalds that he spent the greater part of every day on horseback with his different herds of mares, each led by its own proud piebald stallion. He was perpetually waiting and watching with anxious interest for the appearance of a new foal. If it turned out not a piebald he cared nothing more about it, no matter how beautiful in colour it might be or what good points it had: it was to go as soon as he could get rid of it; but if a piebald, he would rejoice, and if there was anything remarkable in its colouring he would keep a sharp eye on it, to find out later perhaps that he liked it too well to part with it. Eventually, when broken, it would go into his private *tropilla*, and in this way he would always possess three or four times as many saddle-horses as he needed. If you met Gandara every day for a week or two you would see him each time on a different horse, and every one of them would be more or less a surprise to you on account of its colouring.

There was something fantastic in this passion. It reminds one of the famous eighteenth-century miller of Newhaven, described by Mark Antony Lower in his book about the strange customs and quaint characters in the Sussex of the old days. The miller used to pay weekly visits on horseback to his customers in the neighbouring towns and villages, his horse, originally a white one, having first been painted some brilliant colour—blue, green, yellow, orange, purple, or scarlet. The whole village would turn out to look at the miller's wonderful horse and speculate as to the colour he would exhibit on his next appearance. Gandara's horses were strangely coloured by nature aided by artificial selection, and I remember that as a boy I thought them very beautiful. Sometimes it was a black- or brown- or bay-and-white, or a chestnut- or silver-grey- or strawberry-red-and-white, but the main point was the pleasing arrangement and shading of the dark colour. Some of his best selected specimens were iron- or blue-grey-and-white; others, finer still, fawn-and-white and dun-and-white, and the best of all, perhaps, white and a metallic tawny yellow, the colour the natives call bronze or brassy, which I never see in England. Horses of this colour have the ears edged and tipped with black, the muzzle, fetlocks, mane, and tail also black. I do not know if he ever succeeded in breeding a tortoiseshell.

Gandara's pride in the horses he rode himself—the rare blooms selected from his equine garden—showed itself in the way in which he decorated them with silver headstalls and bit and the whole gear sparkling with silver, while he was careless of his own dress, going about in an old rusty hat, unpolished boots, and a frayed old Indian poncho or cloak over his gaucho garments. Probably the most glorious moment of his life was when he rode to a race-meeting or cattle-marking or other gathering of the gaucho population of the district, when all eyes would be turned to him on his arrival. Dismounting, he would hobble his horse, tie the glittering reins to the back of the saddle, and leave him proudly champing his big native bit and tossing his decorated head, while the people gathered round to admire the strangely-coloured animal as if it had been a Pegasus just alighted from the skies to stand for a while exhibiting itself among the horses of the earth.

My latest recollections of La Tapera are concerned more with Demetria than the piebalds. She was not an elegant figure, as was natural in a daughter of the grotesque Don Gregorio, but her countenance, as I have said, was attractive on account of its colour and gentle wistful expression, and being the daughter of a man rich in horses she did not want for lovers. In those far-off days the idle, gay, well-dressed young gambler was always a girl's first and often most successful wooer, but at La Tapera the young lovers had to reckon with one who, incredible as it seemed in a gaucho, hated gambling and kept a hostile and rather terrifying eye on their approaches. Eventually Demetria became engaged to a young stranger from a distance who had succeeded in persuading the father that he was an eligible person and able to provide for a wife.

Now it happened that the nearest priest in our part of the country lived a long distance away, and to get to him and his little thatched chapel one had to cross a swamp two miles wide in which one's horse would sink belly-deep in miry holes at least a dozen times before one could get through. In these circumstances the Gandara family could not go to the priest, but managed to persuade him to come to them, and as La Tapera was not considered a good enough place in which to hold so important a ceremony, my parents invited them to have the marriage in our house. The priest arrived on horseback about noon on a sultry day, hot and tired and well splashed with dried mud, and in a rather bad temper. It must also have gone against him to unite these young people in the house of heretics who were doomed to a dreadful future after their rebellious lives had ended. However, he got through with the business, and presently recovered his good temper and grew quite genial and talkative when he was led into the dining-room and found a grand wedding-breakfast with wine in plenty on the table. During the breakfast I looked often and long at the faces of the newly-married pair, and pitied our nice gentle Demetria, and wished she had not given herself to that man. He was not a bad-looking young man and was well-dressed in the gaucho costume, but he was strangely silent and ill at ease the whole time and did not win our regard. I never saw him again. It soon came out that he was a gambler and had nothing but his skill with a pack of cards to live by, and Don Gregorio in a rage told him to go back to his native place. And go he did very soon, leaving poor Demetria on her parents' hands.

Shortly after this unhappy experience Don Gregorio bought a house in Buenos Ayres for his wife and daughters, so that they could go and spend a month or two when they wanted a change, and I saw them on one or two occasions when in town. He himself would have been out of his element in such a place, shut up in a close room or painfully waddling over the rough boulder-stones of the narrow streets on his bow legs. Life for him was to be on the back of a piebald horse on the wide green plain, looking after his beloved animals.

CHAPTER XII
The Head of a Decayed House

The Estancia Cañada Seca—Low lands and floods—Don
Anastacio, a gaucho exquisite—A greatly respected
man—Poor relations—Don Anastacio a pig-fancier—
Narrow escape from a pig—Charm of the low green
lands—The flower called *mácachina*—A sweet-tasting
bulb—Beauty of the green flower-sprinkled turf—
A haunt of the golden plover—The *Bolas*—My plover-
hunting experience—Rebuked by a gaucho—A green
spot, our playground in summer and lake in winter—
The venomous toad-like Caratophrys—Vocal performance of the toad-like creature—We make war on
them—The great lake battle and its results.

In this chapter I wish to introduce the reader to the
last but one of the half a dozen of our nearest neighbours, selected as typical of the smaller estancieros—
a class of landowners and cattle-breeders then in their
decay and probably now fast vanishing. This was
Don Anastacio Buenavida, who was an original person
too in his little way. He was one of our very nearest
neighbours, his estancia house being no more than two
short miles from us on the south side. Like most
of these old establishments, it was a long low building
with a thatched roof, enclosures for cattle and sheep
close by, and an old grove or plantation of shade-trees
bordered with rows of tall Lombardy poplars. The

whole place had a decayed and neglected appearance, the grounds being weedy and littered with bleached bones and other rubbish: fences and ditches had also been destroyed and obliterated, so that the cattle were free to rub their hides on the tree trunks and gnaw at the bark. The estancia was called Cañada Seca, from a sluggish muddy stream near the house which almost invariably dried up in summer; in winter after heavy rains it overflowed its low banks, and in very wet seasons lake-like ponds of water were formed all over the low-lying plain between Cañada Seca and our house. A rainy season was welcome to us children: the sight of wide sheets of clear shallow water with a vivid green turf beneath excited us joyfully, and also afforded us some adventurous days, one of which will be related by and by.

Don Anastacio Buenavida was a middle-aged man, a bachelor, deeply respected by his neighbours, and even looked on as a person of considerable importance. So much did I hear in his praise that as a child I had a kind of reverential feeling for him, which lasted for years and did not, I think, wholly evaporate until I was in my teens and began to form my own judgments. He was quite a little man, not more than an inch or two over five feet high, slim, with a narrow waist and small ladylike hands and feet. His small oval face was the colour of old parchment; he had large dark pathetic eyes, a beautifully shaped black moustache, and long black hair, worn in symmetrical ringlets to his shoulders. In his dress too he was something of an exquisite. He wore the picturesque gaucho costume; a *camiseta,* or blouse, of the finest black cloth, profusely decorated with silver buttons, puffs and pleats, and scarlet and green embroidery; a *chiripá*, the shawl-like garment worn in place of trousers, of the finest yellow or vicuña-coloured wool, the white *carsoncillos*, or wide drawers, showing below, of the finest linen, with more fringe and lace-work than was usual in that garment. His boots were well polished, and his poncho, or cloak, of the finest blue cloth, lined with scarlet.

It must have taken Don Anastacio a couple of hours each morning to get himself up in this fashion, ringlets and all, and once up he did nothing but sit in the living-room, sipping bitter maté and taking part from time to time in the general conversation, speaking always in low but impressive tones. He would say something about the weather, the lack or superabundance of water, according to the season, the condition of his animals and the condition of the pasture—in fact, just what everybody else was saying but of more importance as coming from him. All listened to his words with the profoundest attention and respect, and no wonder, since most of those who sat in his living-room, sucking maté, were his poor relations who fed on his bounty.

Don Anastacio was the last of a long line of estancieros once rich in land and cattle, but for generations the Cañada Seca estate had been dwindling as land was sold, and now there was little left, and the cattle and horses were few, and only a small flock of sheep kept just to provide the house with mutton. His poor relations living scattered about the district knew that he was not only an improvident but an exceedingly weak and soft-hearted man, in spite of his grand manner, and many of the poorest among them had been allowed to build their ranchos on his land and to keep a few animals for their sustenance: most of these had built their hovels quite close to the estancia house, behind the plantation, so that it was almost like a hamlet at this point. These poor neighbours had the freedom of the kitchen or living-room; it was usually full of them, especially of the women, gossiping, sipping endless maté, and listening with admiring attention to the wise words which fell at intervals from the lips of the head of the family or tribe.

Altogether, Don Anastacio in his ringlets was an ineffectual, colourless, effeminate person, a perfect contrast to his ugly, barrel-shaped, badly-dressed but robust-minded neighbour, Gandara. Yet he too had a taste in animals which distinguished him among his fellow-landowners, and even reminded one of Gandara in a ridiculous way. For just as Gandara was devoted to piebald horses, so Don Anastacio was devoted to pigs. It would not have been like him if these had been pigs for profit: they were not animals fit to be fattened for the market, and no person would have thought of buying such beasts. They were of the wild-pig breed, descended originally from the European animal introduced by the early Spanish colonists, but after two or three centuries of feral life a good deal changed in appearance from their progenitors. This feral pig was called *barráco* in the vernacular, and was about a third less in size than the domestic animal, with longer legs and more pointed face, and of a uniform deep rust-red in colour. Among hundreds I never saw one with any black or white on it.

I believe that before Don Anastacio's time a few of these wild pigs had been kept as a curiosity at the estancia, and that when he came into possession he allowed them to increase and roam in herds all over the place, doing much harm by rooting up many acres of the best grazing land in their search after grubs, earthworms, mole-crickets, and blind snakes, along with certain roots and bulbs which they liked. This was their only provender when there happened to be no carcasses of cows, horses, or sheep for them to feed on in company with the dogs and carrion hawks. He would not allow his pigs to be killed, but probably his poor relations and pensioners were out occasionally by night to stick a pig when beef and mutton were wanting. I never tasted or wanted to taste their flesh. The gaucho is inordinately fond of the two gamiest-flavoured animals in the pampas—the ostrich or rhea and the hairy armadillo. These I could eat and enjoy eating, although I was often told by English friends that they were too strong for their stomachs; but the very thought of this wild pig-flesh produced a sensation of disgust.

One day when I was about eight years old I was riding home at a lonely spot three or four miles out, going at a fast gallop by a narrow path through a dense growth of giant thistles seven or eight feet high, when all at once I saw a few yards before me a big round heap of thistle plants, which had been plucked up entire and built into a shelter from the hot sun about four feet high. As I came close to it a loud savage grunt and the squealing of many little piglets issued from the mound, and out from it rushed a furious red sow and charged me. The pony suddenly swerved aside in terror, throwing me completely over on one side, but luckily I had instinctively gripped the mane with both hands, and with a violent effort succeeded in getting a leg back over the horse, and we swiftly left the dangerous enemy behind. Then, remembering all I had been told about the ferocity of these pigs, it struck me that I had had an extremely narrow escape, since if I had been thrown off the savage beast would have had me at her mercy and would have certainly killed me in a couple of minutes; and as she was probably mad with hunger and thirst in that lonely hot spot, with a lot of young to feed, it would not have taken her long to devour me, bones and boots included.

This set me thinking on the probable effect of my disappearance, of my mother's terrible anxiety, and what they would think and do about it. They would know from the return of the pony that I had fallen somewhere: they would have searched for me all over the surrounding plain, especially in all the wilder, lonelier places where birds breed; on lands where the cardoon thistle flourished most, and in the vast beds of bulrushes in the marshes, but would not have found me. And at length when the searching was all over, some gaucho riding by that cattle-path through the thistles would catch sight of a piece of cloth, a portion of a boy's garment, and the secret of my end would be discovered.

I had never liked the red pigs, on account of the way they ploughed up and disfigured the beautiful green sward with their iron-hard snouts, also because of the powerful and disgusting smell they emitted, but after this adventure with the sow the feeling was much stronger, and I wondered more and more why that beautiful soul, Don Anastacio, cherished an affection for such detestable beasts.

In spring and early summer the low-lying areas about Cañada Seca were pleasant places to see and ride on where the pigs had not defaced them: they kept their bright verdure when the higher grounds were parched and brown; then too, after rain, they were made beautiful with the bright little yellow flower called *mácachina*.

As the *mácachina* was the first wild flower to blossom in the land it had as great an attraction to us children as the wild strawberry, ground-ivy, celandine, and other first blooms for the child in England. Our liking for our earliest flower was all the greater because we could eat it and liked its acid taste, also because it had a bulb very nice to eat—a small round bulb the size of a hazel nut, of a pearly white, which tasted like sugar and water. That little sweetness was enough to set us all digging the bulbs up with tableknives, but even little children can value things for their beauty as well as taste. The *mácachina* was like the wood-sorrel in shape, both flower and leaf, but the leaves were much smaller and grew close to the ground, as the plant flourished most where the grass was close-cropped by the sheep, forming a smooth turf like that of our chalk downs. The flowers were never crowded together like the buttercup, forming sheets of shining yellow, but grew two or three inches apart, each slender stem producing a single flower, which stood a couple of inches above the turf. So fine were the stems that the slightest breath of wind would set the blossoms swaying, and it was then a pretty sight, and often held me motionless in the midst of some green place, when all around me for hundreds of yards the green carpet of grass was abundantly sprinkled with thousands of the little yellow blossoms all swaying to the light wind.

These green level lands were also a favourite haunt of the golden plover on their first arrival in September from their breeding-places many thousands of miles away in the arctic regions. Later in the season, as the water dried up, they would go elsewhere. They came in flocks and were then greatly esteemed as a table-bird, especially by my father, but we could only have them when one of my elder brothers, who was the sportsman of the family, went out to shoot them. As a very small boy I was not allowed to use a gun, but as I had been taught to throw the *bolas* by the little native boys I sometimes associated with, I thought I might be able to procure a few of the birds with it. The *bolas,* used for such an object, is a string a couple of yards long, made from fine threads cut from a colt's hide, twisted or braided, and a leaden ball at each end, one being the size of a hen's egg, the other less than half the size. The small ball is held in the hand, the other swung round three or four times and the *bolas* then launched at the animal or bird one wishes to capture.

I spent many hours on several consecutive days following the flocks about on my pony, hurling the *bolas* at them without bringing down more than one bird. My proceedings were no doubt watched with amusement by the people of the estancia house, who were often sitting out of doors at the everlasting maté-drinking; and perhaps Don Anastacio did not like it, as he was, I imagine, something of a St. Francis with regard to the lower animals. He certainly loved his abominable pigs. At all events on the last day of my vain efforts to procure golden plover, a big, bearded gaucho, with hat stuck on the back of his head, rode forth from the house on a large horse, and was passing at a distance of about fifty yards when he all at once stopped, and turning came at a gallop to within a few feet of me and shouted in a loud voice: "Why do you come here, English boy, frightening and chasing away God's little birds? Don't you know that they do no harm to any one, and it is wrong to hurt them?" And with that he galloped off.

I was angry at being rebuked by an ignorant ruffianly gaucho, who like most of his kind would tell lies, gamble, cheat, fight, steal, and do other naughty things without a qualm. Besides, it struck me as funny to hear the golden plover, which I wanted for the table, called "God's little birds," just as if they were wrens or swallows or humming-birds, or the darling little many-coloured kinglet of the bulrush beds. But I was ashamed, too, and gave up the chase.

The nearest of the moist green low-lying spots I have described as lying south of us, between our house and Cañada Seca, was not more than twenty minutes' walk from the gate. It was a flat, oval-shaped area of about fifty acres, and kept its vivid green colour and freshness when in January the surrounding land was all of a rusty brown colour. It was to us a delightful spot to run about and play on, and though the golden plover did not come there it was haunted during the summer by small flocks of the pretty buff-coloured sandpiper, a sandpiper with the habits of a plover, one, too, which breeds in the arctic regions and spends half the year in southern South America. This green area would become flooded after heavy rains. It was then like a vast lake to us, although the water was not more than about three feet deep, and at such times it was infested with the big venomous toad-like creature called *escuerzo* in the vernacular, which simply means toad, but naturalists have placed it in quite a different family of the batrachians and call it *Ceratophrys ornata* It is toad-like in form but more lumpish, with a bigger head; it is big as a man's fist, of a vivid green with black symmetrical markings on its back, and primrose-yellow beneath. A dreadful looking creature, a toad that preys on the real or common toads, swallowing them alive just as the hamadryad swallows other serpents, venomous or not, and as the Cribo of Martinique, a big non-venomous serpent, kills and swallows the deadly fer-de-lance.

In summer we had no fear of this creature, as it buries itself in the soil and æstivates during the hot, dry season, and comes forth in wet weather. I never knew any spot where these creatures were more abundant than in that winter lake of ours, and at night in the flooded time we used to lie awake listening to their concerts. The *Ceratophrys* croaks when angry, and as it is the most truculent of all batrachians it works itself into a rage if you go near it. Its first efforts at chanting or singing sounds like the deep, harsh, anger-croak prolonged, but as the time goes on they gradually acquire, night by night, a less raucous and a louder, more sustained and far-reaching sound. There was always very great variety in the tones; and while some continued deep and harsh—the harshest sound in nature—others were clearer and not unmusical; and in a large number there were always a few in the scattered choir that out-soared all the others in high, long-drawn notes, almost organ-like in quality.

Listening to their varied performance one night as we lay in bed, my sporting brother proposed that on the following morning we should drag one of the cattle-troughs to the lake to launch it and go on a voyage in quest of these dangerous, hateful creatures and slay them with our javelins. It was not an impossible scheme, since the creatures were to be seen at this season swimming or floating on the surface, and in our boat or canoe we should also detect them as they moved about over the green sward at the bottom.

Accordingly, next morning after breakfast we set out, without imparting our plans to any one, and with great labour dragged the trough to the water. It was a box-shaped thing, about twenty feet long and two feet wide at the bottom and three at the top. We were also provided with three javelins, one for each of us, from my brother's extensive armoury.

He had about that time been reading ancient history, and fired with the story of old wars when men fought hand to hand, he had dropped guns and pistols for the moment and set himself with furious zeal to manufacture the ancient weapons—bows and arrows, pikes,

shield, battle-axes and javelins. These last were sticks
about six feet long, nicely made of pine-wood—he had
no doubt bribed the carpenter to make them for him—
and pointed with old knife-blades six or seven inches
long, ground to a fearful sharpness. Such formidable
weapons were not required for our purpose: they
would have served well enough if we had been going
out against Don Anastacio's fierce and powerful swine;
but it was his order, and to his wild and warlike imagination the toad-like creatures were the warriors of
some hostile tribe opposing us, I forget if in Asia or
Africa, which had to be conquered and extirpated.

No sooner had we got into our long, awkwardly-
shaped boat than it capsized and threw us all into the
water; that was but the first of some dozens of upsets
and fresh drenchings we experienced during the day.
However, we succeeded in circumnavigating the lake
and crossing it two or three times from side to side,
and in slaying seventy or eighty of the enemy with our
javelins.

At length, when the short, mid-winter day was in its
decline, and we were all feeling stiff and cold and half-
famished, our commander thought proper to bring the
great lake battle, with awful slaughter of our barbarian
foes, to an end, and we wearily trudged home in our
soaking clothes and squeaking shoes. We were too
tired to pay much heed to the little sermon we had expected, and glad to get into dry clothes and sit down
to food and tea. Then to sit by the fire as close as we
could get to it, until we all began to sneeze and to feel
our throats getting sore and our faces burning hot.
And, finally, when we went burning and shivering with

cold to bed we could not sleep; and hark! the grand nightly chorus was going on just as usual. No, in spite of the great slaughter we had not exterminated the enemy; on the contrary, they appeared to be rejoicing over a great victory, especially when high above the deep harsh notes the long-drawn, organ-like sounds of the leaders were heard.

How I then wished, when tossing and burning feverishly in bed, that I had rebelled and refused to take part in that day's adventure! I was too young for it, and again and again, when thrusting one of the creatures through with my javeline, I had experienced a horrible disgust and shrinking at the spectacle. Now in my wakeful hours, with that tremendous chanting in my ears, it all came back to me and was like a nightmare.

CHAPTER XIII

A Patriarch of the Pampas

The grand old man of the plains—Don Evaristo Peñalva, the Patriarch—My first sight of his estancia house—Don Evaristo described—A husband of six wives—How he was esteemed and loved by every one—On leaving home I lose sight of Don Evaristo—I meet him again after seven years—His failing health—His old first wife and her daughter, Cipriana—The tragedy of Cipriana—Don Evaristo dies and I lose sight of the family.

PATRIARCHS were fairly common in the land of my nativity: grave, dignified old men with imposing beards, owners of land and cattle and many horses, though many of them could not spell their own names; handsome too, some of them with regular features, descendants of good old Spanish families who colonized the wide pampas in the seventeenth and early eighteenth centuries. I do not think I have got one of this sort in the preceding chapters which treat of our neighbours, unless it be Don Anastacio Buenavida of the corkscrew curls and quaint taste in pigs. Certainly he was of the old landowning class, and in his refined features and delicate little hands and feet gave evidence of good blood, but the marks of degeneration were equally plain; he was an effeminate, futile person, and not properly to be ranked with the patriarchs. His ugly grotesque neighbour of the piebald horses was more like one. I described the people that lived nearest to us, our next-door neighbours so to speak, because I knew them from childhood and followed their fortunes when I grew up, and was thus able to give their complete history. The patriarchs, the grand old gaucho estancieros, I came to know, were scattered all over the land, but, with one exception, I did not know them intimately from childhood, and though I could fill this chapter with their portraits I prefer to give it all to the one I knew best, Don Evaristo Peñalva, a very fine patriarch indeed.

I cannot now remember when I first made his acquaintance, but I was not quite six, though very near it, when I had my first view of his house. In the chapter on "Some Early Bird Adventures," I have described my first long walk on the plains, when two of my brothers took me to a river some distance from home, where I was enchanted with my first sight of that glorious waterfowl, the flamingo. Now, as we stood on the brink of the flowing water, which had a width of about two hundred yards at that spot when the river had overflowed its banks, one of my elder brothers pointed to a long low house, thatched with rushes, about three-quarters of a mile distant on the other side of the stream, and informed me that it was the estancia house of Don Evaristo Peñalva, who was one of the principal landowners in that part.

That was one of the images my mind received on that adventurous day which have not faded—the long, low mud built house, standing on the wide, empty, treeless plain, with three ancient, half-dead, crooked acacia trees growing close to it, and a little further away a corral or cattle-enclosure and a sheep-fold. It was a poor, naked, dreary-looking house without garden or shade, and I dare say a little English boy six years old would have smiled, a little incredulous, to be told that it was the residence of one of the principal land-owners in that part.

Then, as we have seen, I got my horse, and being delivered from the fear of evil-minded cows with long, sharp horns, I spent a good deal of my time on the plain, where I made the acquaintance of other small boys on horseback, who took me to their homes and introduced me to their people. In this way I came to be a visitor to that lonely-looking house on the other side of the river, and to know all the interesting people in it, including Don Evaristo himself, its lord and master. He was a middle-aged man at that date, of medium height, very white-skinned, with long black hair and full beard, straight nose, fine broad forehead, with large dark eyes. He was slow and deliberate in all his movements, grave, dignified, and ceremonious in his manner and speech; but in spite of this lofty air he was known to have a sweet and gentle disposition and was friendly towards every one, even to small boys who are naturally naughty and a nuisance to their elders. And so it came about that even as a very small shy boy, a stranger in the house, I came to know that Don Evaristo was not one to be afraid of.

I hope that the reader, forgetting all he has learnt about the domestic life of the patriarchs of an older time, will not begin to feel disgusted at Don Evaristo when I proceed to say that he was the husband of six wives, all living with him at that same house. The first, the only one he had been permitted to marry in a church, was old as or rather older than himself; she was very dark and was getting wrinkles, and was the mother of several grown-up sons and daughters, some married. The others were of various ages, the youngest two about thirty; and these were twin sisters, both named Ascension, for they were both born on Ascension Day. So much alike were these Ascensions in face and figure that one day, when I was a big boy, I went into the house and finding one of the sisters there began relating something, when she was called out. Presently she came back, as I thought, and I went on with my story just where I had left off, and only when I saw the look of surprise and inquiry on her face did I discover that I was now talking to the other sister.

How was this man with six wives regarded by his neighbours? He was esteemed and beloved above most men in his position. If any person was in trouble or distress, or suffering from a wound or some secret malady, he would go to Don Evaristo for advice and assistance and for such remedies as he knew; and if he was sick unto death he would send for Don Evaristo to come to him to write down his last will and testament. For Don Evaristo knew his letters and had the reputation of a learned man among the gauchos. They considered him better than any one calling himself a doctor. I remember that his cure for shingles, a common and dangerous ailment in that region, was regarded as infallible. The malady took the form of an eruption, like erysipelas, on the middle of the body and extending round the waist till it formed a perfect zone. "If the zone is not complete I can cure the disease," Don Evaristo would say. He would send some one down to the river to procure a good-sized toad, then causing the patient to strip, he would take pen and ink and write on the skin in the space between the two ends of the inflamed region, in stout letters, the words, *In the name of the Father,* etc. This done, he would take the toad in his hand and gently rub it on the inflamed part, and the toad, enraged at such treatment, would swell himself up almost to bursting and exude a poisonous milky secretion from his warty skin. That was all, and the man got well!

If it pleased such a man as that to have six wives instead of one it was right and proper for him to have them; no person would presume to say that he was not a good and wise and religious man on that account. It may be added that Don Evaristo, like Henry VIII, who also had six wives, was a strictly virtuous man. The only difference was that when he desired a fresh wife he did not barbarously execute or put away the one, or the others, he already possessed.

I lost sight of Don Evaristo when I was sixteen, having gone to live in another district about thirty miles from my old home. He was then just at the end of the middle period of life, with a few grey hairs beginning to show in his black beard, but he was still a strong man and more children were being added to his numerous family. Some time later I heard that he had acquired a second estate a long day's journey on horseback from the first, and that some of his wives and children had emigrated to the new esctancia and that he divided his time between the two establishments. But his people were not wholly separated from each other; from time to time some of them would take the long journey to visit the absent ones and there would be an exchange of homes between them. For, incredible as it may seem, they were in spirit, or appeared to be, a united family.

Seven years had passed since I lost sight of them, when it chanced that I was travelling home from the southern frontier with only two horses to carry me. One gave out, and I was compelled to leave him on the road. I put up that evening at a little wayside pulperia, or public-house, and was hospitably entertained by the landlord, who turned out to be an Englishman. But he had lived so long among the gauchos, having left his country when very young, that he had almost forgotten his own language. Again and again during the evening he started talking in English as if glad of the opportunity to speak his native tongue once more; but after a sentence or two a word wanted would not come, and it would have to be spoken in Spanish, and gradually he would relapse into unadulterated Spanish again, then, becoming conscious of the relapse, he would make a fresh start in English.

As we sat talking after supper I expressed my intention of leaving early in the morning so as to get over a few leagues while it was fresh, as the weather was very hot and I had to consider my one horse. He was sorry not to be able to provide me with another, but at one of the large estancias I would come to next morning I would no doubt be able to get one. He then mentioned that in about an hour and a half or two hours I should arrive at an estancia named La Paja Brava, where many riding-horses were kept.

This was good news indeed! La Paja Brava was the name of the estate my ancient friend and neighbour, Don Evaristo, had bought so many years before: no doubt I should find some of the family, and they would give me a horse and anything I wanted.

The house, when I approached it next morning, strongly reminded me of the old home of the family many leagues away, only it was if possible more lonely and dreary in appearance, without even an old half-dead acacia tree to make it less desolate. The plain all round as far as one could see was absolutely flat and treeless, the short grass burnt by the January sun to a yellowish-brown colour; while at the large watering-well, half a mile distant, the cattle were gathering in vast numbers, bellowing with thirst and raising clouds of dust in their struggles to get to the trough.

I found Don Evaristo himself in the house, and with him his first and oldest wife, with several of the grown-up children. I was grieved to see the change in my old friend; he had aged greatly in seven years; his face was now white as alabaster, and his full beard and long hair quite grey. He was suffering from some internal malady, and spent most of the day in the large kitchen and living-room, resting in an easy-chair. The fire burnt all day in the hearth in the middle of the clay floor, and the women served maté and did their work in a quiet way, talking the while; and all day long the young men and big boys came and went, coming in, one or two at a time, to sip maté, smoke, and tell the news—the state of the well, the time the water would last, the condition of the cattle, of horses strayed, and so on.

The old first wife had also aged—her whole dark, anxious face had been covered with little interlacing wrinkles; but the greatest change was in the eldest child, her daughter Cipriana, who was living permanently at La Paja Brava. The old mother had a dash of dark or negrine blood in her veins, and this strain came out strongly in the daughter, a tall woman with lustreless crinkled hair of a wrought-iron colour, large voluptuous mouth, pale dark skin, and large dark sad eyes.

I remembered that they had not always been sad, for I had known her in her full bloom—an imposing woman, her eyes sparkling with intense fire and passion, who, despite her coarse features and dark skin, had a kind of strange wild beauty which attracted men. Unhappily she placed her affections on the wrong person, a dashing young gaucho who, albeit landless and poor in cattle, made a brave appearance, especially when mounted and when man and horse glittered with silver ornaments. I recalled how one of my last sights of her had been on a Sunday morning in summer when I had ridden to a spot on the plain where it was overgrown with giant thistles, standing about ten feet high, in full flower and filling the hot air with their perfume. There, in a small open grassy space I had dismounted to watch a hawk, in hopes of finding its nest concealed somewhere among the thistles close by. And presently two persons came at a swift gallop by the narrow path through the thistles, and bursting out into that small open spot I saw that it was Cipriana, in a white dress, on a big bay horse, and her lover, who was leading the way. Catching sight of me they threw me a "Good morning" and galloped on, laughing gaily at the unexpected encounter. I thought that in her white dress, with the hot sun shining on her, her face flushed with excitement, on her big spirited horse, she looked splendid that morning.

But she gave herself too freely to her lover, and by and by there was a difference, and he rode away to return no more. It was hard for her then to face her neighbours, and eventually she went away with her mother to live at the new estancia; but even now at this distance of time it is a pain to remember her when her image comes back to my mind as I saw her on that chance visit to La Paja Brava.

Every evening during my stay, after maté had been served and there was a long vacant interval before night, she would go out from the gate to a distance of fifty or sixty yards, where an old log was lying on a piece of waste ground overgrown with nettles, burdock, and redweed, now dead and brown, and sitting on the log, her chin resting on her hand, she would fix her eyes on the dusty road half a mile away, and motionless in that dejected attitude she would remain for about an hour. When you looked closely at her you could see her lips moving, and if you came quite near her you could hear her talking in a very low voice, but she would not lift her gaze from the road nor seem to be aware of your presence. The fit or dream over, she would get up and return to the house, where she would quietly set to work with the other women in preparing the great meal of the day—the late supper of roast and boiled meat, when all the men would be back from their work with the cattle.

That was my last sight of Cipriana; what her end was I never heard, nor what was done with the Paja Brava after the death of Don Evaristo, who was gathered to his fathers a year or so after my visit. I only know that the old place where as a child I first knew him, where his cattle and horses grazed and the stream where they were watered was alive with herons and spoonbills, black-necked swans, glossy ibises in clouds, and great blue ibises with resounding voices, is now possessed by aliens, who destroy all wild bird life and grow corn on the land for the markets of Europe.

CHAPTER XIV

The Dovecote

A favourite climbing tree—The desire to fly—Soaring birds
—A peregrine falcon—The dovecote and pigeon-pies—
The falcon's depredations—A splendid aerial feat—A
secret enemy of the dovecote—A short-eared owl in a
loft—My father and birds—A strange flower—The
owls' nesting-place—Great owl visitations.

By the side of the moat at the far end of the enclosed
ground there grew a big red willow, the tree already
mentioned in a former chapter as the second largest
in the plantation. It had a thick round trunk, wide-
spreading horizontal branches, and rough bark. In its
shape, when the thin foliage was gone, it was more
like an old oak than a red willow. This was my favourite tree when I had once mastered the difficult
and dangerous art of climbing. It was farthest from
the house of all the trees, on a waste weedy spot which
no one else visited, and this made it an ideal place for
me, and whenever I was in the wild arboreal mood I
would climb the willow to find a good stout branch
high up on which to spend an hour, with a good view
of the wide green plain before me and the sight of
grazing flocks and herds, and of houses and poplar
groves looking blue in the distance. Here, too, in this

tree, I first felt the desire for wings, to dream of the delight it would be to circle upwards to a great height and float on the air without effort, like the gull and buzzard and harrier and other great soaring land and water birds. But from the time this notion and desire began to affect me I envied most the great crested screamer, an inhabitant then of all the marshes in our vicinity. For here was a bird as big or bigger than a goose, as heavy almost as I was myself, who, when he wished to fly, rose off the ground with tremendous labour, and then as he got higher and higher flew more and more easily, until he rose so high that he looked no bigger than a lark or pipit, and at that height he would continue floating round and round in vast circles for hours, pouring out those jubilant cries at intervals which sounded to us so far below like clarion notes in the sky. If I could only get off the ground like that heavy bird and rise as high, then the blue air would make me as buoyant and let me float all day without pain or effort like the bird! This desire has continued with me through my life, yet I have never wished to fly in a balloon or airship, since I should then be tied to a machine and have no will or soul of my own. The desire has only been gratified a very few times in that kind of dream called levitation, when one rises and floats above the earth without effort and is like a ball of thistledown carried by the wind.

My favourite red willow was also the chosen haunt of another being, a peregrine falcon, a large handsome female that used to spend some months each year with us, and would sit for hours every day in the tree. It was an ideal tree for the falcon, too, not only because it was a quiet spot where it could doze the hot hours away in safety, but also on account of the numbers of pigeons we used to keep. The pigeon-house, a round, tower-shaped building, whitewashed outside, with a small door always kept locked, was usually tenanted by four or five hundred birds. These cost us nothing to keep, and were never fed, as they picked up their own living on the plain, and being strong fliers and well used to the dangers of the open country abounding in hawks, they ranged far from home, going out in small parties of a dozen or more to their various distant feeding-grounds. When out riding we used to come on these flocks several miles from home, and knew they were our birds since no one else in that neighbourhood kept pigeons. They were highly valued, especially by my father, who preferred a broiled pigeon to mutton cutlets for breakfast, and was also fond of pigeon-pies. Once or twice every week, according to the season, eighteen or twenty young birds, just ready to leave the nest, were taken from the dovecote to be put into a pie of gigantic size, and this was usually the grandest dish on the table when we had a lot of people to dinner or supper.

Every day the falcon, during the months she spent with us, took toll of the pigeons, and though these depredations annoyed my father he did nothing to stop them. He appeared to think that one or two birds a day didn't matter much as the birds were so many. The falcon's custom was, after dozing a few hours in the willow, to fly up and circle high in the air above the buildings, whereupon the pigeons, losing their heads in their terror, would rush up in a cloud to escape their deadly enemy. This was exactly what their enemy wanted them to do, and no sooner would they rise to the proper height than she would make her swoop, and singling out her victim strike it down with a blow of her lacerating claws; down like a stone it would fall, and the hawk, after a moment's pause in mid-air, would drop down after it and catch it in her talons before it touched the tree-tops, then carry it away to feed on at leisure out on the plain. It was a magnificent spectacle, and although witnessed so often it always greatly excited me.

One day my father went to the *galpon,* the big barn-like building used for storing wood, hides, and horse-hair, and seeing him go up the ladder I climbed up after him. It was an immense vacant place containing nothing but a number of empty cases on one side of the floor and empty flour-barrels, standing upright, on the other. My father began walking about among the cases, and by and by called me to look at a young pigeon, apparently just killed, which he had found in one of the empty boxes. Now, how came it to be there? he asked. Rats, no doubt, but how strange and almost incredible it seemed that a rat, however big, had been able to scale the pigeon-house, kill a pigeon and drag it back a distance of twenty-five yards, then mount with it to the loft, and after all that labour to leave it uneaten! The wonder grew when he began to find more young pigeons, all young birds almost of an age to have left the nest, and only one or two out of half a dozen with any flesh eaten.

Here was an enemy to the dovecote who went about at night and did his killing quietly, unseen by any one, and was ten times more destructive than the falcon, who killed her adult old pigeon daily in sight of all the world and in a magnificent way!

I left him pondering over the mystery, gradually working himself up into a rage against rats, and went off to explore among the empty barrels standing upright on the other side of the loft.

"Another pigeon!" I shouted presently, filled with pride at the discovery and fishing the bird up from the bottom. He came over to me and began to examine the dead bird, his wrath still increasing; then I shouted gleefully again, "Another pigeon!" and altogether I shouted "Another pigeon!" about five times, and by that time he was in a quite furious temper. "Rats—rats!" he exclaimed, "killing all these pigeons and dragging them up here just to put them away in empty barrels—who ever heard of such a thing!" No stronger language did he use. Like the vicar's wonderfully sober-minded daughter, as described by Marjory Fleming, "he never said a single dam," for that was the sort of man he was, but he went back fuming to his boxes.

Meanwhile I continued my investigations, and by and by, peering into an empty barrel received one of the greatest shocks I had ever experienced. Down at the bottom of the barrel was a big brown-and-yellow mottled owl, one of a kind I had never seen, standing with its claws grasping a dead pigeon and its face turned up in alarm at mine. What a face it was!—a round grey disc, with black lines like spokes radiating from the centre, where the beak was, and the two wide-open staring orange-coloured eyes, the wheel-like head surmounted by a pair of ear- or horn-like black feathers! For a few moments we stared at one another, then recovering myself I shouted, "Father—an owl!" For although I had never seen its like before I knew it was an owl. Not until that moment had I known any owl except the common burrowing-owl of the plain, a small grey-and-white bird, half diurnal in its habits, with a pretty dove-like voice when it hooted round the house of an evening.

In a few moments my father came running over to my side, an iron bar in his hand, and looking into the barrel began a furious assault on the bird. "This then is the culprit!" he cried. "This is the rat that has been destroying my birds by the score! Now he's going to pay for it;" and so on, striking down with the bar while the bird struggled frantically to rise and make its escape; but in the end it was killed and thrown out on the floor.

That was the first and only time I saw my father kill a bird, and nothing but his extreme anger against the robber of his precious pigeons would have made him do a thing so contrary to his nature. He was quite willing to have birds killed—young pigeons, wild ducks, plover, snipe, whimbrel, tinamou or partridge, and various others which he liked to eat— but the killing always had to be done by others. He hated to see any bird killed that was not for the table, and that was why he tolerated the falcon, and even allowed a pair of *caranchos,* or carrrion-eagles—birds destructive to poultry, and killers when they got the chance of newly-born lambs and sucking-pigs—to have their huge nest in one of the old peach-trees for several years. I never saw him angrier than once when a visitor staying in the house, going out with his gun one day suddenly threw it up to his shoulder and brought down a passing swallow.

That was my first encounter with the short-eared owl, a world-wandering species, known familiarly to the sportsman in England as the October or woodcock owl; an inhabitant of the whole of Europe, also of Asia, Africa, America, Australasia, and many Atlantic and Pacific islands. No other bird has so vast a range; yet nobody in the house could tell me anything about it, excepting that it was an owl, which I knew, and no such bird was found in our neighbourhood. Several months later I found out more about it, and this was when I began to ramble about the plain on my pony.

One of the most attractive spots to me at that time, when my expeditions were not yet very extended, was a low-lying moist stretch of ground about a mile and a half from home, where on account of the moisture it was always a vivid green. In spring it was like a moist meadow in England, a perfect garden of wild flowers, and as it was liable to become flooded in wet winters it was avoided by the *vizcachas,* the big rodents that make their warrens or villages of huge burrows all over the plain. Here I used to go in quest of the most charming flowers which were not found in other places; one, a special favourite on account of its delicious fragrance, being the small lily called by the natives *Lagrimas de la Virgin*—Tears of the Virgin. Here at one spot the ground to the extent of an acre or so was occupied by one plant of a peculiar appearance, to the complete exclusion of the tall grasses and herbage in other parts. It grew in little tussocks like bushes, each plant composed of twenty or thirty stalks of a woody toughness and about two and a half feet high. The stems were thickly clothed with round leaves, soft as velvet to the touch and so dark a green that at a little distance they looked almost black against the bright green of the moist turf. Their beauty was in the blossoming season, when every stem produced its dozen or more flowers growing singly among the leaves, in size and shape like dog-roses, the petals of the purest, loveliest yellow. As the flowers grew close to the stalk, to gather them it was necessary to cut the stalk at the root with all its leaves and flowers, and this I sometimes did to take it to my mother, who had a great love of wild flowers. But no sooner would I start with a bunch of flowering stalks in my hand than the lovely delicate petals would begin to drop off, and before I was half way home there would not be a petal left. This extreme frailty or sensitiveness used to infect me with the notion that this flower was something more than a mere flower, something like a sentient being, and that it had a feeling in it which caused it to drop its shining petals and perish when removed from its parent root and home.

One day in the plant's blossoming time, I was slowly walking my pony through the dark bottle-green tufts, when a big yellowish-tawny owl got up a yard or so from the hoofs, and I instantly recognized it as the same sort of bird as our mysterious pigeon-killer. And there on the ground where it had been was its nest, just a slight depression with a few dry bents by way of lining and five round white eggs. From that time I was a frequent visitor to the owls, and for three summers they bred at the same spot in spite of the anxiety they suffered on my account, and I saw and grew familiar with their quaint-looking young, clothed in white down and with long narrow pointed heads more like the heads of aquatic birds than of round-headed flat-faced owls.

Later, I became even better acquainted with the short-eared owl. A year or several years would sometimes pass without one being seen, then all at once they would come in numbers, and this was always when there had been a great increase in field mice and other small rodents, and the owl population all over the country had in some mysterious way become aware of the abundance and had come to get their share of it. At these times you could see the owls abroad in the late afternoon, before sunset, in quest of prey, quartering the ground like harriers, and dropping suddenly into the grass at intervals, while at dark the air resounded with their solemn hooting, a sound as of a deep-voiced mastiff baying at a great distance.

As I have mentioned our famous pigeon-pies, when describing the dovecote, I may as well conclude this chapter with a fuller account of our way of living as to food, a fascinating subject to most persons. The psychologists tell us a sad truth when they say that taste, being the lowest or least intellectual of our five senses, is incapable of registering impressions on the mind; consequently we cannot recall or recover vanished flavours as we can recover, and mentally see and hear, long past sights and sounds. Smells, too, when we cease smelling, vanish and return not, only we remember that blossoming orange grove where we once walked, and beds of wild thyme and pennyroyal when we sat on the grass, also flowering bean and lucerne fields, filled and fed us, body and soul, with delicious perfumes. In like manner we can recollect the good things we consumed long years ago—the things we cannot eat now because we are no longer capable of digesting and assimilating them; it is like recalling past perilous adventures by land and water in the brave young days when we loved danger for its own sake. There was, for example, the salad of cold sliced potatoes and onions, drenched in oil and vinegar, a glorious dish with cold meat to go to bed on! Also hot maize-meal cakes eaten with syrup at breakfast, and other injudicious cakes. As a rule it was a hot breakfast and midday dinner; an afternoon tea, with hot bread and scones and peach-preserve, and a late cold supper. For breakfast, mutton cutlets, coffee, and things made with maize. Eggs were plentiful— eggs of fowl, duck, goose, and wild fowl's eggs—wild duck and plover in their season. In spring—August to October—we occasionally had an ostrich or rhea's egg in the form of a huge omelette at breakfast, and it was very good. The common native way of cooking it by thrusting a rod heated red through the egg, then burying it in the hot ashes to complete the cooking, did not commend itself to us. From the end of July to the end of September we feasted on plovers' eggs at breakfast. In appearance and taste they were precisely like our lapwings' eggs, only larger, the Argentine lapwing being a bigger bird than its European cousin. In those distant days the birds were excessively abundant all over the pampas where sheep were pastured, for at that time there were few to shoot wild birds and nobody ever thought of killing a lapwing for the table. The country had not then been overrun by bird-destroying immigrants from Europe, especially by Italians. Outside of the sheep zone in the exclusively cattle-raising country, where the rough pampas grasses and herbage had not been eaten down, the plover were sparsely distributed.

I remember that one day, when I was thirteen, I went out one morning after breakfast to look for plovers' eggs, just at the beginning of the laying season when all the eggs one found were practically new-laid. My plan was that of the native boys, to go at a fast gallop over the plain and mark the spot far ahead where a lapwing was seen to rise and fly straight away to some distance. For this method some training is necessary to success, as in many cases more birds than one—sometimes as many as three or four—would be seen to rise at various points and distances, and one had to mark and keep in memory the exact spots to visit them successively and find the nests. The English method of going out and quartering the ground in search of a nest in likely places where the birds breed was too slow for us.

The nests I found that morning contained one or two and sometimes three eggs—very rarely the full clutch of four. Before midday I had got back with a bag of sixty-four eggs; and that was the largest number I ever gathered at one time.

Our dinner consisted of meat and pumpkin, boiled

or baked maize "in the milk" in its season and sweet potatoes, besides the other common vegetables and salads. Maize-meal puddings and pumpkin pies and tarts were common with us, but the sweet we loved best was a peach-pie, made like an apple-pie with a crust, and these came in about the middle of February and lasted until April or even May, when our late variety, which we called "winter peach," ripened.

My mother was a clever and thrifty housekeeper, and I think she made more of the peach than any other resident in the country who possessed an orchard. Her peach preserves, which lasted us the year round, were celebrated in our neighbourhood. Peach preserves were in most English houses, but our house was alone in making pickled peaches: I think this was an invention of her own; I do not know if it has taken on, but we always had pickled peaches on the table and preferred them to all other kinds, and so did every person who tasted them.

I here recall an amusing incident with regard to our pickled peaches, and will relate it just because it serves to bring in yet another of our old native neighbours. I never thought of him when describing the others, as he was not so near us and we saw little of him and his people. His name was Bentura Gutierres, and he called himself an estanciero—a landowner and head of a cattle establishment; but there was very little land left and practically no cattle—only a few cows, a few sheep, a few horses. His estate had been long crumbling away and there was hardly anything left; but he was a brave spirit and had a genial, breezy manner, and dressed well in the European mode, with trousers and coat and waistcoat—this last garment being of satin and a very bright blue. And he talked incessantly of his possessions: his house, his trees, his animals, his wife and daughters. And he was immensely popular in the neighbourhood, no doubt because he was the father of four rather good-looking, marriageable girls; and as he kept open house his kitchen was always full of visitors, mostly young men, who sipped maté by the hour, and made themselves agreeable to the girls.

One of Don Ventura's most delightful traits—that is, to us young people—was his loud voice. I think it was a convention in those days for estancieros or cattlemen to raise their voices according to their importance in the community. When several gauchos are galloping over the plain, chasing horses, hunting or marking cattle, the one who is head of the gang shouts his directions at the top of his voice. Probably in this way the habit of shouting at all times by landowners and persons in authority had been acquired. And so it pleased us very much when Don Ventura came one evening to see my father and consented to sit down to partake of supper with us. We loved to listen to his shouted conversation.

My parents apologized for having nothing but cold meats to put before him—cold shoulder of mutton, a bird, and pickles, cold pie and so on. True, he replied, cold meat is never or rarely eaten by man on the plains. People do have cold meat in the house, but that as a rule is where there are children, for when a child is hungry, and cries for food, his mother gives him a bone of cold meat, just as in other countries where bread is common you give a child a piece of bread.

However, he would try cold meat for once. It looked to him as if there were other things to eat on the table. "And what is this?" he shouted, pointing dramatically at a dish of large, very green-looking pickled peaches. Peaches—peaches in winter! This is strange indeed!

It was explained to him that they were pickled peaches, and that it was the custom of the house to have them on the table at supper. He tried one with his cold mutton, and was presently assuring my parents that never in his life had he partaken of anything so good—so tasty, so appetizing, and whether or not it was because of the pickled peaches, or some quality in our mutton which made it unlike all other mutton, he had never enjoyed a meal as much. What he wanted to know was how the thing was done. He was told that large, sound fruit, just ripening, must be selected for pickling; when the finger dents a peach it is too ripe. The selected peaches are washed and dried and put into a cask, then boiling vinegar, with a handful of cloves is poured in till it covers the fruit, the cask closed and left for a couple of months, by which time the fruit would be properly pickled. Two or three casks-full were prepared in this way each season and served us for the entire year.

It was a revelation, he said, and lamented that he and his people had not this secret before. He, too, had a peach orchard, and when the fruit ripened his family, assisted by all their neighbours, feasted from morning till night on peaches, and hardly left room in their stomachs for roast meat when it was dinner-time. The consequence was that in a very few weeks—he could almost say days—the fruit was all gone, and they had to say, "No more peaches for another twelve months!" All that would now be changed. He would command his wife and daughters to pickle peaches—a cask-full, or two or three if one would not be enough. He would provide vinegar—many gallons of it, and cloves by the handful. And when they had got their pickled peaches he would have cold mutton for supper every day all the year round, and enjoy his life as he had never done before!

This amused us very much, as we knew that poor Don Ventura, notwithstanding his loud commanding voice, had little or no authority in his house; that it was ruled by his wife, assisted by a council of four marriageable daughters, whose present objects in life were little dances and other amusements, and lovers with courage enough to marry them or carry them off.

CHAPTER XV

Serpent and Child

My pleasure in bird life—Mammals at our new home—
Snakes and how children are taught to regard them—
A colony of snakes in the house—Their hissing confab-
ulations—Finding serpent sloughs—A serpent's saviour
—A brief history of our English neighbours, the Blakes.

It is not an uncommon thing, I fancy, for a child or
boy to be more deeply impressed and stirred at the
sight of a snake than of any other creature. This at
all events is my experience. Birds certainly gave me
more pleasure than other animals, and this too is no
doubt common with children, and I take the reason of
it to be not only because birds exceed in beauty, but
also on account of the intensity of life they exhibit—a
life so vivid, so brilliant, as to make that of other
beings, such as reptiles and mammals, seem a rather
poor thing by comparison. But while birds were more
than all other beings to me, mammals too had a great
attraction. I have already spoken of rats, opossums,
and armadillos; also of the vizcacha, the big burrowing
rodent that made his villages all over the plain. One
of my early experiences is of the tremendous outcry
these animals would make at night when suddenly
startled by a very loud noise, as by a clap of thunder.

When we had visitors from town, especially persons new to the country who did not know the vizcacha, they would be taken out after supper, a little distance from the house, when the plain was all dark and profoundly silent, and after standing still for a few minutes to give them time to feel the silence, a gun would be discharged, and after two or three seconds the report would be followed by an extraordinary hullabaloo, a wild outcry of hundreds and thousands of voices, from all over the plain for miles round, voices that seemed to come from hundreds of different species of animals, so varied they were, from the deepest booming sounds to the high shrieks and squeals of shrill-voiced birds. Our visitors used to be filled with astonishment.

Another animal that impressed us deeply and painfully was the skunk. They were fearless little beasts and in the evening would come quite boldly about the house, and if seen and attacked by a dog, they would defend themselves with the awful-smelling liquid they discharge at an adversary. When the wind brought a whiff of it into the house, when all the doors and windows stood open, it would create a panic, and people would get up from table feeling a little sea-sick, and go in search of some room where the smell was not. Another powerful-smelling but very beautiful creature was the common deer. I began to know it from the age of five, when we went to our new home, and where we children were sometimes driven with our parents to visit some neighbours several miles away. There were always herds of deer on the lands where the cardoon thistle flourished most, and it was a delight to come upon them and to see their yellow figures standing among the grey-green cardoon bushes, gazing motionless at us, then turning and rushing away with a whistling cry, and sending out gusts of their powerful musky smell, which the wind sometimes brought to our nostrils.

But there was a something in the serpent which produced a quite different and a stronger effect on the mind than bird or mammal or any other creature. The sight of it was always startling, and however often seen always produced a mixed sense of amazement and fear. The feeling was no doubt acquired from our elders. They regarded snakes as deadly creatures, and as a child I did not know that they were mostly harmless, that it was just as senseless to kill them as to kill harmless and beautiful birds. I was told that when I saw a snake I must turn and run for my life until I was a little bigger, and then on seeing a snake I was to get a long stick and kill it; and it was furthermore impressed on me that snakes are exceedingly difficult to kill, that many persons believe that a snake never really dies until the sun sets, therefore when I killed a snake, in order to make it powerless to do any harm between the time of killing it and sunset, it was necessary to pound it to a pulp with the aforesaid long stick.

With such teaching it was not strange that even as a small boy I became a persecutor of snakes.

Snakes were common enough about us; snakes of seven or eight different kinds, green in the green grass, and yellow and dusky-mottled in dry and barren places and in withered herbage, so that it was difficult to detect them. Sometimes they intruded into the dwelling-rooms, and at all seasons a nest or colony of snakes existed in the thick old foundations of the house, and under the flooring. In winter they hibernated there, tangled together in a cluster no doubt; and in summer nights when they were at home, coiled at their ease or gliding ghost-like about their subterranean apartments, I would lie awake and listen to them by the hour. For although it may be news to some closet ophiologists, serpents are not all so mute as we think them. At all events this kind, the *Philodryas æstivus*—a beautiful and harmless colubrine snake, two and a half to three feet long, marked all over with inky black on a vivid green ground—not only emitted a sound when lying undisturbed in his den, but several individuals would hold a conversation together which seemed endless, for I generally fell asleep before it finished. A hissing conversation it is true, but not unmodulated or without considerable variety in it; a long sibilation would be followed by distinctly-heard ticking sounds, as of a husky-ticking clock, and after ten or twenty or thirty ticks another hiss, like a long expiring sigh, sometimes with a tremble in it as of a dry leaf swiftly vibrating in the wind. No sooner would one cease than another would begin; and so it would go on, demand and response, strophe and antistrope; and at intervals several voices would unite in a kind of low mysterious chorus, death-watch and flutter and hiss; while I, lying awake in my bed, listened and trembled. It was dark in the room, and to my excited imagination the serpents were no longer under the floor, but out, gliding hither and thither over it, with uplifted heads in a kind of mystic dance;

and I often shivered to think what my bare feet might touch if I were to thrust a leg out and let it hang down over the bedside.

"I'm shut in a dark room with the candle blown out," pathetically cried old Farmer Fleming, when he heard of his beautiful daughter Dahlia's clandestine departure to a distant land with a nameless lover. "I've heard of a sort of fear you have in that dilemma, lest you should lay your fingers on edges of sharp knives, and if I think a step—if I go thinking a step, and feel my way, I do cut myself, and I bleed, I do." Only in a comparatively snakeless country could such fancies be born and such metaphors used—snakeless and highly civilized, where the blades of Sheffield are cheap and abundant. In ruder lands, where ophidians abound, as in India and South America, in the dark one fears the cold living coil and deadly sudden fang.

Serpents were fearful things to me at that period; but whatsoever is terrible and dangerous, or so reported, has an irresistible attraction for the mind, whether of child or man; it was therefore always a pleasure to have seen a snake in the day's rambles, although the sight was a startling one. Also in the warm season it was a keen pleasure to find the cast slough of the feared and subtle creature. Here was something not the serpent, yet so much more than a mere picture of it; a dead and cast-off part of it, but in its completeness, from the segmented mask with the bright unseeing eyes, to the fine whip-like tail end, so like the serpent itself; I could handle it, handle the serpent as it were, yet be in no danger from venomous tooth or stinging tongue. True, it was colourless, but silvery bright, soft as satin to the touch, crinkling when handled with a sound that to the startled fancy recalled the dangerous living hiss from the dry rustling grass! I would clutch my prize with a fearful joy, as if I had picked up a strange feather dropped in passing from the wing of one of the fallen but still beautiful angels. And it always increased my satisfaction when, on exhibiting my treasure at home, the first sight of it caused a visible start or an exclamation of alarm.

When my courage and strength were sufficient I naturally began to take an active part in the persecution of serpents; for was not I also of the seed of Eve? Nor can I say when my feelings towards our bruised enemy began to change; but an incident which I witnessed at this time, when I was about eight, had, I think, a considerable influence on me. At all events it caused me to reflect on a subject which had not previously seemed one for reflection. I was in the orchard, following in the rear of a party of grown-up persons, mostly visitors to the house; when among the foremost there were sudden screams, gestures of alarm, and a precipitate retreat: a snake had been discovered lying in the path and almost trodden upon. One of the men, the first to find a stick or perhaps the most courageous, rushed to the front and was about to deal a killing blow when his arm was seized by one of the ladies and the blow arrested. Then, stooping quickly, she took the creature up in her hands, and going away to some distance from the others, released it in the long green grass, green in colour as its glittering skin and as cool to the touch. Long ago as this happened it is just as vivid to my mind as if it had happened yesterday. I can see her coming back to us through the orchard trees, her face shining with joy because she had rescued the reptile from imminent death, her return greeted with loud expressions of horror and amazement, which she only answered with a little laugh and the question, "Why should you kill it?" But why was she glad, so innocently glad as it seemed to me, as if she had done some meritorious and no evil thing? My young mind was troubled at the question, and there was no answer. Nevertheless, I think that this incident bore fruit later, and taught me to consider whether it might not be better to spare than to kill; better not only for the animal spared, but for the soul.

And the woman who did this unusual thing and in doing it unknowingly dropped a minute seed into a boy's mind, who was she? Perhaps it would be as well to give a brief account of her, although I thought that I had finished with the subject of our neighbours. She and her husband, a man named Matthew Blake, were our second nearest English neighbours, but they lived a good deal further than the Royds and were seldom visited by us. To me there was nothing interesting in them and their surroundings, as they had no family and no people but the native peons about them, and, above all, no plantation where birds could be seen. They were typical English people of the lower middle class, who read no books and conversed, with considerable misuse of the aspirate, about nothing but their own and their neighbours' affairs. Physically Mr. Blake was a very big man, being six feet three in height and powerfully built. He had a round ruddy face, clean-shaved except for a pair of side-whiskers, and pale-blue shallow eyes. He was invariably dressed in black cloth, his garments being home-made and too large for him, the baggy trousers thrust into his long boots. Mr. Blake was nothing to us but a huge, serious, somewhat silent man who took no notice of small boys, and was clumsy and awkward and spoke very bad Spanish. He was well spoken of by his neighbours, and was regarded as a highly respectable and dignified person, but he had no intimates and was one of those unfortunate persons, not rare among the English, who appear to stand behind a high wall and, whether they desire it or not, have no power to approach and mix with their fellow-beings.

I think he was about forty-five to fifty years old when I was eight. His wife looked older and was a short ungraceful woman with a stoop, wearing a sunbonnet and sack and a faded gown made by herself. Her thin hair was of a yellowish-grey tint, her eyes pale blue, and there was a sunburnt redness on her cheeks, but the face had a faded and weary look. But she was better than her giant husband and was glad to associate with her fellows, and was also a lover of animals—horses, dogs, cats, and any and every wild creature that came in her way.

The Blakes had been married a quarter of a century or longer and had spent at least twenty years of their childless solitary life in a mud-built ranch, sheep-farming on the pampas, and had slowly accumulated a small fortune, until now they were possessed of about a square league of land with 25,000 or 30,000 sheep, and had built themselves a big ugly brick house to live in. They had thus secured the prize for which they had gone so many thousands of miles and had toiled for so many years, but they were certainly not happy. Poor Mr. Blake, cut off from his fellow-creatures by that wall that stood before him, had found companionship in the bottle, and was seen less and less of by his neighbours; and when his wife came to us to spend two or three days "for a change," although her home was only a couple of hours' ride away, the reason probably was that her husband was in one of his bouts and had made the place intolerable to her. I remember that she always came to us with a sad, depressed look on her face, but after a few hours she would recover her spirits and grow quite cheerful and talkative. And of an evening when there was music she would sometimes consent, after some persuasion, to give the company a song. That was a joy to us youngsters, as she had a thin cracked voice that always at the high notes went off into a falsetto. Her favourite air was "Home, sweet Home," and her rendering in her wailing cracked voice was as great a feast to us as the strange laugh of our grotesque neighbour Gandara.

And that is all I can say about her. But now when I remember that episode of the snake in the orchard, she looks to me not unbeautiful in memory, and her voice in the choir invisible sounds sweet enough.

CHAPTER XVI
A Serpent Mystery

A new feeling about snakes—Common snakes of the country
—A barren weedy patch—Discovery of a large black
snake—Watching for its reappearance—Seen going to
its den—The desire to see it again—A vain search—
Watching a bat—The black serpent reappears at my
feet—Emotions and conjectures—Melanism—My baby
sister and a strange snake—The mystery solved.

IT was not until after the episode related in the last
chapter and the discovery that a serpent was not neces-
sarily dangerous to human beings, therefore a creature
to be destroyed at sight and pounded to a pulp lest it
should survive and escape before sunset, that I began
to appreciate its unique beauty and singularity. Then,
somewhat later, I met with an adventure which produced another and a new feeling in me, that sense of
something supernatural in the serpent which appears
to have been universal among peoples in a primitive
state of culture and still survives in some barbarous or
semi-barbarous countries, and in others, like Hindustan,
which have inherited an ancient civilization.

The snakes I was familiar with as a boy up to this
time were all of comparatively small size, the largest
being the snake-with-a-cross, described in an early

chapter. The biggest specimen I have ever found of this ophidian was under four feet in length; but the body is thick, as in all the pit vipers. Then, there was the green-and-black snake described in the last chapter, an inhabitant of the house, which seldom exceeded three feet; and another of the same genus, the most common snake in the country. One seldom took a walk or ride on the plain without seeing it. It was in size and shape like our common grass-snake, and was formerly classed by naturalists in the same genus, Coronella. It is quite beautiful, the pale greenish-grey body, mottled with black, being decorated with two parallel bright red lines extending from the neck to the tip of the fine-pointed tail. Of the others the most interesting was a still smaller snake, brightly coloured, the belly with alternate bands of crimson and bright blue. This snake was regarded by every one as exceedingly venomous and most dangerous on account of its irascible temper and habit of coming at you and hissing loudly, its head and neck raised, and striking at your legs. But this was all swagger on the snake's part: it was not venomous at all, and could do no more harm by biting than a young dove in its nest by puffing itself up and striking at an intrusive hand with its soft beak.

Then one day I came upon a snake quite unknown to me: I had never heard of the existence of such a snake in our parts, and I imagine its appearance would have strongly affected any one in any land, even in those abounding in big snakes. The spot, too, in our plantation, where I found it, served to make its singular appearance more impressive.

There existed at that time a small piece of waste ground about half an acre in extent, where there were no trees and where nothing planted by man would grow. It was at the far end of the plantation, adjoining the thicket of fennel and the big red willow tree on the edge of the moat described in another chapter. This ground had been ploughed and dug up again and again, and planted with trees and shrubs of various kinds which were supposed to grow on any soil, but they had always languished and died, and no wonder, since the soil was a hard white clay resembling china clay. But although trees refused to grow there it was always clothed in a vegetation of its own; all the hardiest weeds were there, and covered the entire barren area to the depth of a man's knees. These weeds had thin wiry stalks and small sickly leaves and flowers, and would die each summer long before their time. This barren piece of ground had a great attraction for me as a small boy, and I visited it daily and would roam about it among the miserable half-dead weeds with the sun-baked clay showing between the brown stalks, as if it delighted me as much as the alfalfa field, blue and fragrant in its flowering-time and swarming with butterflies.

One hot day in December I had been standing perfectly still for a few minutes among the dry weeds when a slight rustling sound came from near my feet, and glancing down I saw the head and neck of a large black serpent moving slowly past me. In a moment or two the flat head was lost to sight among the close-growing weeds, but the long body continued moving slowly by—so slowly that it hardly appeared to move, and as the creature must have been not less than six feet long, and probably more, it took a very long time, while I stood thrilled with terror, not daring to make the slightest movement, gazing down upon it. Although so long it was not a thick snake, and as it moved on over the white ground it had the appearance of a coal-black current flowing past me—a current not of water or other liquid but of some such element as quicksilver moving on in a rope-like stream. At last it vanished, and turning I fled from the ground, thinking that never again would I venture into or near that frightfully dangerous spot in spite of its fascination.

Nevertheless I did venture. The image of that black mysterious serpent was always in my mind from the moment of waking in the morning until I fell asleep at night. Yet I never said a word about the snake to any one: it was my secret, and I knew it was a dangerous secret, but I did not want to be told not to visit that spot again. And I simply could not keep away from it; the desire to look again at that strange being was too strong. I began to visit the place again, day after day, and would hang about the borders of the barren weedy ground watching and listening, and still no black serpent appeared. Then one day I ventured, though in fear and trembling, to go right in among the weeds, and still finding nothing began to advance step by step until I was right in the middle of the weedy ground and stood there a long time, waiting and watching. All I wanted was just to see it once more, and I had made up my mind that immediately on its appearance, if it did appear, I would take to my heels. It was when standing in this central spot that once again that slight rustling sound, like that of a few days before, reached my straining sense and sent an icy chill down my back. And there, within six inches of my toes, appeared the black head and neck, followed by the long, seemingly endless body. I dared not move, since to have attempted flight might have been fatal. The weeds were thinnest here, and the black head and slow-moving black coil could be followed by the eye for a little distance. About a yard from me there was a hole in the ground about the circumference of a breakfast-cup at the top, and into this hole the serpent put his head and slowly, slowly drew himself in, while I stood waiting until the whole body to the tip of the tail had vanished and all danger was over.

I had seen my wonderful creature, my black serpent unlike any serpent in the land, and the excitement following the first thrill of terror was still on me, but I was conscious of an element of delight in it, and I would not now resolve not to visit the spot again. Still, I was in fear, and kept away three or four days. Thinking about the snake I formed the conclusion that the hole he had taken refuge in was his den, where he lived, that he was often out roaming about in search of prey, and could hear footsteps at a considerable distance, and that when I walked about at that spot my footsteps disturbed him and caused him to go straight to his hole to hide himself from a possible danger. It struck me that if I went to the middle of the ground and stationed myself near the hole, I would be sure to see him. It would indeed be difficult to see him any other way, since one could never know in which direction he had gone out to seek for food.

But no, it was too dangerous: the serpent might come upon me unawares and would probably resent always finding a boy hanging about his den. Still, I could not endure to think I had seen the last of him, and day after day I continued to haunt the spot, and going a few yards into the little weedy wilderness would stand and peer, and at the slightest rustling sound of an insect or falling leaf would experience a thrill of fearful joy, and still the black majestical creature failed to appear.

One day in my eagerness and impatience I pushed my way through the crowded weeds right to the middle of the ground and gazed with a mixed delight and fear at the hole: would he find me there, as on a former occasion? Would he come? I held my breath, I strained my sight and hearing in vain, the hope and fear of his appearance gradually died out, and I left the place bitterly disappointed and walked to a spot about fifty yards away, where mulberry trees grew on the slope of the mound inside the moat.

Looking up into the masses of big clustering leaves over my head I spied a bat hanging suspended from a twig. The bats, I must explain, in that part of the world, that illimitable plain where there were no caverns and old buildings and other dark places to hide in by day, are not so intolerant of the bright light as in other lands. They do not come forth until evening, but by day they are content to hitch themselves to the twig of a tree under a thick cluster of leaves and rest there until it is dark.

Gazing up at this bat suspended under a big green leaf, wrapped in his black and buff-coloured wings as in a mantle, I forgot my disappointment, forgot the serpent, and was so entirely taken up with the bat that I paid no attention to a sensation like a pressure or a dull pain on the instep of my right foot. Then the feeling of pressure increased and was very curious and was as if I had a heavy object like a crowbar lying across my foot, and at length I looked down at my feet, and to my amazement and horror spied the great black snake slowly drawing his long coil across my instep! I dared not move, but gazed down fascinated with the sight of that glistening black cylindrical body drawn so slowly over my foot. He had come out of the moat, which was riddled at the sides with rat-holes, and had most probably been there hunting for rats when my wandering footsteps disturbed him and sent him home to his den; and making straight for it, as his way was, he came to my foot, and instead of going round drew himself over it. After the first spasm of terror I knew I was perfectly safe, that he would not turn upon me so long as I remained quiescent, and would presently be gone from sight. And that was my last sight of him; in vain I watched and waited for him to appear on many subsequent days: but that last encounter had left in me a sense of a mysterious being, dangerous on occasion as when attacked or insulted, and able in some cases to inflict death with a sudden blow, but harmless and even friendly or beneficent towards those who regarded it with kindly and reverent feelings in place of hatred. It is in part the feeling of the Hindoo with regard to the cobra which inhabits his house and may one day accidently cause his death, but is not to be persecuted.

Possibly something of that feeling about serpents has survived in me; but in time, as my curiosity about all wild creatures grew, as I looked more on them with the naturalist's eyes, the mystery of the large black snake pressed for an answer. It seemed impossible to believe that any species of snake of large size and black as jet or anthracite coal in colour could exist in any inhabited country without being known, yet no person I interrogated on the subject had ever seen or heard of such an ophidian. The only conclusion appeared to be that this snake was the sole one of its kind in the land. Eventually I heard of the phenomenon of melanism in animals, less rare in snakes perhaps than in animals of other classes, and I was satisfied that the problem was partly solved. My serpent was a black individual of a species of some other colour. But it was not one of our common species—not one of those I knew. It was not a thick blunt-bodied serpent like our venomous pit-viper, our largest snake, and though in shape it conformed to our two common harmless species it was twice as big as the biggest specimens I had ever seen of them. Then I recalled that two years before my discovery of the black snake, our house had been visited by a large unknown snake which measured two or three inches over six feet and was similar in form to my black serpent. The colour of this strange and unwelcome visitor was a pale greenish grey, with numerous dull black mottlings and small spots. The story of its appearance is perhaps worth giving.

It happened that I had a baby sister who could just toddle about on two legs, having previously gone on all-fours. One midsummer day she was taken up and put on a rug in the shade of a tree, twenty-five yards from the sitting-room door, and left alone there to amuse herself with her dolls and toys. After half an hour or so she appeared at the door of the sitting-room where her mother was at work, and standing there with wide-open astonished eyes and moving her hand and arm as if to point to the place she came from, she uttered the mysterious word *kú-ku*. It is a wonderful word which the southern South American mother teaches her child from the moment it begins to toddle, and is useful in a desert and sparsely inhabited country where biting, stinging, and other injurious creatures are common. For babies when they learn to crawl and to walk are eager to investigate and have no natural sense of danger. Take as an illustration the case of the gigantic hairy brown spider, which is excessively abundant in summer and has the habit of wandering about as if always seeking something— "something it cannot find, it knows not what"; and in these wanderings it comes in at the open door and rambles about the room. At the sight of such a creature the baby is snatched up with the cry of *kú-ku* and the intruder slain with a broom or other weapon and thrown out. *Kú-ku* means dangerous, and the terrified gestures and the expression of the nurse or mother when using the word sink into the infant mind, and when that sound or word is heard there is an instant response, as in the case of a warning note or cry uttered by a parent bird which causes the young to fly away or crouch down and hide.

The child's gestures and the word it used caused

her mother to run to the spot where it had been left in the shade, and to her horror she saw there a huge serpent coiled up in the middle of the rug. Her cries brought my father on the scene, and seizing a big stick he promptly dispatched the snake.

The child, said everybody, had had a marvellous escape, and as she had never previously seen a snake and could not intuitively know it as dangerous, or *kú-ku,* it was conjectured that she had made some gesture or attempted to push the snake away when it came on to the rug, and that it had reared its head and struck viciously at her.

Recalling this incident I concluded that this unknown serpent, which had been killed because it wanted to share my baby sister's rug, and my black serpent were one and the same species—possibly they had been mates—and that they had strayed a distance away from their native place or else were the last survivors of a colony of their kind in our plantation. It was not until twelve or fourteen years later that I discovered that it was even as I had conjectured. At a distance of about forty miles from my home, or rather from the home of my boyhood where I no longer lived, I found a snake that was new to me, the *Philodryas scotti* of naturalists, a not uncommon Argentine snake, and recognized it as the same species as the one found coiled up on my little sister's rug and presumably as my mysterious black serpent. Some of the specimens which I measured exceeded six feet in length.

CHAPTER XVII
A Boy's Animism

The animistic faculty and its survival in us—A boy's animism
and its persistence—Impossibility of seeing our past
exactly as it was—Serge Aksakoff's history of his childhood—The child's delight in nature purely physical—
First intimations of animism in the child—How it
affected me—Feeling with regard to flowers—A flower
and my mother—History of a flower—Animism with
regard to trees—Locust-trees by moonlight—Animism
and nature-worship—Animistic emotion not uncommon—Cowper and the Yardley oak—The religionist's
fear of nature—Pantheistic Christianity—Survival of
nature-worship in England—The feeling for nature—
Wordsworth's pantheism and animistic emotion in poetry.

THESE serpent memories, particularly the enduring
image of that black serpent which when recalled restores
most vividly the emotion experienced at the time, serve
to remind me of a subject not yet mentioned in my
narrative: this is animism, or that sense of something
in nature which to the enlightened or civilized man is
not there, and in the civilized man's child, if it be
admitted that he has it at all, is but a faint survival
of a phase of the primitive mind. And by animism I
do not mean the theory of a soul in nature, but the
tendency or impulse or instinct, in which all myth
originates, to *animate* all things; the projection of our-

selves into nature; the sense and apprehension of an intelligence like our own but more powerful in all visible things. It persists and lives in many of us, I imagine, more than we like to think, or more than we know, especially in those born and bred amidst rural surroundings, where there are hills and woods and rocks and streams and waterfalls, these being the conditions which are most favourable to it—the scenes which have "inherited associations" for us, as Herbert Spencer has said. In large towns and all populous places, where nature has been tamed until it appears like a part of man's work, almost as artificial as the buildings he inhabits, it withers and dies so early in life that its faint intimations are soon forgotten and we come to believe that we have never experienced them. That such a feeling can survive in any man, or that there was ever a time since his infancy when he could have regarded this visible world as anything but what it actually is—the stage to which he has been summoned to play his brief but important part, with painted blue and green scenery for background—becomes incredible. Nevertheless, I know that in me, old as I am, this same primitive faculty which manifested itself in my early boyhood, still persists, and in those early years was so powerful that I am almost afraid to say how deeply I was moved by it.

It is difficult, impossible I am told, for any one to recall his boyhood exactly as it was. It could not have been what it seems to the adult mind, since we cannot escape from what we are, however great our detachment may be; and in going back we must take our present selves with us: the mind has taken a different colour, and this is thrown back upon our past. The poet has reversed the order of things when he tells us that we come trailing clouds of glory, which melt away and are lost as we proceed on our journey. The truth is that unless we belong to the order of those who crystallize or lose their souls on their passage, the clouds gather about us as we proceed, and as cloud-compellers we travel on to the very end.

Another difficulty in the way of those who write of their childhood is that unconscious artistry will steal or sneak in to erase unseemly lines and blots, to re-touch, and colour, and shade and falsify the picture. The poor, miserable autobiographer naturally desires to make his personality as interesting to the reader as it appears to himself. I feel this strongly in reading other men's recollections of their early years. There are, however, a few notable exceptions, the best one I know being Serge Aksakoff's *History of His Childhood;* and in his case the picture was not falsified, simply because the temper, and tastes, and passions of his early boyhood—his intense love of his mother, of nature, of all wildness, and of sport—endured un-changed in him to the end and kept him a boy in heart, able after long years to revive the past mentally, and picture it in its true, fresh, original colours.

And I can say of myself with regard to this primi-tive faculty and emotion—this sense of the supernatural in natural things, as I have called it—that I am on safe ground for the same reason; the feeling has never been wholly outlived. And I will add, probably to the disgust of some rigidly orthodox reader, that these are childish things which I have no desire to put away.

The first intimations of the feeling are beyond recall; I only know that my memory takes me back to a time when I was unconscious of any such element in nature, when the delight I experienced in all natural things was purely physical. I rejoiced in colours, scents, sounds, in taste and touch: the blue of the sky, the verdure of earth, the sparkle of sunlight on water, the taste of milk, of fruit, of honey, the smell of dry or moist soil, of wind and rain, of herbs and flowers; the mere feel of a blade of grass made me happy; and there were certain sounds and perfumes, and above all certain colours in flowers, and in the plumage and eggs of birds, such as the purple polished shell of the tinamou's egg, which intoxicated me with delight. When, riding on the plain, I discovered a patch of scarlet verbenas in full bloom, the creeping plants covering an area of several yards, with a moist, green sward sprinkled abundantly with the shining flower-bosses, I would throw myself from my pony with a cry of joy to lie on the turf among them and feast my sight on their brilliant colour.

It was not, I think, till my eighth year that I began to be distinctly conscious of something more than this mere childish delight in nature. It may have been there all the time from infancy—I don't know; but when I began to know it consciously it was as if some hand had surreptitiously dropped something into the honeyed cup which gave it at certain times a new flavour. It gave me little thrills, often purely pleasurable, at other times startling, and there were occasions when it became so poignant as to frighten me. The sight of a magnificent sunset was sometimes almost more than I could endure and made me wish to hide myself away. But when the feeling was roused by the sight of a small and beautiful or singular object, such as a flower, its sole effect was to intensify the object's loveliness. There were many flowers which produced this effect in but a slight degree, and as I grew up and the animistic sense lost its intensity, these too lost their magic and were almost like other flowers which had never had it. There were others which never lost what for want of a better word I have just called their magic, and of these I will give an account of one.

I was about nine years old, perhaps a month or two more, when during one of my rambles on horseback I found at a distance of two or three miles from home, a flower that was new to me. The plant, a little over a foot in height, was growing in the shelter of some large cardoon thistle, or wild artichoke, bushes. It had three stalks clothed with long, narrow, sharply-pointed leaves, which were downy, soft to the feel like the leaves of our great mullein, and pale green in colour. All three stems were crowned with clusters of flowers, the single flower a little larger than that of the red valerian, of a pale red hue and a peculiar shape, as each small pointed petal had a fold or twist at the end. Altogether it was slightly singular in appearance and pretty, though not to be compared with scores of other flowers of the plains for beauty. Nevertheless it had an extraordinary fascination for me, and from the moment of its discovery it became one of my sacred flowers. From that time onwards, when riding on the plain, I was always on the look-out for it, and as a rule I found three or four plants in a season, but never more than one at any spot. They were usually miles apart.

On first discovering it I took a spray to show to my mother, and was strangely disappointed that she admired it merely because it was a pretty flower, seen for the first time. I had actually hoped to hear from her some word which would have revealed to me why I thought so much of it: now it appeared as if it was no more to her than any other pretty flower and even less than some she was peculiarly fond of, such as the fragrant little lily called Virgin's Tears, the scented pure white and the rose-coloured verbenas, and several others. Strange that she who alone seemed always to know what was in my mind and who loved all beautiful things, especially flowers, should have failed to see what I had found in it!

Years later, when she had left us and when I had grown almost to manhood and we were living in another place, I found that we had as neighbour a Belgian gentleman who was a botanist. I could not find a specimen of my plant to show him, but gave him a minute description of it as an annual, with very large, tough, permanent roots, also that it exuded a thick milky juice when the stem was broken, and produced its yellow seeds in a long, cylindrical, sharply-pointed pod full of bright silvery down, and I gave him sketches of flower and leaf. He succeeded in finding it in his books: the species had been known upwards of thirty years, and the discoverer, who happened to be an Englishman, had sent seed and roots to the Botanical Societies abroad he corresponded with; the species had been named after him, and it was to be found now growing in some of the Botanical Gardens of Europe.

All this information was not enough to satisfy me; there was nothing about the man in his books. So I went to my father to ask him if he had ever known or heard of an Englishman of that name in the country. Yes, he said, he had known him well; he was a merchant in Buenos Ayres, a nice gentle-mannered man, a bachelor and something of a recluse in his private house, where he lived alone and spent all his week-ends and holidays roaming about the plains with his vasculum in search of rare plants. He had been long dead—oh, quite twenty or twenty-five years.

I was sorry that he was dead, and was haunted with a desire to find out his resting-place so as to plant the flower that bore his name on his grave. He, surely, when he discovered it, must have had that feeling which I had experienced when I first beheld it and could never describe. And perhaps the presence of those deep ever-living roots near his bones, and of the flower in the sunshine above him, would bring him a beautiful memory in a dream, if ever a dream visited him, in his long unawakening sleep.

No doubt in cases of this kind, when a first impression and the emotion accompanying it endures through life, the feeling changes somewhat with time; imagination has worked on it and has had its effect; nevertheless the endurance of the image and emotion serves to show how powerful the mind was moved in the first instance.

I have related this case because there were interesting circumstances connected with it; but there were other flowers which produced a similar feeling, which, when recalled, bring back the original emotion; and I would gladly travel many miles any day to look again at any one of them. The feeling, however, was evoked more powerfully by trees than by even the most supernatural of my flowers; it varied in power according to time and place and the appearance of the tree or trees, and always affected me most on moonlight nights. Frequently, after I had first begun to experience it consciously, I would go out of my way to meet it, and I used to steal out of the house alone when the moon was at its full to stand, silent and motionless, near some group of large trees, gazing at the dusky green foliage silvered by the beams; and at such times the sense of mystery would grow until a sensation of delight would change to fear, and the fear increase until it was no longer to be borne, and I would hastily escape to recover the sense of reality and safety indoors, where there was light and company. Yet on the very next night I would steal out again and go to the spot where the effect was strongest, which was usually among the large locust or white acacia trees, which gave the name of Las Acacias to our place. The loose feathery foliage on moonlight nights had a peculiar hoary aspect that made this tree seem more intensely alive than others, more conscious of my presence and watchful of me.

I never spoke of these feelings to others, not even to my mother, notwithstanding that she was always in perfect sympathy with me with regard to my love of nature. The reason of my silence was, I think, my powerlessness to convey in words what I felt; but I imagine it would be correct to describe the sensation experienced on those moonlight nights among the trees as similar to the feeling a person would have if visited by a supernatural being, if he was perfectly convinced that it was there in his presence, albeit silent and unseen, intently regarding him, and divining every thought in his mind. He would be thrilled to the marrow, but not terrified if he knew that it would take no visible shape nor speak to him out of the silence.

This faculty or instinct of the dawning mind is or has always seemed to me essentially religious in character; undoubtedly it is the root of all nature-worship, from fetishism to the highest pantheistic development. It was more to me in those early days than all the religious teaching I received from my mother. Whatever she told me about our relations with the Supreme Being I believed implicitly, just as I believed everything else she told me, and as I believed that two and two make four and that the world is round in spite of its flat appearance; also that it is travelling through space and revolving round the sun instead of standing still, with the sun going round it, as one would imagine. But apart from the fact that the powers above would save me in the end from extinction, which was a great consolation, these teachings did not touch my heart as it was touched and thrilled by something nearer, more intimate, in nature, not only in moonlit trees or in a flower or serpent, but, in certain exquisite moments and moods and in certain aspects of nature, in "every grass" and in all things, animate and inanimate.

It is not my wish to create the impression that I am a peculiar person in this matter; on the contrary, it is my belief that the animistic instinct, if a mental faculty can be so called, exists and persists in many persons, and that I differ from others only in looking steadily at it and taking it for what it is, also in exhibiting it to the reader naked and without a fig-leaf expressed, to use a Baconian phrase.   When the religious Cowper confesses in the opening lines of his address to the famous Yardley oak, that the sense of awe and reverence it inspired in him would have made him bow himself down and worship it but for the happy fact that his mind was illumined with the knowledge of the truth, he is but saying what many feel without in most cases recognizing the emotion for what it is—the sense of the supernatural in nature.   And if they have grown up, as was the case with Cowper, with the image of an implacable anthropomorphic deity in their minds, a being who is ever jealously watching them to note which way their wandering thoughts are tending, they rigorously repress the instinctive feeling as a temptation of the evil one, or as a lawless thought born of their own inherent sinfulness.   Nevertheless it is not uncommon to meet with instances of persons who appear able to reconcile their faith in revealed religion with their animistic emotion.   I will give an instance.   One of the most treasured memories of an old lady friend of mine, recently deceased, was of her visits, some sixty years or more ago, to a great country-house where she met many of the distinguished people of that time, and of her host, who was then old, the head of an ancient and distinguished family, and of his reverential feeling for his trees. His greatest pleasure was to sit out of doors of an evening in sight of the grand old trees in his park, and before going in he would walk round to visit them, one by one, and resting his hand on the bark he would whisper a good-night. He was convinced, he confided to his young guest, who often accompanied him in these evening walks, that they had intelligent souls and knew and encouraged his devotion.

There is nothing surprising to me in this; it is told here only because the one who cherished this feeling and belief was an orthodox Christian, a profoundly religious person; also because my informant herself, who was also deeply religious, loved the memory of this old friend of her early life mainly because of his feeling for trees, which she too cherished, believing, as she often told me, that trees and all living and growing things have souls. What has surprised me is that a form of tree-worship is still found existing among a few of the inhabitants in some of the small rustic villages in out-of-the-world districts in England. Not such survivals as the apple tree folk-songs and ceremonies of the west, which have long become meaningless, but something living, which has a meaning for the mind, a survival such as our anthropologists go to the end of the earth to seek among barbarous and savage tribes.

The animism which persists in the adult in these scientific times has been so much acted on and changed by dry light that it is scarcely recognizable in what is somewhat loosely or vaguely called a "feeling for nature": it has become intertwined with the æsthetic feeling and may be traced in a good deal of our poetic literature, particularly from the time of the first appearance of *Lyrical Ballads,* which put an end to the eighteenth-century poetic convention and made the poet free to express what he really felt. But the feeling, whether expressed or not, was always there. Before the classic period we find in Traherne a poetry which was distinctly animistic, with Christianity grafted on it. Wordsworth's pantheism is a subtilized animism, but there are moments when his feeling is like that of the child or savage when he is convinced that the flower enjoys the air it breathes.

I must apologize to the reader for having gone beyond my last, since I am not a student of literature, nor catholic in my literary tastes, and on such subjects can only say just what I feel. And this is, that the survival of the sense of mystery, or of the supernatural, in nature, is to me in our poetic literature like that ingredient of a salad which "animates the whole"; that the absence of that emotion has made a great portion of the eighteenth century poetic literature almost intolerable to me, so that I wish the little big man who dominated his age (and till a few months ago still had in Mr. Courthope one follower among us) had emigrated west when still young, leaving *Windsor Forest* as his only monument and sole and sufficient title to immortality.

CHAPTER XVIII
The New Schoolmaster

Mr. Trigg recalled—His successor—Father O'Keefe—His mild rule and love of angling—My brother is assisted in his studies by the priest—Happy fishing afternoons —The priest leaves us—How he had been working out his own salvation—We run wild once more—My brother's plan for a journal to be called *The Tin Box*—Our imperious editor's exactions—My little brother revolts —*The Tin Box* smashed up—The loss it was to me.

THE account of our schooling days under Mr. Trigg was given so far back in this history that the reader will have little recollection of it. Mr. Trigg was in a small way a sort of Jekyll and Hyde, all pleasantness in one of his states and all black looks and truculence in the other; so that out of doors and at table we children would say to ourselves in astonishment, "Is this our schoolmaster?" but when in school we would ask, "Is this Mr. Trigg?" But, as I have related, he had been forbidden to inflict corporal punishment on us, and was finally got rid of because in one of his demoniacal moods he thrashed us brutally with his horsewhip. When this occurred we, to our regret, were not permitted to go back to our aboriginal condition of young barbarians: some restraint, some teaching was still imposed upon us by our mother, who took, or rather tried to take, this additional burden on herself. Accordingly, we had to meet with our lesson-books and spend three or four hours every morning with her, or in the schoolroom without her, for she was constantly being called away, and when present a portion of the time was spent in a little talk which was not concerned with our lessons. For we moved and breathed and had our being in a strange moral atmosphere, where lawless acts were common and evil and good were scarcely distinguishable, and all this made her more anxious about our spiritual than our mental needs.

My two elder brothers did not attend, as they had long discovered that their only safe plan was to be their own schoolmasters, and it was even more than she could manage very well to keep the four smaller ones to their tasks. She sympathized too much with our impatience at confinement when sun and wind and the cries of wild birds called insistently to us to come out and be alive and enjoy ourselves in our own way.

At this stage a successor to Mr. Trigg, a real schoolmaster, was unexpectedly found for us in the person of Father O'Keefe, an Irish priest without a cure and with nothing to do. Some friends of my father, on one of his periodical visits to Buenos Ayres, mentioned this person to him—this priest who in his wanderings about the world had drifted hither and was anxious to find some place to stay at out on the plains while waiting for something to turn up. As he was without means he said he would be glad of the position of schoolmaster in the house for a time, that it would exactly suit him.

Father O'Keefe, who now appeared on the scene, was very unlike Mr. Trigg; he was a very big man in black but rusty clerical garments. He also had an extraordinarily big head and face, all of a dull, reddish colour, usually covered with a three or four days' growth of grizzly hair. Although his large face was unmistakably, intensely Irish, it was not the gorilla-like countenance so common in the Irish peasant-priest —the priest one sees every day in the streets of Dublin. He was, perhaps, of a better class, as his features were all good. A heavy man as well as a big one, he was not so amusing and so fluent a talker out of school as his predecessor, nor, as we were delighted to discover, so exacting and tyrannical in school. On the contrary, in and out of school he was always the same, mild and placid in temper, with a gentle sort of humour, and he was also very absent-minded. He would forget all about school hours, roam about the gardens and plantations, get into long conversations with the workmen, and eventually, when he found that he was somewhat too casual to please his employer, he enjoined us to "look him up" and let him know when it was school-time. Looking him up usually took a good deal of time. His teaching was not very effective. He could not be severe nor even passably strict, and never punished us in any way. When lessons were not learned he would sympathize with and comfort us by saying we had done our best and more could not be expected. He was also glad of any excuse to let us off for half-a-day. We found out that he was exceedingly fond of fishing—that with a rod and line in his hand he would spend hours of perfect happiness, even without a bite to cheer him, and on any fine day that called us to the plain we would tell him that it was a perfect day for fishing, and ask him to let us off for the afternoon. At dinner time he would broach the subject and say the children had been very hard at their studies all the morning, and that it would be a mistake to force their young minds too much, that all work and no play makes Jack a dull boy, and so on and so forth, and that he considered it would be best for them, instead of going back to more lessons in the afternoon, to go for a ride. He always gained his point, and dinner over we would rush out to catch and saddle our horses, and one for Father O'Keefe.

The younger of our two elder brothers, the sportsman and fighter, and our leader and master in all our outdoor pastimes and peregrinations, had taken to the study of mathematics with tremendous enthusiasm, the same temper which he displayed in every subject and exercise that engaged him—fencing, boxing, shooting, hunting, and so on; and on Father O'Keefe's engagement he was anxious to know if the new master would be any use to him. The priest had sent a most satisfactory reply; he would be delighted to assist the young gentleman with his mathematics, and to help him over all his difficulties; it was accordingly arranged that my brother was to have an early hour each morning with the master before school hours, and an hour or two in the evening. Very soon it began to appear that the studies were not progressing smoothly; the priest would come forth as usual with a smiling, placid countenance, my brother with a black scowl on his face, and gaining his room, he would hurl his books down and protest in violent language that the O'Keefe was a perfect fraud, that he knew as much of the infinitesimal calculus as a gaucho on horseback or a wild Indian. Then, beginning to see it in a humorous light, he would shout with laughter at the priest's pretentions to know anything, and would say he was only fit to teach babies just out of the cradle to say their A B C. He only wished the priest had also pretended to some acquaintance with the manly art, so that they could have a few bouts with the gloves on, as it would have been a great pleasure to bruise that big humbugging face black and blue.

The mathematical lessons soon ceased altogether, but whenever an afternoon outing was arranged my brother would throw aside his books to join us and take the lead. The ride to the river, he would say, would give us the opportunity for a little cavalry training and lance-throwing exercise. In the cane-brake he would cut long, straight canes for lances, which at the fishing-ground would be cut down to a proper length for rods. Then, mounting, we would set off, O'Keefe ahead, absorbed as usual in his own thoughts, while we at a distance of a hundred yards or so would form in line and go through our evolutions, chasing the flying enemy, O'Keefe; and at intervals our commander would give the order to charge, whereupon we would dash forward with a shout, and when about forty yards from him we would all hurl our lances so as to make them fall just at the feet of his horse. In this way we would charge him a dozen or twenty times before getting to our destination, but never once would he turn his head or have any inkling of our carryings-on

in the rear, even when his horse lashed out viciously
with his hind legs at the lances when they fell too near
his feet.

We enjoyed the advantage of the O'Keefe regime
for about a year, then one day, in his usual casual
manner, without a hint as to how his private affairs
were going, he said that he had to go somewhere to see
some one about something, and we saw him no more.
However, news of his movements and a good deal of
information about him reached us incidentally, from all
which it appeared that during his time with us, and for
some months previously, Father O'Keefe had been
working out his own salvation in a quiet way in accord-
ance with a rather elaborate plan which he had devised.
Before he became our teacher he had lived in some
priestly establishment in the capital, and had been a
hanger-on at the Bishop's palace, waiting for a benefice
or for some office, and at length, tired of waiting in
vain, he had quietly withdrawn himself from this
society and had got into communication with one of
the Protestant clergymen of the town. He intimated
or insinuated that he had long been troubled with
certain scruples, that his conscience demanded a little
more liberty than his church would allow its followers,
and this had caused him to cast a wistful eye on that
other church whose followers were, alas! accorded a
little more liberty than was perhaps good for their
souls. But he didn't know, and in any case he would
like to correspond on these important matters with
one on the other side. This letter met with a warm
response, and there was much correspondence and
meetings with other clerics—Anglican or Episcopalian,

I forget which. But there were also Presbyterians, Lutherans, and Methodist ministers, all with churches of their own in the town, and he may have flirted a little with all of them. Then he came for his year of waiting to us, during which he amused himself by teaching the little ones, smoothing the way for my mathematical brother, and fishing. But the authorities of the church had not got rid of him; they heard not infrequently from him, and it was not pleasant hearing. He had come, he told them, a Roman Catholic priest to a Roman Catholic country, and had found himself a stranger in a strange land. He had waited patiently for months, and had been put off with idle promises or thrust aside, while every greedy pushing priest that arrived from Spain and Italy was received with open arms and a place provided for him. Then, when his patience and private means had been exhausted, he had accidently been thrown among those who were not of the Faith, yet had received him with open arms. He had been humiliated and pained at the disinterested hospitality and Christian charity shown to him by those outside the pale, after the treatment he had received from his fellow-priests.

Probably he said more than this: for it is a fact that he had been warmly invited to preach in one or two of the Protestant churches in the town. He did not go so far as to accept that offer: he was wise in his generation, and eventually got his reward.

Our schoolmaster gone, we were once more back in the old way; we did just what we liked. Our parents probably thought that our life would be on the plains, with sheep and cattle-breeding for only vocations, and that should any one of us, like my mathematical-minded brother, take some line of his own, he would find out the way of it for himself: his own sense, the light of nature, would be his guide. I had no inclination to do anything with books myself: books were lessons, therefore repellent, and that any one should read a book for pleasure was inconceivable. The only attempt to improve our minds at this period came, oddly enough, from my masterful brother who despised our babyish intellects—especially mine. However, one day he announced that he had a grand scheme to put before us. He had heard or read of a family of boys living just like us in some wild isolated land where there were no schools or teachers and no newspapers, who amused themselves by writing a journal of their own, which was issued once a week. There was a blue pitcher on a shelf in the house, and into this pitcher every boy dropped his contribution, and one of them—of course the most intelligent one—carefully went through them, selected the best, and copied them all out in one large sheet, and this was their weekly journal called *The Blue Pitcher,* and it was read and enjoyed by the whole house. He proposed that we should do the same; he, of course, would edit the paper and write a large portion of it: it would occupy two or four sheets of quarto paper, all in his beautiful handwriting, which resembled copper-plate, and it would be issued for all of us to read every Saturday. We all agreed joyfully, and as the title had taken our fancy we started hunting for a blue pitcher all over the house, but couldn't find such a thing, and finally had to put up with a tin box with a wooden lid and a lock and key. The contributions were to be dropped in through a slit in the lid which the carpenter made for us, and my brother took possession of the key. The title of the paper was to be *The Tin Box,* and we were instructed to write about the happenings of the week and anything in fact which had interested us, and not to be such little asses as to try to deal with subjects we knew nothing about. I was to say something about birds: there was never a week went by in which I didn't tell them a wonderful story of a strange bird I had seen for the first time: well, I could write about that strange bird and make it just as wonderful as I liked.

We set about our task at once with great enthusiasm, trying for the first time in our lives to put our thoughts into writing. All went well for a few days. Then our editor called us together to hear an important communication he wished to make. First he showed us, but would not allow us to read or handle, a fair copy of the paper, or of the portion he had done, just to enable us to appreciate the care he was taking over it. He then went on to say that he could not give so much time to the task and pay for stationery as well without a small weekly contribution from us. This would only be about three-halfpence or twopence from our pocket-money, and would not be much missed. To this we all agreed at once except my younger brother, aged about seven at that time. Then, he was told, he would not be allowed to contribute to the paper. Very well, he wouldn't contribute to it, he said. In vain we all tried to coax him out of his stubborn resolve: he would not part with a copper of his money and would have nothing to do with *The Tin Box*. Then the Editor's wrath broke out, and he said he had already written his editorial, but would now, as a concluding article, write a second one in order to show up the person who had tried to wreck the paper, in his true colours. He would exhibit him as the meanest, most contemptible insect that ever crawled on the surface of the earth.

In the middle of this furious tirade my poor little brother burst out crying. "Keep your miserable tears till the paper is out," shouted the other, "as you will have good reason to shed them then. You will be a marked being, every one will then point the finger of scorn at you and wonder how he could ever have thought well of such a pitiful little wretch."

This was more than the little fellow could stand, and he suddenly fled from the room, still crying; then we all laughed, and the angry editor laughed too, proud of the effect his words had produced.

Our little brother did not join us at play that afternoon: he was in hiding somewhere, keeping watch on the movements of his enemy, who was no doubt engaged already in writing that dreadful article which would make him a marked being for the rest of his life.

In due time the editor, his task finished, came forth, and mounting his horse, galloped off; and the little watcher came out, and stealing into the room where the Tin Box was kept, carried it off to the carpenter's shop. There with chisel and hammer he broke the lid to pieces, and taking out all the papers, set to work to tear them up into the minutest fragments, which were carried out and scattered all over the place.

When the big brother came home and discovered what had been done he was in a mighty rage, and went off in search of the avaricious little rebel who had dared to destroy his work. But the little rebel was not to be caught; at the right moment he fled from the coming tempest to his parents and claimed their protection. Then the whole matter had to be inquired into, and the big boy was told that he was not to thrash his little brother, that he himself was to blame for everything on account of the extravagant language he had used, which the poor little fellow had taken quite seriously. If he actually believed *The Tin Box* article was going to have that disastrous effect on him, who could blame him for destroying it?

That was the end of *The Tin Box;* not a word about starting it afresh was said, and from that day my elder brother never mentioned it. But years later I came to think it a great pity that the scheme had miscarried. I believe, from later experience, that even if it had lasted but a few weeks it would have given me the habit of recording my observations, and that is a habit without which the keenest observation and the most faithful memory are not sufficient for the field naturalist. Thus, through the destruction of the Tin Box, I believe I lost a great part of the result of six years of life with wild nature, since it was not until six years after my little brother's rebellious act that I discovered the necessity of making a note of every interesting thing I witnessed.

CHAPTER XIX

Brothers

Our third and last schoolmaster—His many accomplishments
—His weakness and final breakdown—My important
brother—Four brothers, unlike in everything except
the voice—A strange meeting—Jack the Killer, his life
and character—A terrible fight—My brother seeks
instructions from Jack—The gaucho's way of fighting
and Jack's contrasted—Our sham fight with knives—
A wound and the result—My feeling about Jack and
his eyes—Bird-lore—My two elder brothers' practical
joke.

THE vanishing of the unholy priest from our ken
left us just about where we had been before his large
red face had lifted itself above our horizon. At all
events the illumination had not been great. And
thereafter it was holiday once more for a goodish time
until yet a third tutor came upon the scene:—yet
another stranger in a strange land who had fallen into
low (and hot) water and was willing to fill a vacant
time in educating us. Just as in the case of the O'Keefe,
he was thrust upon my good-natured and credulous father by his friends in the capital, who had this gentleman with them and were anxious to get him off their
hands. He was, they assured my father, just the man
he wanted, a fine fellow of good family, highly educated
and all that; but he had been a bit wild, and all that

was wanted to bring him round was to get him out a good distance from the capital and its temptations and into a quiet, peaceful home like ours. Strange to say, he actually turned out to be all they had said, and more. He had studied hard at college and when reading for a profession; he was a linguist, a musician, he had literary tastes, and was well read in science, and above all he was a first-rate mathematician. Naturally, to my studious brother he came as an angel beautiful and bright, with no suggestion of the fiend in him; for not only was he a mathematician, but he was also an accomplished fencer and boxer. And so the two were soon fast friends, and worked hard together over their books, and would then repair for an hour or two every day to the plantation to fence and box and practise with pistol and rifle at the target. He also took to the humbler task of teaching the rest of us with considerable zeal, and succeeded in rousing a certain enthusiasm in us. We were, he told us, grossly ignorant—simply young barbarians; but he had penetrated beneath the thick crust that covered our minds, and was pleased to find that there were possibilities of better things; that if we would but second his efforts and throw ourselves, heart and soul, into our studies, we should eventually develop from the grub condition to that of purple-winged butterflies.

Our new teacher was tremendously eloquent, and it looked as if he had succeeded in conquering that wildness or weakness or whatever it was which had been his undoing in the past. Then came a time when he would ask for a horse and go for a long ride. He would make a call at some English estancia, and drink

freely of the wine or spirits hospitably set on the table.
And the result would be that he would come home
raving like a lunatic:—a very little alcohol would
drive him mad. Then would follow a day or two of
repentance and black melancholy; then recovery and
a fresh fair start.

All this was somewhat upsetting to all of us: to my
mother it was peculiarly distressing, and became more
so when, in one of his repentant fits and touched by
her words, he gave her a packet of his mother's letters
to read:—the pathetic letters of a broken-hearted
woman to her son, her only and adored child, lost to
her for ever in a distant country, thousands of miles
from home. These sad appeals only made my mother
more anxious to save him, and it was no doubt her
influence that for a while did save and make him able
to succeed in his efforts to overcome his fatal weakness.
But he was of too sanguine a temper, and by and by
began to think that he had conquered, that he was safe,
that it was time for him to do something great; and
with some brilliant scheme he had hatched in his mind,
he left us and went back to the capital to work it out.
But alas! before many months, when he was getting
seriously to work, with friends and money to help him
and every prospect of success, he broke down once
more, so hopelessly that once more he had to be got
rid of, and he was sent out of the country, but whether
back to his own people or to some other remote district in Argentina I do not remember, nor do I know
what became of him.

Thus disastrously ended the third and last attempt
my father made to have us instructed at home. Nor

could he send us to town, where there was but one English school for boys, run by a weak, sickly gentleman, whose house was a nest of fevers and every sort of ailment incidental to boys herded together in an unhealthy boarding-school. Prosperous English people sent their children home to be educated at that time, but it was enormously expensive and we were not well off enough. A little later an exception had to be made in the case of my elder brother, who would not settle down to sheep-farming or any other occupation out on the pampas, but had set his heart on pursuing his studies abroad.

At this period of my life this brother was so important a person to me that I shall have to give even more space to him in this chapter than he had in the last one. Yet of my brothers he was not the one nearest to my heart. He was five full years my senior, and naturally associated with an elder brother, while we two smaller ones were left to amuse ourselves together in our own childish way. With a younger brother for only playmate, I prolonged my childhood, and when I was ten my brother of fifteen appeared a young man to me. We were all four extremely unlike in character as well as appearance, and alike in one thing only—the voice, inherited from our father; but just as our relationship appeared in that one physical character, so I think that under all the diversities in our minds and temperaments there was a hidden quality, a something of the spirit, which made us one; and this, I believe, came from the mother's side.

That family likeness in the voice was brought home to us in a curious way just about this time, when I was in my tenth year. My brother went one day to Buenos Ayres, and arriving at the stable where our horses were always put up, long after dark, he left his horse, and on going out called to the stableman, giving him some direction. As soon as he had spoken, a feeble voice was heard from the open door of a dark room near the gate, calling, "That's a Hudson that spoke! Father or son—who is it?"

My brother turned back and groped his way into the dark room, and replied: "Yes, I'm a Hudson—Edwin's my name. Who are you?"

"Oh, I'm glad you're here! I'm your old friend Jack," returned the other, and it was a happy meeting between the boy in his sixteenth year and the grey-headed old battered vagabond and fighter, known far and wide in our part of the country as Jack the Killer, and by other dreadful nicknames, both English and Spanish. Now he was lying there alone, friendless, penniless, ill, on a rough bed the stableman had given him in his room. My brother came home full of the subject, sad at poor old Jack's broken-down condition and rejoicing that he had by chance found him there and had been able to give him help.

Jack the Killer was one of those strange Englishmen frequently to be met with in those days, who had taken to the gaucho's manner of life, when the gaucho had more liberty and was a more lawless being than he is now or can ever be again, unless that vast level area of the pampas should at some future time become dispeopled and go back to what it was down to half a century ago. He had drifted into that outlandish place when young, and finding the native system of life congenial had made himself as much of a native as he could, and dressed like them and talked their language, and was horse-breaker, cattle-drover, and many other things by turn, and like any other gaucho he could make his own bridle and whip and horse-gear and lasso and bolas out of raw hide. And when not working he could gamble and drink like any gaucho to the manner born—and fight too. But here there was a difference. Jack could affiliate with the natives, yet could never be just like them. The stamp of the foreigner, of the Englishman, was never wholly eradicated. He retained a certain dignity, a reserve, almost a stiffness, in his manner which made him a marked man among them, and would have made him a butt to the wits and bullies among his comrades but for his pride and deadly power. To be mocked as a foreigner, a gringo, an inferior being, was what he could not stand, and the result was that he had to fight, and it then came as a disagreeable revelation that when Jack fought he fought to kill. This was considered bad form; for though men were often killed when fighting, the gaucho's idea is that you do not fight with that intention, but rather to set your mark upon and conquer your adversary, and so give yourself fame and glory. Naturally, they were angry with Jack and became anxious to get rid of him, and by and by he gave them an excuse. He fought with and killed a man, a famous young fighter, who had many relations and friends, and some of these determined to avenge his death. And one night a band of nine men came to the rancho where Jack was sleeping, and leaving two of their number at the door to kill him if he attempted to escape that way, the others burst into his room, their long knives in their hands. As the door was thrown open Jack woke, and instantly divining the cause of the intrusion, he snatched up the knife near his pillow and sprang like a cat out of his bed; and then began a strange and bloody fight, one man, stark naked, with a short-bladed knife in his hand, against seven men with their long facons, in a small pitch-dark room. The advantage Jack had was that his bare feet made no sound on the clay floor, and that he knew the exact position of a few pieces of furniture in the room. He had, too, a marvellous agility, and the intense darkness was all in his favour, as the attackers could hardly avoid wounding one another. At all events, the result was that three of them were killed and the other four wounded, all more or less seriously. And from that time Jack was allowed to live among them as a harmless, peaceful member of the community, so long as no person twitted him with being a gringo.

Quite naturally, my brother regarded Jack as one of his greatest heroes, and whenever he heard of his being in our neighbourhood he would mount his horse and go off in search of him, to spend long hours in his company and persuade him to talk about that awful fight in a dark room with so many against him. One result of his intimacy with Jack was that he became dissatisfied with his own progress in the manly art of self-defence. It was all very well to make himself proficient with the foils and as a boxer, and to be a good shot, but he was living among people who had the knife for sole weapon, and if by chance he were attacked by a man with a knife, and had no pistol or other weapon, he would find himself in an exceedingly awkward position. There was then nothing to do but to practise with the knife, and he wanted Jack, who had been so successful with that weapon, to give him some lessons in its use.

Jack shook his head. If his boy friend wanted to learn the gaucho way of fighting he could easily do so. The gaucho wrapped his poncho on his left arm to use it as a shield, and flourished his facon, or knife with a sword-like blade and a guard to the handle. This whirling about of the knife was quite an art, and had a fine look when two accomplished fighters stood up to each other and made their weapons look like shining wheels or revolving mirrors in the sun. Meanwhile, the object of each man was to find his opportunity for a sweeping blow which would lay his opponent's face open. Now all that was pretty to look at, but it was mere playing at fighting and he never wanted to practise it. He was not a fighter by inclination; he wanted to live with and be one with the gauchos, but not to fight. There were numbers of men among them who never fought and were never challenged to fight, and he would be of those if they would let him. He never had a pistol, he wore a knife like everybody else, but a short knife for use and not to fight. But when he found that, after all, he had to fight or else exist on sufferance as a despised creature among them, the butt of every fool and bully, he did fight in a way which he had never been taught and could not teach to another. It was nature: it was in him. When the dangerous moment came and knives flashed out, he was instantly transformed into a different being. He was on springs, he couldn't keep still or in one place for a second, or a fraction of a second; he was like a cat, like indiarubber, like steel—like anything you like, but something that flew round and about his opponent and was within striking distance one second and a dozen yards away the next, and when an onset was looked for it never came where it was expected but from another side, and in two minutes his opponent became confused, and struck blindly at him, and his opportunity came, not to slash and cut but to drive his knife with all his power to the heart in the other's body and finish him for ever. That was how he had fought and had killed, and because of that way of fighting he had got his desire and had been permitted to live in peace and quiet until he had grown grey, and no fighter or swashbuckler had said to him, "Do you still count yourself a killer of men? then kill me and prove your right to the title," and no one had jeered at or called him "gringo."

In spite of this discouragement my brother was quite determined to learn the art of defending himself with a knife, and he would often go out into the plantation and practise for an hour with a tree for an opponent, and try to capture Jack's unpremeditated art of darting hither and thither about his enemy and making his deadly strokes. But as the tree stood still and had no knife to oppose him, it was unsatisfactory, and one day he proposed to me and my younger brother to have a fight with knives, just to find out if he was making any progress. He took us out to the far end of the plantation, where no one would see us, and produced three very big knives, with blades like butchers' knives, and asked us to attack him with all our might and try our best to wound him, while he would act solely on the defensive. At first we declined, and reminded him that he had punished us terribly with gloves and foils and singlestick, and that it would be even worse with knives—he would cut us in pieces! No, he said, he would not dream of hurting us: it would be absolutely safe for us, and for him too, as he didn't for a moment believe that we could touch him with our weapons, no matter how hard we tried. And at last we were persuaded, and taking off our jackets and wrapping them, gaucho-fashion, on our left arms as a protection, we attacked him with the big knives, and getting excited we slashed and lunged at him with all our power, while he danced and jumped and flew about *à la* Jack the Killer, using his knife only to guard himself and to try and knock ours out of our hands; but in one such attempt at disarming me his weapon went too far and wounded my right arm about three inches below the shoulder. The blood rushed out and dyed my sleeve red, and the fight came to an end. He was greatly distressed, and running off to the house, quickly returned with a jug of water, sponge, towel, and linen to bind the wounded arm. It was a deep long cut, and the scar has remained to this day, so that I can never wash in the morning without seeing it and remembering that old fight with knives. Eventually he succeeded in stopping the flow of blood, and binding my arm tightly round; and then he made the desponding remark, "Of course they will have to know all about it now."

"Oh no," I returned, "why should they? My arm has stopped bleeding, and they won't find out. If they notice that I can't use it—well, I can just say I had a knock."

He was immensely relieved, and so pleased that he patted me on the back—the first time he had ever done so—and praised me for my manliness in taking it that way; and to be praised by him was such a rare and precious thing that I felt very proud, and began to think I was almost as good as a fighter myself. And when all traces of blood had been removed and we were back in the house and at the supper-table, I was unusually talkative and hilarious, not only to prevent any one from suspecting that I had just been seriously wounded in a fight with knives, but also to prove to my brother that I could take these knocks with proper fortitude. No doubt he was amused; but he didn't laugh at me, he was too delighted to escape being found out.

There were no more fights with knives, although when my wound was healed he did broach the subject again on two or three occasions, and was anxious to convince me that it would be greatly to our advantage to know how to defend ourselves with a knife while living among people who were always as ready on any slight provocation to draw a knife on you as a cat was to unsheathe its claws. Nor could all he told us about the bloody and glorious deeds of Jack *el Matador* arouse any enthusiasm in me; and though in his speech and manner Jack was as quiet and gentle a being as one could meet, I could never overcome a curious shrinking, an almost uncanny feeling, in his presence, particularly when he looked straight at me with those fine eyes of his. They were light grey in colour, clear and bright as in a young man, but the expression pained me; it was too piercing, too concentrated, and it reminded me of the look in a cat's eyes when it crouches motionless just before making its dash at a bird.

Nevertheless, the fight and wound had one good result for me; my brother had all at once become less masterful, or tyrannical, towards me, and even began to show some interest in my solitary disposition and tastes. A little bird incident brought out this feeling in a way that was very agreeable to me. One evening I told him and our eldest brother that I had seen a strange thing in a bird which had led me to find out something new. Our commonest species was the parasitic cowbird, which laid its eggs anywhere in the nests of all the other small birds. Its colour was a deep glossy purple, almost black; and seeing two of these birds flying over my head, I noticed that they had a small chestnut-coloured spot beneath the wing, which showed that they were not the common species. It had then occurred to me that I had heard a peculiar note or cry uttered by what I took to be the cowbird, which was unlike any note of that bird; and following this clue, I had discovered that we had a bird in our plantation which was like the cowbird in size, colour, and general appearance, but was a different species. They appeared amused by my story, and a few days later they closely interrogated me on three consecutive evenings as to what I had seen that was remarkable that day, in birds especially, and were disappointed because I had nothing interesting to tell them.

The next day my brother said he had a confession

to make to me. He and the elder brother had agreed to play a practical joke on me, and had snared a common cowbird and dyed or painted its tail a brilliant scarlet, then liberated it, expecting that I should meet with it in my day's rambles and bird-watching in the plantation and would be greatly excited at the discovery of yet a third purple cowbird, with a scarlet tail, but otherwise not distinguishable from the common one. Now, on reflection, he was glad I had not found their bird and given them their laugh, and he was ashamed at having tried to play such a mean trick on me!

CHAPTER XX

Birding in the Marshes

Visiting the marshes—Pajonales and Juncales—Abundant
bird life—A Coots' metropolis—Frightening the Coots—
Grebe and Painted Snipe colonies—The haunt of the
Social Marsh Hawk—The beautiful Jacana and its eggs—
The colony of Marsh Trupials—The bird's music—
The aquatic plant Durasmillo—The Trupial's nest and
eggs—Recalling a beauty that has vanished—Our
games with gaucho boys—I am injured by a bad boy—
The shepherd's advice—Getting my revenge in a
treacherous manner—Was it right or wrong?—The
game of Hunting the Ostrich.

AT this time of my boy-life most of the daylight hours
were spent out of doors, as when not watching the
birds in our plantation or asked to go and look at the
flock grazing somewhere a mile or so from home, in
the absence of the shepherd or his boy, I was always
away somewhere on the plain with my small brother on
egg-hunting or other expeditions. In the spring and
summer we often visited the lagoons or marshes, the
most fascinating places I knew on account of their
abundant wild bird life. There were four of these
lagoons, all in different directions and all within two or
three miles from home. They were shallow lakelets,
called *lagunas,* each occupying an area of three or four
hundred acres, with some open water and the rest over-

grown with bright green sedges in dense beds, called *pajonales,* and immense beds of bulrushes, called *juncales.* These last were always the best to explore when the water was not deeper than the saddle-girth, and where the round dark polished stems, crowned with their bright brown tufts, were higher than our heads when we urged our horses through them. These were the breeding-places of some small birds that had their beautifully-made nests a couple of feet or so above the water, attached in some cases to single, in others to two or three, rush stems. And here, too, we found the nests of several large species—egret, night-heron, cormorant, and occasionally a hawk—birds which build on trees in forest districts, but here on the treeless region of the pampas they made their nests among the rushes. The fourth lakelet had no rush- or sedge-beds and no reeds, and was almost covered with a luxuriant growth of the floating *camaloté,* a plant which at a distance resembles the wild musk or mimulus in its masses of bright green leaves and brilliant yellow blossoms. This, too, was a fascinating spot, as it swarmed with birds, some of them being kinds which did not breed in the reeds and rushes. It was a sort of metropolis of the coots, and before and after the breeding season they would congregate in flocks of many hundreds on the low wet shore, where their black forms had a singular appearance on the moist green turf. It looked to me like a reproduction in small size of a scene I had witnessed—the vast level green pampa with a scattered herd of two or three thousand black cattle grazing on it, on a large cattle estate where only black beasts were bred. We always thought it great fun when we found a big assembly of coots at some distance from the margin. Whipping up our horses, we would suddenly charge the flock to see them run and fly in a panic to the lake and rush over the open water, striking the surface with their feet and raising a perfect cloud of spray behind them.

Coots, however, were common everywhere, but this water was the only breeding-place of the grebe in our neighbourhood; yet here we could find scores of nests any day—scores with eggs and a still greater number of false nests, and we could never tell which had eggs in it before pulling off the covering of wet weeds. Another bird rarely seen at any other spot than this was the painted snipe, a prettily-marked species with a green curved bill. It has curiously sluggish habits, rising only when almost trodden upon, and going off in a wild sacred manner like a nocturnal species, then dropping again into hiding at a short distance. The natives call it *dormilon*—sleepy-head. On one side of the lagoon, where the ground was swampy and wet, there was always a breeding-colony of these quaint birds; at every few yards one would spring up close to the hoofs, and dismounting we would find the little nest on the wet ground under the grass, always with two eggs so thickly blotched all over with black as to appear almost entirely black.

There were other rushy lagoons at a greater distance which we visited only at long intervals, and one of these I must describe, as it was almost more attractive than any one of the others on account of its bird life. Here, too, there were some kinds which we never found breeding elsewhere.

It was smaller than the other lagoons I have described and much shallower, so that the big birds, such as the stork, wood-ibis, crested screamer, and the great blue ibis, called *vanduria,* and the roseate spoonbill, could wade almost all over it without wetting their feathers. It was one of those lakes which appear to be drying up, and was pretty well covered with a growth of *camaloté* plant, mixed with reed, sedge, and bulrush patches. It was the only water in our part of the country where the large water-snail was found, and the snails had brought the bird that feeds on them—the large social marsh hawk, a slate-coloured bird resembling a buzzard in its size and manner of flight. But being exclusively a feeder on snails, it lives in peace and harmony with the other bird inhabitants of the marsh. There was always a colony of forty or fifty of these big hawks to be seen at this spot. A still more interesting bird was the jacana, as it is spelt in books, but pronounced yä-sä-nä′ by the Indians of Paraguay, a quaint rail-like bird supposed to be related to the plover family : black and maroon-red in colour, the wing-quills a shining greenish yellow, it has enormously long toes, spurs on its wings, and yellow wattles on its face. Here I first saw this strange beautiful fowl, and here to my delight I found its nest in three consecutive summers, with three or four clay-coloured eggs spotted with chestnut-red.

Here, too, was the breeding-place of the beautiful black-and-white stilt, and of other species too many to mention. But my greatest delight was in finding breeding in this place a bird I loved more than all the others I have named—a species of marsh trupial, a bird about

the size of the common cowbird, and like it, of a
uniform deep purple, but with a cap of chestnut-coloured feathers on its head. I loved this bird for its
song—the peculiar delicate tender opening notes and
trills. In spring and autumn large flocks would occasionally visit our plantation, and the birds in hundreds
would settle on a tree and all sing together, producing
a marvellous and beautiful noise, as of hundreds of
small bells all ringing at one time. It was by the
water I first found their breeding-place, where about
three or four hundred birds had their nests quite near
together, and nests and eggs and the plants on which
they were placed, with the solicitous purple birds flying
round me, made a scene of enchanting beauty. The
nesting-site was on a low swampy piece of ground
grown over with a semi-aquatic plant called *durasmillo*
in the vernacular. It has a single white stalk, woody
in appearance, two to three feet high, and little thicker
than a man's middle finger, with a palm-like crown of
large loose lanceolate leaves, so that it looks like a
miniature palm, or rather an ailanthus tree, which has
a slender perfectly white bole. The solanaceous flowers
are purple, and it bears fruit the size of cherries, black
as jet, in clusters of three to five or six. In this forest
of tiny palms the nests were hanging, attached to the
boles, where two or three grew close together; it was
a long and deep nest, skilfully made of dry sedge
leaves woven together, and the eggs were white or
skim-milk blue spotted with black at the large end.

That enchanting part of the marsh, with its forest of
graceful miniature trees, where the social trupials sang
and wove their nests and reared their young in company

—that very spot is now, I dare say, one immense field of corn, lucerne, or flax, and the people who now live and labour there know nothing of its former beautiful inhabitants, nor have they ever seen or even heard of the purple-plumaged trupial, with its chestnut cap and its delicate trilling song. And when I recall these vanished scenes, those rushy and flowery meres, with their varied and multitudinous wild bird life—the cloud of shining wings, the heart-enlivening wild cries, the joy unspeakable it was to me in those early years—I am glad to think I shall never revisit them, that I shall finish my life thousands of miles removed from them, cherishing to the end in my heart the image of a beauty which has vanished from earth.

My elder brother occasionally accompanied us on our egg-hunting visits to the lagoons, and he also joined us in our rides to the two or three streams where we used to go to bathe and fish; but he took no part in our games and pastimes with the gaucho boys: they were beneath him. We ran races on our ponies, and when there were race-meetings in our neighbourhood my father would give us a little money to go and enter our ponies in a boys' race. We rarely won when there were any stakes, as the native boys were too clever on horseback for us, and had all sorts of tricks to prevent us from winning, even when our ponies were better than theirs. We also went tinamou, or partridge, catching, and sometimes we had sham fights with lances, or long canes with which we supplied the others. These games were very rough, and one day when we were armed, not with canes but long straight pliant green poplar boughs we had cut for the purpose, we were having a running fight, when one of the boys got in a rage with me for some reason and, dropping behind, then coming quietly up, gave me a blow on the face and head with his stick which sent me flying off my pony. They all dashed on, leaving me there to pick myself up, and mounting my pony I went home crying with pain and rage. The blow had fallen on my head, but the pliant stick had come down over my face from the forehead to the chin, taking the skin off. On my way back I met our shepherd and told him my story, and said I would go to the boy's parents to tell them. He advised me not to do so; he said I must learn to take my own part, and if any one injured me and I wanted him punished I must do the punishing myself. If I made any fuss and complaint about it I should only get laughed at, and he would go scot free. What, then, was I to do? I asked, seeing that he was older and stronger than myself, and had his heavy whip and knife to defend himself against attack.

"Oh, don't be in a hurry to do it," he returned. "Wait for an opportunity, even if you have to wait for days; and when it comes, do to him just what he did to you. Don't warn him, but simply knock him off his horse, and then you will be quits."

Now this shepherd was a good man, much respected by every one, and I was glad that in his wisdom and sympathy he had put such a simple, easy plan into my head, and I dried my tears and went home and washed the blood from my face, and when asked how I had got that awful wound that disfigured me I made light of it. Two days later my enemy appeared on the scene. I heard his voice outside the gate calling to some one, and peering out I saw him sitting on his horse. His guilty conscience made him afraid to dismount, but he was anxious to find out what was going to be done about his treatment of me, also, if he could see me, to discover my state of mind after two days.

I went out to the timber pile and selected a bamboo cane about twenty feet long, not too heavy to be handled easily, and holding it up like a lance I marched to the gate and started swinging it round as I approached him, and showing a cheerful countenance. "What are you going to do with that cane?" he shouted, a little apprehensively. "Wait and see," I returned. "Something to make you laugh." Then, after whirling it round half a dozen times more, I suddenly brought it down on his head with all my force, and did exactly what I had been counselled to do by the wise shepherd—knocked him clean off his horse. But he was not stunned, and starting up in a screeching fury, he pulled out his knife to kill me. And I, for strategic reasons, retreated, rather hastily. But his wild cries quickly brought several persons on the scene, and, recovering courage, I went back and said triumphantly, "Now we are quits!" Then my father was called and asked to judge between us, and after hearing both sides he smiled and said his judgment was not needed, that we had already settled it all ourselves, and there was nothing now between us. I laughed, and he glared at me, and mounting his horse, rode off without another word. It was, however, only because he was suffering from the blow on his head; when I next met him we were good friends again.

More than once during my life, when recalling that episode, I have asked myself if I did right in taking the shepherd's advice? Would it have been better, when I went out to him with the bamboo cane, and he asked me what I was going to do with it, if I had gone up to him and shown him my face with that broad band across it from the chin to the temple, where the skin had come off and a black crust had formed, and had said to him: "This is the mark of the blow you gave me the day before yesterday, when you knocked me off my horse; you see it is on the right side of my face and head; now take the cane and give me another blow on the left side"? Tolstoy (my favourite author, by the way) would have answered: "Yes, certainly it would have been better for you—better for your soul." Nevertheless, I still ask myself: "Would it?" and if this incident should come before me half a second before my final disappearance from earth, I should still be in doubt.

One of our favourite games at this period—the only game on foot we ever played with the gaucho boys—was hunting the ostrich. To play this game we had bolas, only the balls at the end of the thong were not of lead like those with which the grown-up gaucho hunter captures the real ostrich or rhea. We used light wood to make balls, so as not to injure each other. The fastest boy was chosen to play the ostrich, and would be sent off to roam ostrich-fashion on the plain, pretending to pick clover from the ground as he walked in a stooping attitude, or making little runs and waving his arms about like wings, then standing erect and mimicking the hollow booming sounds the cock bird emits when calling the flock together.

The hunters would then come on the scene and the chase begin, the ostrich putting forth all his speed, doubling to this side and that, and occasionally thinking to escape by hiding, dropping upon the ground in the shelter of a cardoon thistle, only to jump up again when the shouts of the hunters drew near, to rush on as before. At intervals the bolas would come whirling through the air, and he would dodge or avoid them by a quick turn, but eventually he would be hit and the thong would wind itself about his legs and down he would come.

Then the hunters would gather round him, and pulling out their knives begin operations by cutting off his head; then the body would be cut up, the wings and breast removed, these being the best parts for eating, and there would be much talk about the condition and age of the bird, and so on. Then would come the most exciting part of the proceedings—the cutting the gizzard open and the examination of its varied contents; and by and by there would be an exultant shout, and one of the boys would pretend to come on a valuable find—a big silver coin perhaps, a *patacon,* and there would be a great gabble over it and perhaps a fight for its possession, and they would wrestle and roll on the grass, struggling for the imaginary coin. That finished, the dead ostrich would get up and place himself among the hunters, while the boy who had captured him with his bolas would then play ostrich, and the chase would begin anew.

When this game was played I was always chosen as

first ostrich, as at that time I could easily outrun and out-jump any of my gaucho playmates, even those who were three or four years older than myself. Nevertheless, these games—horse-racing, sham fights, and ostrich-hunting, and the like—gave me no abiding satisfaction; they were no sooner over than I would go back, almost with a sense of relief, to my solitary rambles and bird-watching, and to wishing that the day would come when my masterful brother would allow me to use a gun and practise the one sport of wild-duck shooting I desired.

That was soon to come, and will form the subject of the ensuing chapter.

CHAPTER XXI
Wild-Fowling Adventures

My sporting brother and the armoury—I attend him on his
shooting expeditions—Adventure with Golden Plover—
A morning after Wild Duck—Our punishment—I
learn to shoot—My first gun—My first wild duck—
My ducking tactics—My gun's infirmities—Duck-shooting with a blunderbus—Ammunition runs out—An
adventure with Rosy-bill Duck—Coarse gunpowder and
home-made shot—The war danger comes our way—
We prepare to defend the house—The danger over and
my brother leaves home.

I HAVE said I was not allowed to shoot before the age
of ten, but the desire had come long before that; I
was no more than seven when I used to wish to be a
big, or at all events a bigger, boy, so that, like my
brother, I too might carry a gun and shoot big wild
birds. But he said "No" very emphatically, and there
was an end of it.

He had virtually made himself the owner of all the
guns and weapons generally in the house. These included three fowling-pieces, a rifle, an ancient Tower
musket with a flint-lock—doubtless dropped from the
dead hands of a slain British soldier in one of the
fights in Buenos Ayres in 1807 or 1808; a pair of heavy
horse pistols, and a ponderous, formidable-looking old
blunderbuss, wide at the mouth as a tea-cup saucer.

His, too, were the swords. To our native neighbours this appeared an astonishingly large collection of weapons, for in those days they possessed no fire-arm except, in some rare instances, a carbine, brought home by a runaway soldier and kept concealed lest the authorities should get wind of it.

As the next best thing to doing the shooting myself, I attended my brother in his expeditions, to hold his horse or to pick up and carry the birds, and was deeply grateful to him for allowing me to serve him in this humble capacity. We had some exciting adventures together. One summer day he came rushing home to get his gun, having just seen an immense flock of golden plover come down at a spot a mile or so from home. With his gun and a sack to put the birds in, he mounted his pony, I with him, as our ponies were accustomed to carry two and even three at a pinch. We found the flock where he had seen it alight—thousands of birds evenly scattered, running about busily feeding on the wet level ground.

The bird I speak of is the *Charadrius dominicana,* which breeds in Arctic America and migrates in August and September to the plains of La Plata and Patagonia, so that it travels about sixteen thousand miles every year. In appearance it is so like our golden plover, *Charadrius pluvialis,* as to be hardly distinguishable from it. The birds were quite tame: all our wild birds were if anything too tame, although not *shockingly* so as Alexander Selkirk found them on his island —the poet's, not the real Selkirk. The birds being so scattered, all he could do was to lie flat down and fire with the barrel of his fowling-piece level with

the flock, and the result was that the shot cut through
the loose flock to a distance of thirty or forty yards,
dropping thirty-nine birds, which we put into the sack,
and remounting our pony set off home at a fast gallop.
We were riding barebacked, and as our pony's back
had a forward slope we slipped further and further
forward until we were almost on his neck, and I, sitting behind my brother, shouted for him to stop. But
he had his gun in one hand and the sack in the other,
and had lost the reins; the pony, however, appeared
to have understood, as he came to a dead stop of his
own accord on the edge of a rain-pool, into which
we were pitched headlong. When I raised my head
I saw the bag of birds at my side, and the gun lying
under water at a little distance; about three yards
further on my brother was just sitting up, with the
water streaming from his long hair, and a look of
astonishment on his face. But the pool was quite clean,
with the soft grass for bottom, and we were not hurt.

However, we did sometimes get into serious trouble.
On one occasion he persuaded me and the little brother
to accompany him on a secret shooting expedition he
had planned. We were to start on horseback before
daybreak, ride to one of the marshes about two miles
from home, shoot a lot of duck, and get back about
breakfast-time. The main thing was to keep the plan
secret, then it would be all right, since the sight of the
number of wild duck we should have to show on our
return would cause our escapade to be overlooked.

In the evening, instead of liberating our ponies as
usual, we took and tethered them in the plantation,
and next morning about three o'clock we crept cau-

tiously out of the house and set off on our adventure. It was a winter morning, misty and cold when the light came, and the birds were excessively wild at that hour. In vain we followed the flocks, my brother stalking them through the sedges, above his knees in the water; not a bird could he get, and at last we were obliged to go back empty-handed to face the music. At half-past ten we rode to the door, wet and hungry and miserable, to find the whole house in a state of commotion at our disappearance. When we were first missed in the morning, one of the workmen reported that he had seen us taking our horses to conceal them in the plantation at a little after dark, and it was assumed that we had run away—that we had gone south where the country was more thinly settled and wild animals more abundant, in quest of new and more stirring adventures. They were greatly relieved to see us back, but as we had no ducks to placate them we could not be forgiven, and as a punishment we had to go breakfastless that day, and our leader was in addition sternly lectured and forbidden to use a gun for the future.

We thought this a very hard thing, and for the following days were inclined to look at life as a rather tame, insipid business; but soon, to our joy, the ban was removed. In forbidding us the use of the guns my father had punished himself as well as us, since he never thoroughly enjoyed a meal—breakfast, dinner, or supper—unless he had a bird on the table, wild duck, plover, or snipe. A cold roast duck was his favourite breakfast dish, and he was never quite happy when he didn't get it.

Still, I was not happy, and could not be so long as I was not allowed to shoot. It was a privilege to be allowed to attend, but it seemed to me that at the age of ten I was quite old enough to have a gun. I had been a rider on horseback since the age of six, and in some exercises I was not much behind my brother, although when we practised with the foils or with the gloves he punished me in rather a barbarous manner. He was my guide and philosopher, and had also been a better friend ever since our fight with knives and the cow-bird episode; nevertheless he still managed to dissemble his love, and when I revolted against his tyranny I generally got well punished for it.

About that time an old friend of the family, who took an interest in me and wished to do something to encourage me in my natural history tastes, made me a present of a set of pen-and-ink drawings. There was, however, nothing in these pictures to help me in the line I had taken: they were mostly architectural drawings made by himself of buildings—houses, churches, castles, and so on, but my brother fell in love with them and began to try to get them from me. He could not rest without them, and was continually offering me something of his own in exchange for them; but though I soon grew tired of looking at them I refused to part with them, either because his anxiety to have them gave them a fictitious value in my sight, or because it was pleasing to be able to inflict a little pain on him in return for the many smarts I had suffered at his hands. At length one day, finding me still unmoved, he all at once offered to teach me to shoot and to allow me the use of one of the guns in exchange for the pictures. I could hardly believe my good fortune: it would have surprised me less if he had offered to give me his horse with "saddle and bridle also."

As soon as the drawings were in his hand he took me to our gun-room and gave me a quite unneeded lesson in the art of loading a gun—first so much powder, then a wad well rammed down with the old obsolete ramrod; then so much shot and a second wad and ramming down; then a percussion cap on the nipple. He then led the way to the plantation, and finding two wild pigeons sitting together in a tree, he ordered me to fire. I fired, and one fell, quite dead, and that completed my education, for now he declared he was not going to waste any more time on my instruction.

The gun he had told me to use was a single-barrel fowling-piece, an ancient converted flintlock, the stock made of an iron-hard black wood with silver mountings. When I stood it up and measured myself by it I found it was nearly two inches taller than I was, but it was light to carry and served me well: I became as much attached to it as to any living thing, and it was like a living being to me, and I had great faith in its intelligence.

My chief ambition was to shoot wild duck. My brother shot them in preference to anything else: they were so much esteemed and he was so much commended when he came in with a few in his bag that I looked on duck-shooting as the greatest thing I could go in for. Ducks were common enough with us and in great variety; I know not in what country more kinds are to be found. There were no fewer than five species of teal, the commonest a dark brown bird with black mottlings; another, very common, was pale grey, the plumage beautifully barred and pencilled with brown and black; then we had the blue-winged teal, a maroon-red duck which ranges from Patagonia to California; the ringed teal, with salmon-coloured breast and velvet-black collar; the Brazilian teal, a lovely olive-brown and velvet-black duck, with crimson beak and legs. There were two pintails, one of which was the most abundant species in the country; also a widgeon, a lake duck, a shoveller duck, with red plumage, grey head and neck, and blue wings; and two species of the long-legged whistling or tree duck. Another common species was the rosy-billed duck, now to be seen on ornamental waters in England; and occasionally we saw the wild Muscovy duck, called Royal duck by the natives, but it was a rare visitor so far south. We also had geese and swans: the upland geese from the Megellanic Straits that came to us in winter—that is to say, our winter from May to August. And there were two swans, the black-necked, which has black flesh and is unfit to eat, and the white or Coscoroba Swan, as good a table bird as there is in the world. And oddly enough this bird has been known to the natives as a "goose" since the discovery of America, and now after three centuries our scientific ornithologists have made the discovery that it is a link between the geese and swans, but is more goose than swan. It is a beautiful white bird, with bright red bill and legs, the wings tipped with black; and has a loud musical cry of three notes, the last prolonged note with a falling inflection.

These were the birds we sought after in winter; but we could shoot for the table all the year round, for no sooner was it the duck's pairing and breeding season than another bird-population from their breeding-grounds in the arctic and sub-arctic regions came on the scene—plover, sandpiper, godwit, curlew, whimbrel, —a host of northern species that made the summer-dried pampas their winter abode.

My first attempt at duck-shooting was made at a pond not many minutes' walk from the house, where I found a pair of shoveller ducks, feeding in their usual way in the shallow water with head and neck immersed. Anxious not to fail in this first trial, I got down flat on the ground and crawled snake-fashion for a distance of fifty or sixty yards, until I was less than twenty yards from the birds, when I fired and killed one.

That first duck was a great joy, and having succeeded so well with my careful tactics, I continued in the same way, confining my attention to pairs or small parties of three or four birds, when by patiently creeping a long distance through the grass I could get very close to them. In this way I shot teal, widgeon, pintail, shovellers, and finally the noble rosy-bill, which was esteemed for the table above all the others.

My brother, ambitious of a big bag, invariably went a distance from home in quest of the large flocks, and despised my way of duck-shooting; but it sometimes vexed him to find on his return from a day's expedition that I had succeeded in getting as many birds as himself without having gone much more than a mile from home.

Some months after I had started shooting I began to have trouble with my beloved gun, owing to a weakness it had developed in its lock—one of the infirmities incidental to age which the gunsmiths of Buenos Ayres were never able to cure effectually. Whenever it got bad I was permitted to put it into the cart sent to town periodically, to have it repaired, and would then go gunless for a week or ten days. On one of these occasions I one day saw a party of shoveller duck dibbling in a small rain-pool at the side of the plantation, within a dozen yards of the old moat which surrounded it. Ducks always appeared to be exceptionally tame and bold when I was without a gun, but the boldness of those shovellers was more than I could stand, and running to the house I got out the old blunderbuss, which I had never been forbidden to use, since no one had ever thought it possible that I should want to use such a monster of a gun. But I was desperate, and loading it for the first (and last) time, I went after those shovellers.

I had once been told that it would be impossible to shoot wild duck or anything with the blunderbuss unless one could get within a dozen yards of them, on account of its tremendous scattering power. Well, by going along the bottom of the moat, which was luckily without water just then, I could get as near the birds as I liked and kill the whole flock. When I arrived abreast of the pool I crept up the grassy crumbling outside bank, and resting the ponderous barrel on the top of the bank, fired at the shovellers at a distance of about fifteen yards, and killed nothing, but received a kick which sent me flying to the bottom of the foss. It was several days before I got over that pain in my shoulder.

Later on there was a period of trouble and scarcity in the land. There was war, and the city from which we obtained our supplies was besieged by an army from the "upper provinces" which had come down to break the power and humble the pride of Buenos Ayres. Our elders missed their tea and coffee most, but our anxiety was that we should soon be without powder and shot. My brother constantly warned me not to be so wasteful, although he fired half a dozen shots to my one without getting more birds for the table. At length there came a day when there was little shot left—just about enough to fill one shot-pouch—and knowing it was his intention to have a day out, I sneaked into the gun-room and loaded my fowling-piece just to have one shot more. He was going to try for upland geese that day, and, as I had expected, carried off all the shot.

After he had gone I took my gun, and being determined to make the most of my one shot, refused to be tempted by any of the small parties of duck I found in the pools near home, even when they appeared quite tame. At length I encountered a good-sized flock of rosy-bills by the side of a marshy stream about two miles from home. It was a still, warm day in mid-winter, and the ducks were dozing on the green bank in a beautiful crowd, and as the land near them was covered with long grass, I saw it would be possible to get quite close to them. Leaving my pony at a good distance, I got down flat on the ground and began my long laborious crawl, and got within twenty-five yards of the flock. Never had I had such a chance before! As I peeped through the grass and herbage I imagined all sorts of delightful things—my brother far away vainly firing long shots at the wary geese, and his return and disgust at the sight of my heap of noble rosy-bills, all obtained near home at one shot!

Then I fired just as the birds, catching sight of my cap, raised their long necks in alarm. Bang! Up they rose with a noise of wings, leaving not one behind! Vainly I watched the flock, thinking that some of the birds I must have hit would soon be seen to waver in their course and then drop to earth. But none wavered or fell. I went home as much puzzled as disappointed. Late in the day my brother returned with one upland goose and three or four ducks, and inquired if I had had any luck. I told him my sad story, whereupon he burst out laughing and informed me that he had taken care to draw the shot from my gun before going out. He was up to my little tricks, he said; he had seen what I had done, and was not going to allow me to waste the little shot we had left!

Our duck-shooting was carried on under difficulties during those days. We searched for ammunition at all the houses for some leagues around, and at one house we found and purchased a quantity of exceedingly coarse gunpowder, with grain almost the size of canary-seed. They told us it was cannon-powder, and to make it fit for use in our fowling-pieces we ground it fine with glass and stone bottles for rollers on a tin plate. Shot we could not find, so had to make it for ourselves by cutting up plates of lead into small square bits with a knife and hammer.

Eventually the civil war, which had dragged on for a long time, brought an unexpected danger to our house and caused us to turn our minds to more important things than ducks. I have said that the city was besieged by an army from the provinces, but away on the southern frontier of the province of Buenos Ayres the besieged party, or faction, had a powerful friend in an estanciero in those parts who was friendly with the Indians, and who collected an army of Indians hungry for loot, and gauchos, mostly criminals and deserters, who in those days were accustomed to come from all parts of the country to put themselves under the protection of this good man.

This horde of robbers and enthusiasts was now advancing upon the capital to raise the siege, and each day brought us alarming reports—whether true or false we could not know—of depredations they were committing on their march. The good man, their commander, was not a soldier, and there was no pretence of discipline of any kind; the men, it was said, did what they liked, swarming over the country on the line of march in bands, sacking and burning houses, killing or driving off the cattle, and so on. Our house was unfortunately on the main road running south from the capital, and directly in the way of the coming rabble. That the danger was a real and very great one we could see in the anxious faces of our elders; besides, nothing was now talked of but the coming army and of all we had to fear.

At this juncture my brother took it upon himself to

make preparations for the defence of the house. Our oldest brother was away, shut up in the besieged city, but the three of us at home determined to make a good fight, and we set to work cleaning and polishing up our firearms—the Tower musket, the awful blunderbuss, the three fowling-pieces, double and single-barrelled, and the two big horse-pistols and an old revolver. We collected all the old lead we could find about the place and made bullets in a couple of bullet-moulds we had found—one for ounce and one for small bullets, three to the ounce. The fire to melt the lead was in a shelter we had made behind an outhouse, and here one day, in spite of all our precautions, we were discovered at work, with rows and pyramids of shining bullets round us, and our secret was out. We were laughed at as a set of young fools for our pains. "Never mind," said my brother. "Let them mock now; by and by when it comes to choosing between having our throats cut and defending ourselves, they will probably be glad the bullets were made."

But though they laughed, our work was not interfered with, and some hundreds of bullets were turned out and made quite a pretty show.

Meanwhile the besiegers were not idle: they had in their army a cavalry officer who had had a long experience of frontier warfare and had always been successful in his fights with the pampas Indians; and this man, with a picked force composed of veteran fighters, was dispatched against the barbarians. They had already crossed the Salado river and were within two or three easy marches of us, when the small disciplined force met and gave them battle and utterly routed them.

Indians and gauchos were sent flying south like thistle-down before the wind; but all being well-mounted, not many were killed.

So ended that danger, and I think we boys were all a little disappointed that no use had been made of our bright beautiful bullets. I am sure my brother was; but soon after that he left home for a distant country, and our shooting and other adventures together were ended for ever.

CHAPTER XXII
Boyhood's End

The book—The Saledero, or killing-grounds, and their
smell—Walls built of bullocks' skulls—A pestilential
city—River water and Aljibe water—Days of lassitude
—Novel scenes—Home again—Typhus—My first day
out—Birthday reflections—What I asked of life—A
boy's mind—A brother's resolution—End of our thousand and one nights—A reading spell—My boyhood
ends in disaster.

THIS book has already run to a greater length than
was intended; nevertheless there must be yet another
chapter or two to bring it to a proper ending, which I
can only find by skipping over three years of my life,
and so getting at once to the age of fifteen. For that
was a time of great events and serious changes, bodily
and mental, which practically brought the happy time
of my boyhood to an end.

On looking back over the book, I find that on three
or four occasions I have placed some incident in the
wrong chapter or group, thus making it take place a
year or so too soon or too late. These small errors
of memory are, however, not worth altering now: so
long as the scene or event is rightly remembered and
pictured it doesn't matter much whether I was six or
seven, or eight years old at the time. I find, too, that
I have omitted many things which perhaps deserved a

place in the book—scenes and events which are vividly remembered, but which unfortunately did not come up at the right moment, and so were left out.

Of these scenes unconsciously omitted, I will now give one which should have appeared in the chapter describing my first visit to Buenos Ayres city: placed here it will serve very well as an introduction to this last chapter.

In those days, and indeed down to the 'seventies of last century, the south side of the capital was the site of the famous Saladero, or killing-grounds, where the fat cattle, horses and sheep brought in from all over the country were slaughtered every day, some to supply the town with beef and mutton and to make *charque,* or sun-dried beef, for exportation to Brazil, where it was used to feed the slaves, but the greater number of the animals, including all the horses, were killed solely for their hides and tallow. The grounds covered a space of three or four square miles, where there were cattle enclosures made of upright posts placed close together, and some low buildings scattered about. To this spot were driven endless flocks of sheep, half or wholly wild horses and dangerous-looking, long-horned cattle in herds of a hundred or so to a thousand, each moving in its cloud of dust, with noise of bellowings and bleatings and furious shouting of the drovers as they galloped up and down, urging the doomed animals on. When the beasts arrived in too great numbers to be dealt with in the buildings, you could see hundreds of cattle being killed in the open all over the grounds in the old barbarous way the gauchos use, every animal being first lassoed, then hamstrung, then its throat cut

—a hideous and horrible spectacle, with a suitable accompaniment of sounds in the wild shouts of the slaughterers and the awful bellowings of the tortured beasts. Just where the animal was knocked down and killed, it was stripped of its hide and the carcass cut up, a portion of the flesh and the fat being removed and all the rest left on the ground to be devoured by the pariah dogs, the carrion hawks, and a multitude of screaming black-headed gulls always in attendance. The blood so abundantly shed from day to day, mixing with the dust, had formed a crust half a foot thick all over the open space: let the reader try to imagine the smell of this crust and of tons of offal and flesh and bones lying everywhere in heaps. But no, it cannot be imagined. The most dreadful scenes, the worst in Dante's *Inferno*, for example, can be visualized by the inner eye; and sounds, too, are conveyed to us in a description so that they can be heard mentally; but it is not so with smells. The reader can only take my word for it that *this* smell was probably the worst ever known on the earth, unless he accepts as true the story of Tobit and the "fishy fumes" by means of which that ancient hero defended himself in his retreat from the pursuing devil.

It was the smell of carrion, of putrifying flesh, and of that old and ever-newly moistened crust of dust and coagulated blood. It was, or seemed, a curiously substantial and stationary smell; travellers approaching or leaving the capital by the great south road, which skirted the killing-grounds, would hold their noses and ride a mile or so at a furious gallop until they got out of the abominable stench.

One extraordinary feature of the private *quintas* or orchards and plantations in the vicinity of the Saladeros was the walls or hedges. These were built entirely of cows' skulls, seven, eight, or nine deep, placed evenly like stones, the horns projecting. Hundreds of thousands of skulls had been thus used, and some of the old, very long walls, crowned with green grass and with creepers and wild flowers growing from the cavities in the bones, had a strangely picturesque but somewhat uncanny appearance. As a rule there were rows of old Lombardy poplars behind these strange walls or fences.

In those days bones were not utilized: they were thrown away, and those who wanted walls in a stoneless land, where bricks and wood for palings were dear to buy, found in the skulls a useful substitute.

The abomination I have described was but one of many—the principal and sublime stench in a city of evil smells, a populous city built on a plain without drainage and without water-supply beyond that which was sold by watermen in buckets, each bucketful containing about half a pound of red clay in solution. It is true that the best houses had *algibes,* or cisterns, under the courtyard, where the rainwater from the flat roofs was deposited. I remember that water well: you always had one or two to half-a-dozen scarlet wrigglers, the larvæ of mosquitoes, in a tumblerful, and you drank your water, quite calmly, wrigglers and all!

All this will serve to give an idea of the condition of the city of that time from the sanitary point of view, and this state of things lasted down to the 'seventies of the last century, when Buenos Ayres came to be the chief pestilential city of the globe and was obliged to call in engineers from England to do something to save the inhabitants from extinction.

When I was in my fifteenth year, before any changes had taken place and the great outbreaks of cholera and yellow fever were yet to come, I spent four or five weeks in the city, greatly enjoying the novel scenes and new life. After about ten or twelve days I began to feel tired and languid, and this feeling grew on me day by day until it became almost painful to exert myself to visit even my most favoured haunts—the great South Market, where cage-birds were to be seen in hundreds, green paroquets, cardinals, and bishop-birds predominating; or to the river front, where I spent much time fishing for little silvery king-fishes from the rocks; or further away to the quintas and gardens on the cliff, where I first feasted my eyes on the sight of orange groves laden with golden fruit amidst the vivid green polished foliage, and old olive trees with black egg-shaped fruit showing among the grey leaves.

And through it all the feeling of lassitude continued, and was, I thought, due to the fact that I was on foot instead of on horseback, and walking on a stony pavement instead of on a green turf. It never occurred to me that there might be another cause, that I was breathing in a pestilential atmosphere and that the poison was working in me.

Leaving town I travelled by some conveyance to spend a night at a friend's house, and next morning set out for home on horseback. I had about twenty-seven miles across country to ride and never touched a road, and I was no sooner on my way than my spirits revived; I was well and unspeakably happy again, on horseback on the wide green plain, drinking in the pure air like a draught of eternal life. It was autumn, and the plain as far as one could see on every side a moist brilliant green, with a crystal blue sky above, over which floated shining white clouds. The healthy glad feeling lasted through my ride and for a day or two after, during which I revisited my favourite haunts in the grounds, rejoicing to be with my beloved birds and trees once more.

Then the hateful town feeling of lassitude returned on me and all my vigour was gone, all pleasure in life ended. Thereafter for a fortnight I spent the time moping about the house; then there was a spell of frosty weather with a bleak cutting wind to tell us that it was winter, which even in those latitudes can be very cold. One day after early dinner my mother and sisters went in the carriage to pay a visit to a neighbouring estancia, and my brothers being out or absent from home I was left alone. The verandah appeared to me the warmest place I could find, as the sun shone on it warm and bright, and there I settled down on a chair placed against the wall at the side of a heap of sacks of meal or something which had been left there, and formed a nice shelter from the wind.

The house was strangely quiet, and the westering sun shining full on me made me feel quite comfortable, and in a little while I fell asleep. The sun set and it grew bitterly cold, but I did not wake, and when my mother returned and inquired for me I could not be found. Finally the whole household turned out with lanterns and searched for me up and down through the plantation, and the hunt was still going on when, about ten o'clock at night, some one hurrying along the verandah stumbled on me in my sheltered corner by the sacks, still in my chair but unconscious and in a burning fever. It was the dread typhus, an almost obsolete malady in Europe, and in fact in all civilized countries, but not uncommon at that date in the pestilential city. It was wonderful that I lived through it in a place where we were out of reach of doctors and apothecaries, with only my mother's skill in nursing and her knowledge of such drugs as were kept in the house to save me. She nursed me day and night for the three weeks during which the fever lasted, and when it left me, a mere shadow of my former self, I was dumb—not even a little Yes or No could I articulate however hard I tried, and it was at last concluded that I would never speak again. However, after about a fortnight, the lost faculty came back, to my mother's inexpressible joy.

Winter was nearing its end when one morning in late July I ventured out of doors for the first time, though still but a skeleton, a shadow of my former self. It was a windy day of brilliant sunshine, a day I shall never forget, and the effect of the air and the sun and smell of earth and early flowers, and the sounds of wild birds, with the sight of the intensely green young grass and the vast crystal dome of heaven above, was like deep draughts of some potent liquor that made the blood dance in my veins. Oh what an inexpressible, immeasurable joy to be alive and not dead, to have my feet still on the earth, and drink in the wind and sunshine once more! But the pleasure was more than I could endure in that feeble state; the chilly wind pierced me like needles of ice, my senses swam, and I would have fallen to the ground if my elder brother had not caught me in his arms and taken me back to the house.

In spite of that fainting fit I was happy again with the old happiness, and from day to day I regained strength, until one day in early August I was suddenly reminded that it was my anniversary by my brothers and sisters all coming to me with birthday presents, which they had been careful to provide beforehand, and congratulations on my recovery.

Fifteen years old! This was indeed the most memorable day of my life, for on that evening I began to think about myself, and my thoughts were strange and unhappy thoughts to me—what I was, what I was in the world for, what I wanted, what destiny was going to make of me! Or was it for me to do just what I wished, to shape my own destiny, as my elder brothers had done? It was the first time such questions had come to me, and I was startled at them. It was as though I had only just become conscious; I doubt that I had ever been fully conscious before. I had lived till now in a paradise of vivid sense-impressions in which all thoughts came to me saturated with emotion, and in that mental state reflection is well-nigh impossible. Even the idea of death, which had come as a surprise, had not made me reflect. Death was a person, a monstrous being who had sprung upon me in my flowery paradise and had inflicted a wound with a poisoned dagger in my flesh. Then had come the knowledge of immortality for the soul, and the wound was healed, or partly so, for a time at all events; after which the one thought that seriously troubled me was that I could not always remain a boy. To pass from boyhood to manhood was not so bad as dying; nevertheless it was a change painful to contemplate. That everlasting delight and wonder, rising to rapture, which was in the child and boy would wither away and vanish, and in its place there would be that dull low kind of satisfaction which men have in the set task, the daily and hourly intercourse with others of a like condition, and in eating and drinking and sleeping. I could not, for example, think of so advanced an age as fifteen without the keenest apprehension. And now I was actually at that age—at that parting of the ways, as it seemed to me.

What, then, did I want?—what did I ask to have? If the question had been put to me then, and if I had been capable of expressing what was in me, I should have replied: I want only to keep what I have; to rise each morning and look out on the sky and the grassy dew-wet earth from day to day, from year to year. To watch every June and July for spring, to feel the same old sweet surprise and delight at the appearance of each familiar flower, every new-born insect, every bird returned once more from the north. To listen in a trance of delight to the wild notes of the golden plover coming once more to the great plain, flying, flying south, flock succeeding flock the whole day long. Oh, those wild beautiful cries of the golden plover! I could exclaim with Hafiz, with but one word changed: "If after a thousand years that sound should float o'er my tomb, my bones uprising in their gladness would dance in the sepulchre!" To climb trees and put my hand down in the deep hot nest of the Bien-te-veo and feel the hot eggs—the five long pointed cream-coloured eggs with chocolate spots and splashes at the larger end. To lie on a grassy bank with the blue water between me and beds of tall bulrushes, listening to the mysterious sounds of the wind and of hidden rails and coots and courlans conversing together in strange human-like tones; to let my sight dwell and feast on the *camaloté* flower amid its floating masses of moist vivid green leaves—the large alamanda-like flower of a purest divine yellow that when plucked sheds its lovely petals, to leave you with nothing but a green stem in your hand. To ride at noon on the hottest days, when the whole earth is a-glitter with illusory water, and see the cattle and horses in thousands, covering the plain at their watering-places; to visit some haunt of large birds at that still, hot hour and see storks, ibises, grey herons, egrets of a dazzling whiteness, and rose-coloured spoonbills and flamingoes, standing in the shallow water in which their motionless forms are reflected. To lie on my back on the rust-brown grass in January and gaze up at the wide hot whitey-blue sky, peopled with millions and myriads of glistening balls of thistle-down, ever, ever floating by; to gaze and gaze until they are to me living things and I, in an ecstasy, am with them, floating in that immense shining void!

And now it seemed that I was about to lose it—this glad emotion which had made the world what it was to me, an enchanted realm, a nature at once natural and supernatural; it would fade and lessen imperceptibly day by day, year by year, as I became more and more absorbed in the dull business of life, until it would be lost as effectually as if I had ceased to see and hear and palpitate, and my warm body had grown cold and stiff in death, and, like the dead and the living, I should be unconscious of my loss.

It was not a unique nor a singular feeling: it is known to other boys, as I have read and heard; also I have occasionally met with one who, in a rare moment of confidence, has confessed that he has been troubled at times at the thought of all he would lose. But I doubt that it was ever more keenly felt than in my case; I doubt, too, that it is common or strong in English boys, considering the conditions in which they exist. For restraint is irksome to all beings, from a black-beetle or an earthworm to an eagle, or, to go higher still in the scale, to an orang-u-tan or a man; it is felt most keenly by the young, in our species at all events, and the British boy suffers the greatest restraint during the period when the call of nature, the instincts of play and adventure, are most urgent. Naturally, he looks eagerly forward to the time of escape, which he fondly imagines will be when his boyhood is over and he is free of masters.

To come back to my own case: I did not and could not know that it was an exceptional case, that my feeling for nature was something more than the sense of pleasure in sun and rain and wind and earth and water and in liberty of motion, which is universal in children, but was in part due to a faculty which is not universal or common. The fear, then, was an idle one, but I had good reason for it when I considered how it had been with my elder brothers, who had been as little restrained as myself, especially that masterful adventurous one, now in a distant country thousands of miles from home, who, at about the age at which I had now arrived, had made himself his own master, to do what he liked with his own life. I had seen him at *his* parting of the ways, how resolutely he had abandoned his open-air habits, everything in fact that had been his delight, to settle down to sheer hard mental work, and this at our home on the pampas where there were no masters, and even the books and instruments required for his studies could only be procured with great difficulty and after long delays. I remember one afternoon when we were gathered in the dining-room for tea, he was reading, and my mother coming in looked over his shoulder and said, "You are reading a novel: don't you think all that romantic stuff will take your mind off your studies?"

Now he'll flare up, said I to myself; he's so confoundedly independent and touchy no one can say a word to him. It surprised me when he answered quietly, "Yes, mother, I know, but I must finish this book now; it will be the last novel I shall read for some years." And so it was, I believe.

His resolution impressed us even more in another matter. He had an extraordinary talent for inventing stories, mostly of wars and wild adventures with plenty of fighting in them, and whenever we boys were all together, which was usually after we had gone to bed and put the candle out, he would begin one of his wonderful tales and go on for hours, we all wide awake, listening in breathless silence. At length towards midnight the flow of the narrative would suddenly stop, and after an interval we would all begin to cry out to him to go on. "Oh, you *are* awake!" he would exclaim, with a chuckle of laughter. "Very well, then, you know just where we are in our history, to be resumed another day. Now you can go to sleep." On the following evening he would take up the tale, which would often last an entire week, to be followed by another just as long, then another, and so on—our thousand and one nights. And this delightful yarn-spinning was also dropped as he became more and more absorbed in his mathematical and other studies.

To this day I can recall portions of those tales, especially those in which birds and beasts instead of men were the actors, and so much did we miss them that sometimes when we were all assembled of an afternoon we would start begging him for a story— "just one more, and the longer the better," we would say to tempt him. And he, a little flattered at our keen appreciation of his talent as a yarn-spinner, would appear inclined to yield. "Well, now, what story shall I tell you?" he would say; and then, just when we were settling down to listen, he would shout, "No, no, no more stories," and to put the matter from him he would snatch up a book and order us to hold our tongues or clear out of the room!

It was not for me to follow his lead; I had not the intellect or strength of will for such tasks, and not only on that memorable evening of my anniversary, but for days afterwards I continued in a troubled state of mind, ashamed of my ignorance, my indolence, my disinclination to any kind of mental work—ashamed even to think that my delight in nature and wish for no other thing in life was merely due to the fact that while the others were putting away childish things as they grew up, I alone refused to part with them.

The result of all these deliberations was that I temporized: I would not, I could not, give up the rides and rambles that took up most of my time, but I would try to overcome my disinclination to serious reading. There were plenty of books in the house—it was always a puzzle to me how we came to have so many. I was familiar with their appearance on the shelves—they had been before me since I first opened my eyes— their shape, size, colour, even their titles, and that was all I knew about them. A general Natural History and two little works by James Rennie on the habits and faculties of birds was all the literature suited to my wants in the entire collection of three or four hundred volumes. For the rest, I had read a few story-books and novels: but we had no novels; when one came into the house it would be read and lent to our next neighbour five or six miles away, and he in turn would lend to another, twenty miles further on, and so on until it disappeared in space.

I made a beginning with Rollin's *Ancient History* in two huge quarto volumes; I fancy it was the large clear type and numerous plates which illustrated it that determined my choice. Rollin, the good old priest, opened a new wonderful world to me, and instead of the tedious task I had feared the reading would prove, it was as delightful as it had formerly been to listen to my brother's endless histories of imaginary heroes and their wars and adventures.

Still athirst for history, after finishing Rollin I began fingering other works of that kind: there was Whiston's *Josephus,* too ponderous a book to be held in the hands when read out of doors; and there was Gibbon in six stately volumes. I was not yet able to appreciate the lofty artificial style, and soon fell on something better suited to my boyish taste in letters— a *History of Christianity* in, I think, sixteen or eighteen volumes of a convenient size. The simple natural diction attracted me, and I was soon convinced that I could not have stumbled on more fascinating reading than the lives of the Fathers of the Church included in some of the earlier volumes, especially that of Augustine, the greatest of all: how beautiful and marvellous his life was, and his mother Monica's! what wonderful books he wrote!—his *Confessions* and *City of God* from which long excerpts were given in this volume.

These biographies sent me to another old book, *Leland on Revelation,* which told me much I was curious to know about the mythologies and systems of philosophy of the ancients—the innumerable false cults which had flourished in a darkened world before the dawn of the true religion.

Next came Carlyle's *French Revolution* and at last Gibbon, and I was still deep in the *Decline and Fall* when disaster came to us: my father was practically ruined, owing, as I have said in a former chapter, to his childlike trust in his fellow-men, and we quitted the home he had counted as a permanent one, which in due time would have become his property had he but made his position secure by a proper deed on first consenting to take over the place in its then ruinous condition.

Thus ended, sadly enough, the enchanting years of my boyhood; and here, too, the book should finish: but having gone so far, I will venture a little further and give a brief account of what followed and the life which, for several succeeding years, was to be mine—the life, that is to say, of the mind and spirit.

CHAPTER XXIII

A Darkened Life

A severe illness—Case pronounced hopeless—How it affected me—Religious doubts and a mind distressed—Lawless thoughts—Conversation with an old gaucho about religion—George Combe and the desire for immortality.

AFTER we had gone back impoverished to our old home where I first saw the light—which was still my father's property and all he had left—I continued my reading, and was so taken up with the affairs of the universe, seen and unseen, that I did not feel the change in our position and comforts too greatly. I took my share in the rough work and was much out-of-doors on horseback looking after the animals, and not unhappy. I was already very tall and thin at that time, in my sixteenth year, still growing rapidly, and though athletic, it was probable that some weakness had been left in me by the fever. At all events, I had scarcely settled down to the new way of life before a fresh blow fell upon me, a malady which, though it failed to kill me, yet made shipwreck of all my new-born earthly hopes and dreams, and a dismal failure of my after life.

One day I undertook, unaided, to drive home a small troop of cattle we had purchased at a distance of a good many leagues, and was in the saddle from morning till after dark in a continuous flooding rain and violent wind. The wind was against me, and the beasts were incessantly trying to turn and rush back to the place they had been taken from, and the fight with wind and cattle went wearily on, the driving rain gradually soaking through my woollen poncho, then through my clothes to my skin, and trickling down until my long boots were full and slopping over at the knees. For the last half of that midwinter day my feet and legs were devoid of feeling. The result of it was rheumatic fever and years of bad health, with constant attacks of acute pain and violent palpitation of the heart which would last for hours at a stretch. From time to time I was sent or taken to consult a doctor in the city, and in that way from first to last I was in the hands of pretty well all the English doctors in the place, but they did me no permanent good, nor did they say anything to give me a hope of complete recovery. Eventually we were told that it was a practically hopeless case, that I had "outgrown my strength," and had a permanently bad heart and might drop down at any moment.

Naturally this pronouncement had a most disastrous effect on me. That their diagnosis proved in the end to be wrong mattered nothing, since the injury had been done and could not be undone if I lived a century. For the blow had fallen at the most critical period in life, the period of transition when the newly-awakened mind is in its freshest, most receptive stage, and is most curious, most eager, when knowledge is most readily assimilated, and, above everything, when the foundations of character and the entire life of the man are laid.

I speak, it will be understood, of a mind that had not been trained or pressed into a mould or groove by schoolmasters and schools—of a mind that was a forest wilding rather than a plant, one in ten thousand like it, grown under glass in a prepared soil, in a nursery.

That I had to say good-bye to all thoughts of a career, all bright dreams of the future which recent readings had put into my mind, was not felt as the chief loss, it was in fact a small matter compared with the dreadful thought that I must soon resign this earthly life which was so much more to me, as I could not help thinking, than to most others. I was like that young man with a ghastly face I had seen bound to a post in our barn; or like any wretched captive, tied hand and foot and left to lie there until it suited his captor to come back and cut his throat or thrust him through with a spear, or cut him into strips with a sword, in a leisurely manner so as to get all the satisfaction possible out of the exercise of his skill and the spectacle of gushing blood and his victim's agony.

Nor was this all nor even the worst which had befallen me; I now discovered that in spite of all my strivings after the religious mind, that old dread of annihilation which I had first experienced as a small child was not dead as I had fondly imagined, but still lived and worked in me. This visible world—this paradise of which I had had so far but a fleeting glimpse—the sun and moon and other worlds peopling all space with their brilliant constellations, and still other suns and systems, so utterly remote, in such inconceivable numbers as to appear to our vision as a faint luminous mist in the sky—all this universe which had existed for millions and billions of ages, or from eternity, would have existed in vain, since now it was doomed with my last breath, my last gleam of consciousness, to come to nothing. For that was how the thought of death presented itself to me.

Against this appalling thought I struggled with all my power, and prayed and prayed again, morning, noon and night, wrestling with God, as the phrase was, trying as it were to wring something from His hands which would save me, and which He, for no reason that I could discover, withheld from me.

It was not strange in these circumstances that I became more and more absorbed in the religious literature of which we had a good amount on our bookshelves— theology, sermons, meditations for every day in the year, *The Whole Duty of Man, A Call to the Unconverted,* and many other old works of a similar character.

Among these I found one entitled, if I remember rightly, *An Answer to the Infidel,* and this work, which I took up eagerly in the expectation that it would allay those maddening doubts perpetually rising in my mind and be a help and comfort to me, only served to make matters worse, at all events for a time. For in this book I was first made acquainted with many of the arguments of the freethinkers, both of the Deists who were opposed to the Christian creed, and of those who denied the truth of all supernatural religion. And the answers to the arguments were not always convincing. It was idle, then, to seek for proofs in the books. The books themselves, after all their arguments, told me as much when they said that only by faith could a man be saved. And to the sad question: "How was it to be attained?" the only answer was, by striving and striving until it came. And as there was nothing else to do I continued striving, with the result that I believed and did not believe, and my soul, or rather my hope of immortality, trembled in the balance.

This, from first to last, was the one thing that mattered; so much was it to me that in reading one of the religious books entitled *The Saints' Everlasting Rest,* in which the pious author, Richard Baxter, expatiates on and labours to make his readers realize the condition of the eternally damned, I have said to myself: "If an angel, or one returned from the dead, could come to assure me that life does not end with death, that we mortals are destined to live for ever, but that for me there can be no blessed hereafter on account of my want of faith, and because I loved or worshipped Nature rather than the Author of my being, it would be, not a message of despair, but of consolation; for in that dreadful place to which I should be sent, I should be alive and not dead, and have my memories of earth, and perhaps meet and have communion there with others of like mind with myself, and with recollections like mine."

This was but one of many lawless thoughts which assailed me at this time. Another, very persistent, was the view I took of the sufferings of the Saviour of mankind. Why, I asked, were they made so much of? —why was it said that He suffered as no man had suffered? It was nothing but the physical pain which thousands and millions have had to endure! And if

I could be as sure of immortality as Jesus, death would be to me no more than the prick of a thorn. What would it matter to be nailed to a cross and perish in a slow agony if I believed that, the agony over, I should sit down refreshed to sup in paradise? The worst of it was that when I tried to banish these bitter, rebellious ideas, taking them to be the whisperings of the Evil One, as the books taught, the quick reply would come that the supposed Evil One was nothing but the voice of my own reason striving to make itself heard.

But the contest could not be abandoned; devil or reason, or whatever it was, must be overcome, else there was no hope for me; and such is the powerful effect of fixing all one's thoughts on one object, assisted no doubt by the reflex effect on the mind of prayer, that in due time I did succeed in making myself believe all I wished to believe, and had my reward, since after many days or weeks of mental misery there would come beautiful intervals of peace and of more than peace, a new and surprising experience, a state of exaltation, when it would seem to me that I was lifted or translated into a purely spiritual atmosphere and was in communion and one with the unseen world.

It was wonderful. At last and for ever my Dark Night of the Soul was over; no more bitter broodings and mocking whispers and shrinkings from the awful phantom of death continually hovering near me; and, above all, no more "difficulties"—the rocky barriers I had vainly beat and bruised myself against. For I had been miraculously lifted over them and set safely down on the other side, where it was all plain walking.

Unhappily, these blissful intervals would not last

long. A recollection of something I had heard or read would come back to startle me out of the confident happy mood; reason would revive as from a benumbed or hypnotized condition, and the mocking voice would be heard telling me that I had been under a delusion. Once more I would abhor and shudder at the black phantom, and when the thought of annihilation was most insistent, I would often recall the bitter, poignant words about death and immortality spoken to me about two years before by an old gaucho landowner who had been our neighbour in my former home.

He was a rough, rather stern-looking man, with a mass of silver-white hair and grey eyes; a gaucho in his dress and primitive way of life, the owner of a little land and a few animals—the small remnant of the estancia which had once belonged to his people. But he was a vigorous old man, who spent half of his day on horseback, looking after the animals, his only living. One day he was at our house, and coming out to where I was doing something in the grounds, he sat down on a bench and called me to him. I went gladly enough, thinking that he had some interesting bird news to give me. He remained silent for some time, smoking a cigar, and staring at the sky as if watching the smoke vanish in the air. At length he opened fire.

"Look," he said, "you are only a boy, but you can tell me something I don't know. Your parents read books, and you listen to their conversation and learn things. We are Roman Catholics, and you are Protestants. We call you heretics and say that for such there is no salvation. Now I want you to tell me what is the difference between our religion and yours."

I explained the matter as well as I knew how, and added, somewhat maliciously, that the main difference was his religion was a corrupt form of Christianity and ours a pure one.

This had no effect on him; he went on smoking and staring at the sky as if he hadn't heard me. Then he began again: "Now I know. These differences are nothing to me, and though I was curious to know what they were, they are not worth talking about, because, as I know, all religions are false."

"What did he mean—how did he know?" I asked, very much surprised.

"The priests tell us," he replied, "that we must believe and live a religious life in this world to be saved. Your priests tell you the same, and as there is no other world and we have no souls, all they say must be false. You see all this with your eyes," he continued, waving his hands to indicate the whole visible world. "And when you shut them or go blind you see no more. It is the same with our brains. We think of a thousand things and remember, and when the brain decays we forget everything, and we die, and everything dies with us. Have not the cattle eyes to see and brains to think and remember too? And when they die no priest tells us that they have a soul and have to go to purgatory, or wherever he likes to send them. Now, in return for what you told me, I've told you something you didn't know."

It came as a great shock to me to hear this. Hitherto I had thought that what was wrong with our native friends was that they believed too much, and this man —this good honest old gaucho we all respected—believed nothing! I tried to argue with him and told him he had said a dreadful thing, since every one knew in his heart that he had an immortal soul and had to be judged after death. He had distressed and even frightened me, but he went on calmly smoking and appeared not to be listening to me, and as he refused to speak I at last burst out: "How do you know? Why do you say you know?"

At last he spoke. "Listen. I was once a boy too, and I know that a boy of fourteen can understand things as well as a man. I was an only child, and my mother was a widow, and I was more than all the world to her, and she was more than everything else to me. We were alone together in the world—we two. Then she died, and what her loss was to me—how can I say it?—how could you understand? And after she was taken away and buried, I said: 'She is not dead, and wherever she now is, in heaven or in purgatory, or in the sun, she will remember and come to me and comfort me.' When it was dark I went out alone and sat at the end of the house, and spent hours waiting for her. 'She will surely come,' I said, 'but I don't know whether I shall see her or not. Perhaps it will be just a whisper in my ear, perhaps a touch of her hand on mine, but I shall know that she is with me.' And at last, worn out with waiting and watching, I went to my bed and said she will come to-morrow. And the next night and the next it was the same. Sometimes I would go up the ladder, always standing against the gable so that one could go up, and standing on the roof, look out over the plain and see where our horses were grazing. There I would sit or lie on the thatch for hours. And I would cry: 'Come to me, my mother! I cannot live without you! Come soon—come soon, before I die of a broken heart!' That was my cry every night, until worn out with my vigil I would go back to my room. And she never came, and at last I knew that she was dead and that we were separated for ever—that there is no life after death."

His story pierced me to the heart, and without another word I left him, but I succeeded in making myself believe that grief for his mother had made him mad, that as a boy he had got these delusions in his mind and had kept them all his life. Now this recollection haunted me. Then one day, with my mind in this troubled state, in reading George Combe's *Physiology* I came on a passage in which the question of the desire for immortality is discussed, his contention being that it is not universal, and as a proof of this he affirms that he himself had no such desire.

This came as a great shock to me, since up to the moment of reading it I had in my ignorance taken it for granted that the desire is inherent in every human being from the dawn of consciousness to the end of life, that it is our chief desire, and is an instinct of the soul like that physical instinct of the migratory bird which calls it annually from the most distant regions back to its natal home. I had also taken it for granted that our hope of immortality, or rather our belief in it, was founded on this same passion in us and in its universality. The fact that there were those who had no such desire was sufficient to show that it was no spiritual instinct or not of divine origin.

There were many more shocks of this kind—when I go back in memory to that sad time, it seems almost incredible to me that that poor doubtful faith in revealed religion still survived, and that the struggle still went on, but go on it certainly did.

To many of my readers, to all who have interested themselves in the history of religion and its effect on individual minds—its psychology—all I have written concerning my mental condition at that period, will come as a twice-told tale, since thousands and millions of men have undergone similar experiences and have related them in numberless books. And here I must beg my reader to bear in mind that in the days of my youth we had not yet fallen into the indifference and scepticism which now infects the entire Christian world. In those days people still believed; and here in England, in the very centre and mind of the world, many thousands of miles from my rude wilderness, the champions of the Church were in deadly conflict with the Evolutionists. I knew nothing about all that: I had no modern books—those we had were mostly about a hundred years old. My fight up to this period was all on the old lines, and on this account I have related it as briefly as possible; but it had to be told, since it comes into the story of the development of my mind at that period. I have no doubt that my sufferings through these religious experiences were far greater than in the majority of cases, and this for the special reason which I have already intimated.

CHAPTER XXIV

Loss and Gain

The soul's loneliness—My mother and her death—A mother's love for her son—Her character—Anecdotes—A mystery and a revelation—The autumnal migration of birds—Moonlight vigils—My absent brother's return—He introduces me to Darwin's works—A new philosophy of life—Conclusion.

THE mournful truth that a man—every man—must die alone, had been thrust sharply into my mind and kept there by the frequent violent attacks of my malady I suffered at that time, every one of which threatened to be the last. And this sense and apprehension of loneliness at the moment of the severance of all earthly ties and parting with light and life, was perhaps the cause of the idea or notion which possessed me, that in all our most intimate thoughts and reflections concerning our destiny and our deepest emotions, we are and must be alone. Anyhow, in so far as these matters are concerned, I never had nor desired a confidant. In this connection I recall the last words spoken to me by my younger brother, the being I loved best on earth at that time and the one I had been more intimate with than with any other person I have ever known. This was after the dark days and years had been overpast, when I had had long periods of fairly good

health and had known happiness in the solitary places
I loved to haunt, communing with wild nature, with
wild birds for company.

He was with me in the ship in which I had taken
my passage "home," as I insisted on calling England,
to his amusement, and when we had grasped hands for
the last time and had said our last good-bye, he added
this one more last word: "Of all the people I have
ever known you are the only one I don't know."

It was a word, I imagine, never spoken by a mother
of a loved son, her insight, born of her exceeding love,
being so much greater than that of the closest friend
and brother. I never breathed a word of my doubts
and mental agonizings to my mother; I spoke to her
only of my bodily sufferings; yet she knew it all, and
I knew that she knew. And because she knew and
understood the temper of my mind as well, she never
questioned, never probed, but invariably when alone
with me she would with infinite tenderness in her manner touch on spiritual things and tell me of her own
state, the consolations of her faith which gave her peace
and strength in all our reverses and anxieties.

I knew, too, that her concern at my state was the
greater because it was not her first experience of a trouble of this kind. My elder long-absent brother had
scarcely ceased to be a boy before throwing off all belief
in the Christian creed and congratulating himself on having got rid of old wives' fables, as he scornfully expressed it. But never a word did he say to her of this
change, and without a word she knew it, and when she
spoke to us on the subject nearest to her heart and he
listened in respectful silence, she knew the thought and

feeling that was in him—that he loved her above everybody but was free of her creed.

He had been able to cast it off with a light heart because of his perfect health, since in that condition death is not in the mind—the mind refuses to admit the thought of it, so remote is it in that state that we regard ourselves as practically immortal. And, untroubled by that thought, the mind is clear and vigorous and unfettered. What, I have asked myself, even when striving after faith, would faith in another world have mattered to me if I had not been suddenly sentenced to an early death, when the whole desire of my soul was life, nothing but life—to live for ever!

Then my mother died. Her perfect health failed her suddenly, and her decline was not long. But she suffered much, and on the last occasion of my being with her at her bedside she told me that she was very tired and had no fear of death, and would be glad to go but for the thought of leaving me in such a precarious state of health and with a mind distressed. Even then she put no questions to me, but only expressed the hope that her prayers for me would be answered and that at the last we should be together again.

I cannot say, as I might say in the case of any other relation or friend, that I had lost her. A mother's love for the child of her body differs essentially from all other affections, and burns with so clear and steady a flame that it appears like the one unchangeable thing in this earthly mutable life, so that when she is no

longer present it is still a light to our steps and a
consolation.

It came to me as a great surprise a few years ago
to have my secret and most cherished feelings about
my own mother expressed to me as I had never heard
them expressed before by a friend who, albeit still
young, has made himself a name in the world, one
who had never known a mother, she having died during his infancy. He lamented that it had been so,
not only on account of the motherless childhood and
boyhood he had known, but chiefly because in after
life it was borne in on him that he had been deprived of
something infinitely precious which others have—the
enduring and sustaining memory of a love which is
unlike any other love known to mortals, and is almost
a sense and prescience of immortality.

In reading, nothing goes to my heart like any true
account of a mother and son's love for one another,
such as we find in that true book I have already spoken
of in a former chapter, Serge Aksakoff's *History of
my Childhood*. Of other books I may cite Leigh
Hunt's *Autobiography* in the early chapters. Reading
the incidents he records of his mother's love and pity
for all in trouble and her self-sacrificing acts, I have
exclaimed: "How like my mother! It is just how
she would have acted!" I will give an instance here
of her loving-kindness.

Some days after her death I had occasion to go to
the house of one of our native neighbours—the humble
rancho of poor people. It was not in my mind at the
moment that I had not seen these people since my
mother died, and on coming into the living-room the

old mother of the family, who had grandchildren of my age, rose from her seat with tottering steps to meet me, and taking my hand in hers, with tears streaming from her eyes, cried: "She has left us! She who called me mother on account of my years and her loving heart. It was she who was my mother and the mother of us all. What shall we do without her?"

Only after going out and getting on my horse it occurred to me that the old woman's memory went back to the time when she first knew my mother, a girl-wife, many years before I was born. She could remember numerous acts of love and compassion: that when one of her daughters died in childbirth in that very house, my mother, who was just then nursing me, went to give them whatever aid and comfort she could, and finding the child alive, took it home and nursed it, with me, at her own breasts for several days until a nurse was found.

From the time when I began to think for myself I used to wonder at her tolerance; for she was a saint in her life, spiritually-minded in the highest degree. To her, a child of New England parents and ancestors, reared in an intensely religious atmosphere, the people of the pampas among whom her lot was cast must have appeared almost like the inhabitants of another world. They were as strange to her soul, morally and spiritually, as they were unlike her own people outwardly in language, dress, and customs. Yet she was able to affiliate with them, to visit and sit at ease with them in their lowliest ranchos, interesting herself as much in their affairs as if she belonged to them. This sympathy and freedom endeared her to them, and it was a grief to some who were much attached to her that she was not of their faith. She was a Protestant, and what that exactly meant they didn't know, but they supposed it was something very bad. Protestants, some of them held, had been concerned in the crucifixion of the Saviour; at all events, they would not go to mass or confessional, and despised the saints, those glorified beings who, under the Queen of Heaven, and with the angels, were the guardians of Christian souls in this life and their intercessors in the next. They were anxious to save her, and when I was born, the same old dame I have told about a page or two back, finding that I had come into the world on St. Dominic's Day, set herself to persuade my mother to name me after that saint, that being the religious custom of the country. For if they should succeed in this it would be taken as a sign of grace, that she was not a despiser of the saints and her case hopeless. But my mother had already fixed on a name for me and would not change it for another, even to please her poor neighbours—certainly not for such a name as Dominic; perhaps there is not one in the calendar more obnoxious to heretics of all denominations.

They were much hurt—it was the only hurt she ever caused them—and the old dame and some of her people, who had thought the scheme too good to be dropped altogether, insisted always on calling me Dominic!

My mother's sympathy and love for everybody appeared, too, in the hospitality she delighted to exercise. That, indeed, was the common virtue of the country, especially in the native population; but from all my experience during my wanderings on these great plains in subsequent years, when every night would find me a guest in a different establishment, I never saw anything quite on a par with my parents' hospitality. Nothing seemed to make them happier than having strangers and travellers taking their rest with us; there were also a good number of persons who were accustomed to make periodical visits to the city from the southern part of the province who, after a night with us, with perhaps half a day's rest to follow, would make our house a regular resting-place. But no distinctions were made. The poorest, even men who would be labelled tramps in England, travellers on foot perhaps where cattle made it dangerous to be on foot, would be made as welcome as those of a better class. Our delight as children, loving fun too well, was when we had a guest of this humble description at the supper-table. Settling down in our places at the long table laden with good things, a stern admonitory glance from our father would let us into the secret of the new guest's status—his unsuitability to his surroundings. It was great fun to watch him furtively and listen to his blundering conversational efforts, but we knew that the least sound of a titter on our part would have been an unpardonable offence. The poor and more uncouth, or ridiculous, from our childish point of view, they appeared, the more anxious my mother would be to put them at their ease. And she would sometimes say to us afterwards that she could not laugh with us because she remembered the poor fellow probably had a mother somewhere in a distant country who was perhaps thinking of him at the very time he was at the table with us, and hoping and praying that in his wanderings he would meet with some who would be kind to him.

I remember many of these chance guests, and will give a particular account of one—the guest and the evening we passed in his company—as this survives with a peculiar freshness in my memory, and it was also a cherished recollection of my mother's.

I was then nine or ten years old, and our guest was a young Spanish gentleman, singularly handsome, with a most engaging expression and manner. He was on a journey from Buenos Ayres to a part in our province some sixty or seventy leagues further south, and after asking permission to pass the night at our house, he explained that he had only one horse, as he liked that way of travelling rather than the native way of driving a *tropilla* before him, going at a furious gallop from dawn to dark, and changing horses every three or four leagues. Having but one horse, he had to go in a leisurely way with many rests, and he liked to call at many houses every day just to talk with the people.

After supper, during which he charmed us with his conversation and pure Castilian, which was like music as he spoke it, we formed a circle before a wood fire in the dining-room and made him take the middle seat. For he had confessed that he performed on the guitar, and we all wanted to sit where we could see as well as listen. He tuned the instrument in a leisurely way, pausing often to continue the conversation with my parents, until at last, seeing how eager we all were, he began to play, and his music and style were strange to us, for he had no jigging tunes with fantastic flights and flourishes so much affected by our native guitarists. It was beautiful but serious music.

Then came another long pause and he talked again, and said the pieces he had been playing were composed by his chief favourite, Sarasate. He said that Sarasate had been one of the most famous guitarists in Spain, and had composed a good deal of music for the guitar before he had given it up for the violin. As a violinist he would win a European reputation, but in Spain they were sorry that he had abandoned the national instrument.

All he said was interesting, but we wanted more and more of his music, and he played less and less and at longer intervals, and at last he put the guitar down, and turning to my parents, said with a smile that he begged to be excused—that he could play no more for thinking. He owed it to them, he said, to tell them what he was thinking about; they would then know how much they had done for his pleasure that evening and how he appreciated it. He was, he continued, one of a large family, very united, all living with their parents at home; and in winter, which was cold in his part of Spain, their happiest time was in the evening when they would gather before a big fire of oak logs in their *sala* and pass the time with books and conversation and a little music and singing. Naturally, since he had left his country years ago, the thought of that time and those evenings had occasionally been in his mind—a passing thought and memory. On this evening it had come in a different way, less like a memory than a revival of the past, so that as he sat there among us, he was a boy back in Spain once more, sitting by the fire with his brothers and sisters and parents. With that feeling in him he could not go on playing. And he thought it most strange that such an experience should have come to him for the first time in that place out on that great naked pampa, sparsely inhabited, where life was so rough, so primitive.

And while he talked we all listened—how eagerly! —drinking in his words, especially my mother, her eyes bright with the moisture rising in them; and she often afterwards recalled that evening guest, who was seen no more by us but had left an enduring image in our hearts.

This is a picture of my mother as she appeared to all who knew her. In my individual case there was more, a secret bond of union between us, since she best understood my feeling for Nature and sense of beauty, and recognized that in this I was nearest to her. Thus, besides and above the love of mother and son, we had a spiritual kinship, and this was so much to me that everything beautiful in sight or sound that affected me came associated with her to my mind. I have found this feeling most perfectly expressed in some lines to the Snowdrop by our lost poet, Dolben. I am in doubt, he wrote,

> If summer brings a flower so lovable
> Of such a meditative restfulness
> As this, with all her roses and carnations.
> The morning hardly stirs their noiseless bells;
> Yet could I fancy that they whispered "Home,"
> For all things gentle, all things beautiful,
> I hold, my mother, for a part of thee.

So have I held. All things beautiful, but chiefly flowers. Her feeling for them was little short of adoration. Her religious mind appeared to regard them as little voiceless messengers from the Author of our beings and of Nature, or as divine symbols of a place and a beauty beyond our power to imagine.

I think it likely that when Dolben penned those lines to the Snowdrop it was in his mind that this was one of his mother's favourites. My mother had her favourites too; not the roses and carnations in our gardens, but mostly among the wild flowers growing on the pampas—flowers which I never see in England. But I remember them, and if by some strange chance I should find myself once more in that distant region, I should go out in search of them, and seeing them again, feel that I was communing with her spirit.

These memories of my mother are a relief to me in recalling that melancholy time, the years of my youth that were wasted and worse, considering their effect and that the very thought of that period, which is to others the fullest, richest, and happiest in life, has always been painful to me. Yet to it I am now obliged to return for the space of two or three pages to relate how I eventually came out of it.

My case was not precisely like that of Cowper's Castaway, but rather like that of a fugitive from his ship on some tropical coast who, on swimming to the shore, finds himself in a mangrove swamp, waist-deep in mire, tangled in rope-like roots, straining frantically to escape his doom.

I have told how after my fifteenth anniversary, when

I first began to reflect seriously on my future life, the idea still persisted that my perpetual delight in Nature was nothing more than a condition or phase of my child's and boy's mind, and would inevitably fade out in time. I might have guessed at an earlier date that this was a delusion, since the feeling had grown in strength with the years, but it was only after I took to reading at the beginning of my sixteenth year that I discovered its true character. One of the books I read then for the first time was White's *Selborne,* given to me by an old friend of our family, a merchant in Buenos Ayres, who had been accustomed to stay a week or two with us once a year when he took his holiday. He had been on a visit to Europe, and one day, he told me, when in London on the eve of his departure, he was in a bookshop, and seeing this book on the counter and glancing at a page or two, it occurred to him that it was just the right thing to get for that bird-loving boy out on the pampas. I read and re-read it many times, for nothing so good of its kind had ever come to me, but it did not reveal to me the secret of my own feeling for Nature—the feeling of which I was becoming more and more conscious, which was a mystery to me, especially at certain moments, when it would come upon me with a sudden rush. So powerful it was, so unaccountable, I was actually afraid of it, yet I would go out of my way to seek it. At the hour of sunset I would go out half a mile or so from the house, and sitting on the dry grass with hands clasped round my knees, gaze at the western sky, waiting for it to take me. And I would ask myself: What does it mean? But there was no answer to that in any book concerning the "life and con-versation of animals." I found it in other works: in Brown's *Philosophy*—another of the ancient tomes on our shelves—and in an old volume containing appre-ciations of the early nineteenth-century poets; also in other works. They did not tell me in so many words that it was the mystical faculty in me which produced those strange rushes or bursts of feeling and lifted me out of myself at moments; but what I found in their words was sufficient to show me that the feeling of delight in Nature was an enduring one, that others had known it, and that it had been a secret source of happiness throughout their lives.

This revelation, which in other circumstances would have made me exceedingly happy, only added to my misery when, as it appeared, I had only a short time to live. Nature could charm, she could enchant me, and her wordless messages to my soul were to me sweeter than honey and the honeycomb, but she could not take the sting and victory from death, and I had perforce to go elsewhere for consolation. Yet even so, in my worst days, my darkest years, when occupied with the laborious business of working out my own salvation with fear and trembling, with that spectre of death always following me, even so I could not rid my mind of its old passion and delight. The rising and setting sun, the sight of a lucid blue sky after cloud and rain, the long unheard familiar call-note of some newly-returned migrant, the first sight of some flower in spring, would bring back the old emotion and would be like a sudden ray of sunlight in a dark place—a momentary intense joy, to be succeeded by ineffable pain. Then there were times when these two opposite feelings mingled and would be together in my mind for hours at a time, and this occurred oftenest during the autumnal migration, when the great wave of bird-life set northwards, and all through March and April the birds were visible in flock succeeding flock from dawn to dark, until the summer visitants were all gone, to be succeeded in May by the birds from the far south, flying from the antarctic winter.

This annual spectacle had always been a moving one, but the feeling it now produced—this mingled feeling—was most powerful on still moonlight nights, when I would sit or lie on my bed gazing out on the prospect, earth and sky, in its changed mysterious aspect. And, lying there, I would listen by the hour to the three-syllable call-note of the upland or solitary plover, as the birds went past, each bird alone far up in the dim sky, winging his way to the north. It was a strange vigil I kept, stirred by strange thoughts and feelings, in that moonlit earth that was strange too, albeit familiar, for never before had the sense of the supernatural in Nature been stronger. And the bird I listened to, that same solitary plover I had known and admired from my earliest years, the most graceful of birds, beautiful to see and hear when it would spring up before my horse with its prolonged wild bubbling cry of alarm and go away with swift, swallow-like flight—what intensity and gladness of life was in it, what a wonderful inherited knowledge in its brain, and what an inexhaustible vigour in its slender frame to enable it to perform that annual double journey of up-wards of ten thousand miles! What a joy it would be to live for ages in a world of such fascinating phenomena! If some great physician, wise beyond all others, infallible, had said to me that all my doctors had been wrong, that, barring accidents, I had yet fifty years to live, or forty, or even thirty, I should have worshipped him and would have counted myself the happiest being on the globe, with so many autumns and winters and springs and summers to see yet.

With these supernatural moonlight nights I finish the story of that dark time, albeit the darkness had not yet gone; to have recalled it and related it briefly as I could once in my life is enough. Let me now go back to the simile of the lost wretch struggling for life in the mangrove swamp. The first sense of having set my foot on a firmer place in that slough of fetid slime, of a wholesome breath of air blown to me from outside the shadow of the black abhorred forest, was when I began to experience intervals of relief from physical pain, when these grew more and more frequent and would extend to entire days, then to weeks, and for a time I would become oblivious of my precarious state. I was still and for a long time subject to attacks, when the pain was intolerable and was like steel driven into my heart, always followed by violent palpitations, which would last for hours. But I found that exercise on foot or horseback made me no worse, and I became more and more venturesome, spending most of my time out of doors, although often troubled with the thought that my passion for Nature was a hindrance to me, a turning aside from the difficult way I had been striving to keep.

Then my elder brother returned, an event of the

greatest importance in my life; and as he had not
been expected so soon, I was for a minute in doubt
that this strange visitor could be my brother, so greatly
had he altered in appearance in those five long years
of absence, which had seemed like an age to me. He
had left us as a smooth-faced youth, with skin tanned
to such a deep colour that with his dark piercing eyes
and long black hair he had looked to me more like an
Indian than a white man. Now his skin was white,
and he had grown a brown beard and moustache. In
disposition, too, he had grown more genial and tolerant,
but I soon discovered that in character he had not
changed.

As soon as an opportunity came he began to inter-
rogate and cross-question me as to my mind—life and
where I stood, and expressed himself surprised to hear
that I still held to the creed in which we had been
reared. How, he demanded, did I reconcile these
ancient fabulous notions with the doctrine of evolution?
What effect had Darwin produced on me? I had to
confess that I had not read a line of his work, that
with the exception of Draper's *History of Civilization,*
which had come by chance in my way, I had during all
those five years read nothing but the old books which
had always been on our shelves. He said he knew
Draper's *History,* and it was not the sort of book for
me to read at present. I wanted a different history,
with animals as well as men in it. He had a store of
books with him, and would lend me the *Origin of
Species* to begin with.

When I had read and returned the book, and he
was eager to hear my opinion, I said it had not hurt

me in the least, since Darwin had to my mind only succeeded in disproving his own theory with his argument from artificial selection. He himself confessed that no new species had ever been produced in that way.

That, he said in reply, was the easy criticism that any one who came to the reading in a hostile spirit would make. They would fasten on that apparently weak point and not pay much attention to the fact that it is fairly met and answered in the book. When he first read the book it convinced him; but he had come to it with an open mind and I with a prejudiced mind on account of my religious ideas. He advised me to read it again, to read and consider it carefully with the sole purpose of getting at the truth. "Take it," he said, "and read it again in the right way for you to read it—as a naturalist."

He had been surprised that I, an ignorant boy or youth on the pampas, had ventured to criticise such a work. I, on my side, had been equally surprised at his quiet way of reasoning with me, with none of the old scornful spirit flaming out. He was gentle with me, knowing that I had suffered much and was not free yet.

I read it again in the way he had counselled, and then refused to think any more on the subject. I was sick of thinking. Like the wretch who long has tossed upon the thorny bed of pain, I only wanted to repair my vigour lost and breathe and walk again. To be on horseback, galloping over the green pampas, in sun and wind. For after all it was only a reprieve, not a commutation of sentence—though one of a kind unknown

in the Courts, in which the condemned man is allowed
out on bail. My pardon was not received until a few
years later. I returned with a new wonderful zest to
my old sports, shooting and fishing, and would spend
days and weeks from home, sometimes staying with
old gaucho friends and former neighbours at their
ranchos, attending cattle-markings and partings, dances,
and other gatherings, and also made longer expeditions
to the southern and western frontiers of the province,
living out of doors for months at a time.

Despite my determination to put the question off,
my mind, or sub-conscious mind, like a dog with a
bone which it refuses to drop in defiance of its master's
command, went on revolving it. It went to bed and
got up with me, and was with me the day long, and
whenever I had a still interval, when I would pull up
my horse to sit motionless watching some creature,
bird or beast or snake, or sat on the ground poring
over some insect occupied with the business of its little
life, I would become conscious of the discussion and
argument going on. And every creature I watched,
from the great soaring bird circling in the sky at a vast
altitude to the little life at my feet, was brought into
the argument, and was a type, representing a group
marked by a family likeness not only in figure and
colouring and language, but in mind as well, in habits
and the most trivial traits and tricks of gesture and so
on; the entire group in its turn related to another
group, and to others, still further and further away,
the likeness growing less and less. What explanation
was possible but that of community of descent? How
incredible it appeared that this had not been seen years

ago—yes, even before it was discovered that the world was round and was one of a system of planets revolving round the sun. All this starry knowledge was of little or no importance compared to that of our relationship with all the infinitely various forms of life that share the earth with us. Yet it was not till the second half of the nineteenth century that this great, almost self-evident truth had won a hearing in the world!

No doubt this is a common experience: no sooner has the inquirer been driven to accept a new doctrine than it takes complete possession of his mind, and has not then the appearance of a strange and unwelcome guest, but rather that of a familiar friendly one, and is like a long-established housemate. I suppose the explanation is that when we throw open the doors to the new importunate visitor, it is virtually a ceremony, since the real event has been already accomplished, the guest having stolen in by some other way and made himself at home in the sub-conscious mind. Insensibly and inevitably I had become an evolutionist, albeit never wholly satisfied with natural selection as the only and sufficient explanation of the change in the forms of life. And again, insensibly and inevitably, the new doctrine has led to modifications of the old religious ideas and eventually to a new and simplified philosophy of life. A good enough one so far as this life is concerned, but unhappily it takes no account of another, a second and perdurable life without change of personality.

This subject has been much in men's minds during the past two or three dreadful years, often reminding me of that shock I received as a boy of fourteen at

the old gaucho's bitter story of his soul; I have also
again been reminded of the theory in which that
younger and greatly-loved brother of mine was able
to find comfort. He had become deeply religious,
and after much reading in Herbert Spencer and other
modern philosophers and evolutionists, he told me he
thought it was idle for Christians to fight against the
argument of the materialists that the mind is a func-
tion of the brain. Undoubtedly it was that, and our
mental faculties perished with the brain; but we had
a soul that was imperishable as well. *He knew it,*
which meant that he too was a mystic, and being
wholly preoccupied with religion, his mystical faculty
found its use and exercise there. At all events, his
notion served to lift him over *his* difficulties and to
get him out of *his* mangrove swamp—a way perhaps
less impossible than the one recently pointed out by
William James.

Thus I came out of the contest a loser, but as a
compensation had the knowledge that my physicians
were false prophets; that, barring accidents, I could
count on thirty, forty, even fifty years with their summers and autumns and winters. And that was the
life I desired—the life the heart can conceive—the
earth life. When I hear people say they have not
found the world and life so agreeable or interesting
as to be in love with it, or that they look with
equanimity to its end, I am apt to think they have
never been properly alive nor seen with clear vision
the world they think so meanly of, or anything in it—
not a blade of grass. Only I know that mine is an
exceptional case, that the visible world is to me more

beautiful and interesting than to most persons, that the delight I experienced in my communings with Nature did not pass away, leaving nothing but a recollection of vanished happiness to intensify a present pain. The happiness was never lost, but owing to that faculty I have spoken of, had a cumulative effect on the mind and was mine again, so that in my worst times, when I was compelled to exist shut out from Nature in London for long periods, sick and poor and friendless, I could yet always feel that it was infinitely better to be than not to be.

THE END